LAURA ASHLEY

By the same author

Samplers: Five Centuries of a Gentle Craft
Enid Bagnold

(For children)
Mother Teresa
Margot Fonteyn

LAURA ASHLEY
A Life by Design

ANNE SEBBA

WEIDENFELD AND NICOLSON
LONDON

First published in Great Britain in 1990 by
George Weidenfeld & Nicolson Ltd,
91 Clapham High Street, London SW4 7TA

This paperback edition published by
George Weidenfeld & Nicolson Ltd 1991

British Library Cataloguing in Publication Data
Sebba, Anne, 1951 –
Laura Ashley: a life by design.
1   English interior design. Ashley, Laura
I.   Title
747.22
ISBN 0–297–81199–1

Printed and bound in Great Britain by
The Guernsey Press Co. Ltd, Guernsey, Channel Islands

Losing an Old Friend
BY
ARABELLA ASHLEY

Oh tailored life of woven paths
You are on loan for nought is ours
Allow no hem to fall and fray
For you may need that suit some day
And if by chance the cloth is torn
In such a way it can't be worn
Say not that it's the tailor's fault
Just think of all the joy it brought.

FOR
ROSALIE AND SAM

Contents

Illustrations

Laura with her first grandchild, Sara Jane, at Rhydoldog in 1984
Clogau, Montgomeryshire
Rhydoldog House, Radnorshire
Château de Remaisnil, Doullens, France
La Pré Verger, a romantic French *manoir* in the South of France

Acknowledgements

My first debt of gratitude is to Sir Bernard Ashley for inviting me to write his late wife's biography. Inevitably it impinged hugely upon his own life and yet he was unflinching in his telling of the story. Laura and Bernard's children, Jane, David, Nick and Emma, have been no less open and painstaking in their attempts to help me write an honest and truthful account. I am most grateful to them all and thank them warmly for making my task so enjoyable.

I have been greatly helped too by Laura's friends, colleagues and family. I should particularly like to thank: Barbara Anderman, Mariel Angel, Arabella Ashley, Caroline Ashley, Geoff Ashley, Erica Bard, Liz Barlow, Liz Barry (Matson), Peter Batty, Michael Belchamber, Amelia Blacker, Malcolm Bland, Hugh Blakeway-Webb, Andrew Bloch, Peggy Booker, Comtesse Sybille de la Borde, Marianne Brace, Moira Braybrooke, Peter Brunn, June Buchanan, Sarah Callander, Jane Carr, Lina Carr-Gomm, Mark Collins, Rosina Corfield, Jane and Timothy Clifford, Mary and David Coates, Sir Terence Conran, Georgina Cooke, Livie and Kevin Cooper, Maria José da Cruz, Dai Davies, Mary Deighton, The Duchess of Devonshire, Susan and Adrian Doull, Geoff Dove, Henrietta and Thomas Dunne, Jean Evans, Father Fletcher, Mother Frances Anne (The Community of S. Denys), Kathleen Freeman, Anne Furniss, Ian Gale, Peter Garbett Edwards, Polly (Devlin) and Andy Garnett, Anna Griffiths, Avril Groom, Sally Gritten, Rosemary Hargreaves (National Federation of Women's Institutes), Martha Harrison, Lady Henderson, Janet Holdsworth, Lord Hooson, Michael Howells, Gwenny Hughes, Deborah James, John James, Brian Jones, Carol Jones, Colin Jones, Dai Jones, Dai Walter

Jones, Dominick Jones, Surapee Karnasuta, Lynda Kee-Scott, Jean Keen, Antonia Kirwan-Taylor, Denise Krusche, Robert Landgrebe, Tony Lambert, Lynda Lee-Potter, Jonathan Leiserach, Wendy Leslie, Patrick Libby, Julia Lubomirska, Anne and Bernard Llewellyn, George Llewellyn (The Dowlais Male Voice Choir), Trevor Maddocks, Anthony Marangos, Margaret Mellor, Bettina and Henry McNulty, Al Maclean, Cliff Michelmore, Heather Mitchell, Phil Morris, Oliver Charles Morton, Catherine di Montezemolo, Sandy Munroe, Jessica and Lionel Ottley, Rev. D. J. Parry, Jane Pocock, the late Venetia Pollock and Philip Pollock, Dr John Rae, Susan Raven, Carol Rayman, Jean and Peter Revers, Janet Roberts, Meirion Rowlands, Joan and Eric Rubinstein, Ceinwen Rymer, Anita Saada, Michael Sandler, Sasha Schwerdt, Rosalie and Sam Sebba, Anthony Sheppard, Jacqui Smale, Dr Penny Sparke, Richard Strong, Francis Thomas, Christine Thompson, Anna Thorne, James Thorne, Adrienne and Andre Tossens, Tom Trevaskis, Countess Walburg, Paddy Wall (Association of Wrens), Anne Wallwork, Liza Wanklyn, Franklyn Warburg, Jenny Warburton-Lee, Carolyn Warrender, Leslie Watts, Jeanne Watters, June Weir, Sally, Duchess of Westminster, Dr Ronald Williams, John Winter, Pauline Wood, Bruce Wright, Joe Yanow, Jill Yate and Pat Yot.

I acknowledge with thanks permission to quote on page 195 from the Dictionary of National Biography 1981–1985 given by the publishers Oxford University Press, and assistance from the Industrial Development Division of the Welsh Office, the Department of Manuscripts and Records at the National Library of Wales, the London Library and the Office of Population Census and Surveys.

In addition I should like to thank all the staff at 'Laura Ashley' who have courteously fielded my telephone calls, letters and queries, made appointments and chased after people on my behalf. I am most grateful to Lord Weidenfeld, who first suggested the idea to me, and to my agent, Gill Coleridge who has been, as ever, a stalwart support. My final thanks – and love – go to my children and to my husband, who discovered the pleasures of Wales with me and shared much else besides during the preparation of this book.

Foreword
BY SIR BERNARD ASHLEY

When I read Anne Sebba's manuscript for the first time I was quite shocked. I could not believe that this Laura had been the same person I had lived and worked with for nearly forty years. Here was another Laura seen through the eyes of her biographer, who had never met her, and perceived by other people who had worked with her. In fact I largely did not believe it. I read it a second time, correcting some facts as I went, and then I read it carefully, fully, without interruption, for a third time. Then I did believe it.

Anne's work is a remarkable insight into Laura's life and work – it shows quite clearly the route of Laura's background and standards and the source of her many strengths, the strongest of which was her Christianity. Call this Christianity Calvinism, Welsh Chapel, narrow-mindedness, or by any other epithet, but to me it was that part of her that I admired and respected most – an unswerving service to standards. As a young girl you could see and feel this quality in her, standing out in the crowd and later as I grew up with her I shaped a lot of my character around this quality and drew enormous strength from it. Compromise was never a part of her nature and when she discovered it was part of mine she would work through me in her relations with people in the company, letting me adjust her disciplines to fit in with theirs as best as I could. This and the other complementary qualities in each of us formed the basis of our partnership.

Living and working together was a form of hardly suppressed excitement. What we were doing completely filled our lives and later the lives of our children and those of the people working with us. We worked, or play-worked, as we called it, sixteen-hour days, walking and talking on the beaches in Wales, endlessly rambling in fields and lanes and in the hills. Most of our ideas, plans and design philosophies were formed on these walks. My ideas, often far-fetched, were never rejected but were always discussed with enormous enthusiasm. Then, as we analysed them her criticism would start to shape them, editing away the unnecessary and measuring them against her standards. All of those who worked with Laura at design meetings were always amazed at her ability to work with such unerring skill and speed to conclusions that were proved to be correct when we went to market.

Through all the excitement of these years Laura always remained a private person – my wife above all. Nearly always she was home first in the evenings to make tea or to have dinner ready before I arrived, and she always wanted to hear about my day, my achievements and prizes, before we talked about hers. Perhaps I should have written this book. I thought about it for a couple of years after she left me but as time drew on I realized I should leave it to someone who had not been so close to her and to tell a more complete story of my wife.

Lyford Cay, Bahamas, January 1990

1

From Wales to Wallington

On 10 September 1985, British newspapers flashed the report across their front pages that Laura Ashley, the founder of the multi-million pound fashion and furnishing empire, was critically ill in hospital after a fall down stairs. For the next two weeks, barely a day passed without a progress bulletin or speculation as to how such a tragic domestic accident could have happened. The British media considered her a public personality, although it was not a role she welcomed. They hungered after every crumb of detail about the accident. Thousands of get-well messages poured in to a disbelieving family. Editors swiftly chased around those who had known her, as well as some who had not, for comments on the person behind the name on the dark green shops. The day of the fall, three days before, had been Laura Ashley's sixtieth birthday. She had returned to Britain from her home abroad for a double celebration as her elder daughter had just given birth to her first child.

Attaining a decade is, for everyone, a cause for reflection. The significance, in 1985, of reaching this particular milestone was well appreciated by Laura, for whom the existence of an inner dialogue was always important. The previous year had been a particularly full one, capping an extraordinary life. But it was not without occasion for taking stock. As a highly spiritual and self-contained person she was sustained by her knowledge that, although external appearances might indicate

1

her freedom was restricted, whether by domestic or business demands, true freedom comes from self-discipline, from being in charge of one's own destiny or from being 'steward of one's own talents'. She recognized at an early stage in life the importance of self-control and this led naturally to a belief in the importance of controlling one's environment. She dedicated her life to this. As she approached sixty, Laura Ashley had managed to quell much of the inner turmoil that had beset her in earlier years and, as if to emphasize her acceptance of a different life ahead, only weeks beforehand she had formally handed over her role as Design Director of the family company to her son, Nick.

There was new life entering the Ashley family and Laura was acutely aware of the blurred distinctions between birth and death. For her, the moment of giving birth was the most poignant ever experienced; 'nearer my God to thee', was how she described it. Now it was her daughter's turn and Laura had been to England several times in the final weeks of her pregnancy to help with the preparations. In addition, her other child, 'Laura Ashley' was launching itself into a new existence. Laura Ashley plc was due to be floated as a public company in just a few weeks time. Two of her babies were quite definitely grown up and able to fend for themselves.

Death held little fear for her. 'I was taught well in childhood that the mystery of life is entwined with the mystery of God,' she once wrote. Thus, when she contemplated mortality, 'to which we all come sooner or later and one never quite knows when,' it was, in a spiritual sense, simply the next stage of being. 'My conclusion is a strengthening of belief that the world is a testing ground and it is so important to keep your values intact . . . because one day we just have to stand up and be counted'.

This book is not intended to be a company history of Laura Ashley plc. Rather is it the story of a remarkably perceptive and determined woman who married a man of unparalleled energy and vision; the friction of their complementary personalities resulted in a creativity with a commercial edge and a psychological base. The story of Laura's life could easily be written as a novel. It is a classic (almost) rags-to-riches story with the happy ending tragically foreshortened for the heroine. It is interwoven with romance at many stages but romance is only one thread. The background weave comprises a toughly practical woman vigorously clinging to her values against the day when she would have to stand up and be counted. For Laura Ashley, that day came on 17 September 1985. She never regained consciousness after her fall.

The story begins, and ends, in Wales.

It was neither by chance nor without portent that Laura was born in Wales. When she spoke of her roots it was the Welsh roots to which she was referring and when she talked of her childhood home, more often than not it was her grandmother's house, a colliery worker's cottage in Merthyr Tydfil, that she had in mind. South Wales has a long history of ironworking, dating back to the Roman occupation of Britain. At the end of the eighteenth century it was one of the most important areas of ironmaking in the country and it was no coincidence that Trevithick's first steam engine ran in Merthyr in 1804. For most of the nineteenth century Merthyr was the major iron-producing town in Europe, and Dowlais, one of its principal ironworks, supplied the rails for systems in India, Russia and parts of South America. But from the 1870s onwards, as the iron and steel industries in Merthyr declined steadily, coal-mining became more important and pits were opened up throughout the borough to produce household and steam coal.

The dramatic geography of South Wales forced many pits to be squeezed into narrow valleys between high hills. To the already steep natural mountains were added man-made mountains of clinker and ash. As the population of Merthyr (and other British towns) virtually doubled during the last century, those who could, chose to locate their homes on as high a point as possible, where the air was freer of fumes. The houses of Station Terrace, Dowlais Top, had therefore, an obvious appeal. They were on the south side of the Brecon Beacons, very exposed and bitterly cold. But they were right at the very top. Although the miners must have cursed the steepness of the hill as, at dawn, they trudged home up its cobbled length, the height ensured a wonderful view of the town, ironworks and Cyfarthfa Castle, the Gothic symbol of Victorian industrial prosperity which was built in 1825 by William Crawshay as his family home. This was the grandest ironmaster's house in South Wales and the setting for much lavish entertaining. More than a world but less than a mile away, Station Terrace wound its way up from the now defunct Dowlais Station at the bottom of the street.

At the turn of the nineteenth century, the inhabitants of Station Terrace were working class but many of them owned their own houses and the street was long known for its aura of lower middle-class respectability reflected in the shining brass and high moral standards. Laura's grandfather, Enoch Davies, who, around 1905 bought 31 Station Terrace, came from a large, farming family in Pembrokeshire; he and his brother had journeyed to Dowlais in search of work. For almost a century agricultural workers from poor rural communities in West Wales had been attracted to Merthyr by the relatively high wages of the iron industry. The industrial cottages, although simple, small and often overcrowded, were in general an improvement on most farmworkers' cottages. However, although Enoch's brother found work as a miner, Enoch himself became a policeman. Three other brothers decided to chance their luck in America and were never heard of again.

Shortly after his move to Dowlais, Enoch met and married Margaret (Maggie) Beynon. The Beynon family were Welsh speakers for whom Wales and being Welsh was of crucial significance. But the 'Welshness' they believed in was less the radical political nonconformist brand, of which there was a strong element in Merthyr, than the self-improving, chapel-in-our-daily-lives strain which put traditional family and home-based values above all. Some twenty years earlier, Margaret's mother (Laura's great-grandmother), who was by all accounts an adventurous spirit, had followed the emigrant trail to America with her first husband in search of work. But when he died in Boston she and her three-year-old daughter, Mary, took the first available boat to return to live in Wales. She soon married again, a Welshman by the name of Beynon, and produced five more daughters, of whom Margaret was the fourth, and two sons. The Beynon girls grew up to be an attractive, well-turned-out bevy and their parents were frightened by the stories they had heard of the steelworks' owners. If a pretty girl were seen out walking alone she might be persuaded to go back and work in the Castle 'with intent', as it was coyly known. Rather than let a daughter suffer this fate, the Beynons preferred to send theirs to London to learn a trade – millinery for Lizzie, cookery for Margaret – or go into service. Thus they were relieved to see Margaret settle quickly into a respectable marriage with Enoch Davies.

Enoch was a big man with a walrus moustache who soon became a well-liked and respected figure in the community; in the home he took his orders from his wife. The Davies' began married life in Dowlais itself but it was Margaret who urged the move to Station Terrace a year after their first child, Margaret Elizabeth (known as Bessie), was born. Although it was no nearer to the Central Police Station where Enoch worked, it was a house they owned themselves. Moreover, within a short space of time three of Maggie's sisters moved to Station Terrace too. The focal point of the house in which young Bessie grew up was the range, with its proliferation of blackened pots and pans but surrounded by a mirror-clean brass fender and other implements. Behind the net curtains were two rooms on the ground floor with a pantry, a narrow hallway and stairs leading to the upstairs bedrooms. For the Davies', as for many Station Terrace families, the principal piece of furniture was kept in the front room; a great high chest of drawers too big to be taken upstairs and packed full of clean sheets and other linen.

Whatever the hardships and shortages, and during World War I there were many, there was a great sense of community and satisfaction in the life of the colliers' row. There was little privacy but much sharing, which undoubtedly added to the warmth of feeling. Most of the households were matriarchal and informed by a strong sense of the rigours of Chapel. Perhaps not surprisingly for a policeman in a mining town, Enoch Davies was a Conservative voter. Merthyr, however, was the cradle of the British Labour movement and four years before the Davies' bought their house, Keir Hardie was elected for Merthyr as the first Labour Member of Parliament.

Meanwhile Mary, who had married a Staffordshire man, Frank Mountney, went to live in London but remained in occasional contact with her step-sister, Maggie. A few years after the war was over, she brought one of her sons down to Wales for a holiday with the half family he barely knew. Lewis Stanley Mountney, always known as Stan, was an intelligent, poetic man who had volunteered at eighteen after his two elder brothers had already been called up. He was badly shell-shocked in the trenches. From the end of the war he constantly suffered from a nervous twitch and his native patience disappeared. But he was struck by the teenage Bessie, a gentle, undemanding, essentially modest girl almost ten years his junior. He wasted little time in proposing and the following year the cousins were married in London. Margaret and Enoch were delighted that Bessie was marrying someone about whose family background they knew so much.

Little, however, was known of the Mountney origins. There are several versions of the name Mountney (Mounteney, Mountenay, etc) and all are believed to originate from Montigni in North-West France. In later years Laura was attracted by a romantic story that her family might have been descended from a French baronial family that had come over with William the Conqueror in 1066 and was rewarded for its support with lands, the 'Mounteney Levels' in the Pevensey district of Britain. There were Mounteneys who went to fight in the Crusades, and in the eighteenth century one Richard Mounteney became Baron of the Exchequer in Ireland. But whatever the historical possibilities there is no proven family connection between the Mountney family known to have been living in England from the early twelfth century and Lewis Stanley Mountney. In any case, on Bessie's wedding day in 1924, Margaret was concerned solely by the thought that her only daughter was going to live so far away in London. This brought on a weeping fit during the ceremony remembered by relatives for years. Margaret had been almost too good a mother to Bessie; at nineteen she was barely domesticated, her mother having spoiled her so. At first, this did not matter because Stan and Bessie began married life living with his parents in a house in Camden Road near Holloway. Stan worked as a clerk in the Civil Service, a job more menial than his potential before the war might have promised. Bessie knew no one in London, which must have intensified her feeling of 'Welshness', and when, within the year, she became pregnant, she knew immediately that she could not trust anyone in London to deliver her baby. She would return to Dowlais in plenty of time to ensure that the baby would be born safely in Wales.

There were two hospitals within walking distance of Station Terrace. But there were also Dr Cresswell and Nurse Harris. Even today in Dowlais Dr Cresswell is spoken of with awe as an almost God-like figure; his midwife assistant, Nurse Harris, hardly less so. That Bessie Mountney would await the arrival of her first child in the bed of the front room of 31 Station Terrace with Dr Cresswell and Nurse Harris in attendance was a foregone conclusion. The child, a girl, arrived without any problems on 7 September 1925, a Friday. She was called, simply, Laura, although there was no one else in the family with that name. It was a name her parents liked the sound of and it gave her the same initials as her father, who was so thrilled with his first child that for the first year of her life he bought her a small present every

6

day. She was dark-haired and flawlessly fair-skinned and so closely resembled her young mother that as she grew up they were often taken for sisters. As soon as Bessie was fit enough she returned to Holloway with her baby.

The family remained in Camden Road for a few years but when Laura was four they decided to move to a more salubrious area. Stan had one surviving elder brother, Ivor, who had recently bought a new house in an area of south London which, he told his brother, was convenient for work and yet still countrified. Beddington Park, near Croydon, in Surrey, was an area of massive development in the Twenties and Ivor persuaded his younger brother to buy a new house in a quiet road of flowering cherry trees near his own.

And so, in 1929 the Mountney family moved to south London to a semi-detached, pebble-dash house on the edge of Beddington Park. The house had a beautiful hundred-foot garden with a cluster of apple trees and lavender bushes and, inside, the best modern conveniences that the Twenties could offer. But as Laura grew up she discovered that one of its main attractions was its proximity to her childless aunt, Elsie. As two noisy brothers and a tomboy sister arrived in quick succession into the Mountney household, Laura learnt that the ability to construct an escape route, to find a means of creating her own sanctuary or place of perfect peace, was a vital element of life. Aunt Elsie was a mystery. Or perhaps not such a mystery. But part of her charm for Laura lay in believing that she had had a mildly exotic or romantically mysterious background.

Young Mrs Mountney, at twenty-eight the mother of four children, found life in Wallington, away from the bosom of her Welsh family, a continual struggle. Her youngest son, Trevor, was a problem baby who suffered from jaundice, a hernia and digestive problems. Mrs Mountney had to take him twice a week to hospital in London for tests and treatment. That was how the visits to Aunt Elsie began. But these soon took on a special meaning for Laura, who developed a close rapport with her aunt and welcomed every opportunity to spend time at her home. Soon Laura had her own bedroom at Aunt Elsie's house where she could revel in the peace and quiet away from the noise, bustle and mound of unfinished washing-up at her own home. Elsie Mountney was an orphan and Laura and her sister often wondered if her passion for fastidiousness, good taste and gentility betrayed an unknown but

7

aristocratic parentage. At all events Laura found that the atmosphere produced by the calm oasis enriched her soul. She was mature enough to realize that while money could be an important instrument to achieve this state, it was merely an instrument, not the source.

Aunt Elsie introduced her to books and brought her occasional frocks from 'Liberty'. At her aunt's house she could sit quietly reading for hours until tea, which was often served by Uncle Ivor from the best china on a tray with a starched traycloth. If Aunt Elsie took up her needlework it would always be very fine work with small, dainty stitches. Sometimes Laura would enjoy helping her aunt and uncle in their garden. Uncle Ivor grew wonderful raspberries because he covered them, plump potatoes because he limed the soil and abundant apples because he regularly sprayed the trees with insect repellent and secured neat, sticky bands around their trunks. In her own garden, no sooner was a trellis erected than her boisterous siblings would tear it down. Then her father, so long-suffering on occasions, would suddenly burst into one of his uncontrollable rages which the family attributed to his shattered nerves. Laura was such a model child that her aunt wanted formally to adopt her. Mrs Mountney drew the line at this.

Laura was no happier at school. The stone floors, dusty smells and small, pokey rooms oppressed her, making her feel acutely uncomfortable. Even at primary school, a small church school around the corner from her home, Laura was unusually aware of the effect of her surroundings. From this time she developed an intense dislike, verging on phobia, of dark, dank, smelly environments where large insects might be lurking. She grew terrified of spiders and mice and was convinced that both flourished in the school. In fact, Laura's school days were a series of agonies for her. Often she would run home at lunch time only to find that lunch was not ready; then Mary would be despatched to the nearest shop to buy potatoes while Laura would be twisted in anguish in case this made her late for afternoon school. On another occasion she wore a dress to school that her mother had very quickly sewn together with large tacking stitches the night before but the sleeve came undone on the way home. Another time her mother was pushing a pram along Croydon High Street when a wheel came off. Laura found these deeply shaming experiences which she never forgot.

In spite of these fears and worries that beset her childhood, Laura was not shy. As the eldest of the family she was often put in charge of the others – her sister Mary was barely allowed anywhere without her – and she took her responsibilities seriously. But she became self-effacing and quietly self-controlled, losing herself and her cares in romantic novels, the genteel world of Aunt Elsie and, increasingly, whenever she went for long breaks to her grandmother, at 31 Station Terrace, Dowlais.

Holidays in Wales were as much part of Laura's education as any formal schooling. She and Mary would be put on the train at Paddington, left in the charge of a guard, and were often met at Dowlais Station by a large party from the Terrace. Anyone from London was considered extremely special and visits from the little Mountney girls – one neatly serene and dark-haired, the other a blonde, blue-eyed tomboy – were eagerly awaited. Laura loved her holidays with Grandma Wales, as the girls called their grandmother. It was here, away from the brash newness of Thirties London suburbia, that she was able to transport herself to the world of late Victorian security. It was a world where neither moral values nor furniture had changed much in the previous fifty years. Sometimes the children went to the large covered market with Grandpa Enoch but, once he retired, he sat by the fire most of the day often making spills out of newspaper for the Robin Hood that sat on the mantelpiece. Uncle Trevor, their mother's much younger brother and at that time still a bachelor, was often at home and he, like the childless great-aunts, spoiled the two little girls gloriously.

But above all, they would watch the women, constantly working and ever cheerful, so unlike their mother. The water had to be carried through the house in a large, heavy pot where it was then kept on the fire boiling all day. Once a week coal was delivered and the women would fetch a small bath to carry it through the house, pack it exactly into the coalshed behind, then scrub the pavement and steps with warm water and a piece of slate to remove all traces of dirt. When this was done there were the fireplace, brass ornaments, implements and stair rods to be cleaned, or the impressive collection of Swansea china to be dusted. The aunts would never sit idly by the fire but always seemed to be mending, sewing patchwork or making rag rugs. Even frail Aunt Jessie, who had a bad chest ever since living in a damp basement while in service in London, had some form of handiwork in her lap. But she could do little more than cough all day long and her elder sister, Annie, would often spend the whole night helping her and comforting her, never knowing if that night might be her last.

The cooking was done by Grandma Wales herself and the girls' favourite was a yellow cake, literally dripping with eggs and butter. Their subsequent insistence that this tasted like nothing they had ever eaten in Wallington is evidence, perhaps, that memory was a potent ingredient. On Sundays the smell of roast Welsh lamb with freshly shelled peas pervaded the cottage for the whole day. There was, however, one job reserved for the children; collecting the milk in a jug which was brought to the door directly from the farm. The boundaries of these women's lives were family, chapel, cleanliness and orderliness; a very simple combination. They never went anywhere, other than for long walks, nor did anything 'exciting'. The excitement came from doing everything to the best of their abilities. Yet far from seeing themselves as domestic drudges, their toiling earned them the right to take decisions. They loved life intensely and wanted nothing more out of it. It was a philosophy Laura found very appealing.

Great-aunt Annie's husband, Uncle John Lloyd, often the only man in a household of women, undertook the young girls' Bible instruction. There was a painting in the front room and Uncle John Lloyd was not able to walk past it without pointing out its moral to the girls. The background to the picture was a darkly violent raging sea but visible through the middle was a path called 'The Straight and Narrow Way'. Women hanging on to crucifixes were trying to reach it and a line of poor people was travelling up towards the rainbow and heaven. But there were others who were drinking on the way up or misbehaving generally and several of their number were being pitchforked into fire. 'The wickedness of the world is entirely due to the wickedness of the people in it,' Uncle John would boom at the children. 'Keep to the straight and narrow.' After this lecture he would sit down at the table and continue reading his Bible. The starkly naive image was never forgotten by the impressionable girls. And the Devil, such a strong element of Laura's Welsh religious teaching, remained for her a real force in a daily battle against the world's many evil temptations.

Religion was a way of life for the Davies family. They attended the nearby Hebron Chapel where Mrs Davies had her own special door and where Laura and Mary were regularly called upon to recite. Their mother, until her marriage, had been a strict Baptist. On the day she was immersed, it was so cold they had to break the ice on the water.

'Weird extremism', Laura called that. Although the Mountney family attended church on Sunday morning in Wallington, Sunday afternoons were often spent walking to Croydon aerodrome where, if you climbed up on the roof, you could see the aeroplanes. Sundays in Dowlais were spent walking on the Brecon Beacons with discussions on the nature of good and evil or making expeditions to cemeteries where the party read headstones for an hour, punctuated by three visits to chapel. The minister called every Monday lunchtime to have a chat with all the family and, on Thursday evenings, The Band of Hope, trying to encourage other volunteers, gave a talk with slides of missionaries working in Africa – the cinema of the time. Yet Laura never resented this enforced religion. In later life she was convinced that her grandmother's trick of giving her, when she was quite young, a large butterscotch to suck during the sermon left her with an abiding taste that being in God's house was a sweet and pleasurable experience. The fact that the entire service was conducted in Welsh and she did not understand a word of it never worried her. It was only a question of creating the right atmosphere in which smell, taste and behaviour all played their part. For Laura, the Welsh 'atmosphere' began as soon as she stepped off the train and saw the bright, white sheets billowing on the wire lines stretched across the mountain side. Not simply Wales, but Victorian Wales, was the essence of Laura's life. For although the Victorian era had been over for at least thirty years, Laura believed that the ideals of cheerfulness and industry, loyalty and obedience were enshrined for ever in that perfect past she never knew but constantly sought to recreate. She went to other places for holidays, Pevensey, the Isle of Wight and Hayling Island for example, but it was in Wales, and Dowlais Top, that she acquired her deepest feelings about life.

In 1937, the Mountney family moved to West Croydon for a year, to look after her paternal grandfather. They did not sell their house but the move meant that Laura and her sister had to change schools. Old Mr Mountney died after six months but never was there any question that uprooting the children was a small price to pay for family duty and responsibility. The next year, 1938, seemed to promise far greater upheaval for the whole country as Europe moved to the brink of war, only to pull back at Munich in September. World politics may not have been a regular subject for discussion in the Mountney household but the Mountney brothers, working in Whitehall, were well aware that Wallington, with its proximity to Croydon aerodrome, was a prime target for German bombers. Lewis and Ivor had taken the precaution of erecting an electrically-heated Anderson shelter in their garden. Nonetheless on Friday, 1 September 1939, as the entire nation waited for Neville Chamberlain's announcement on the forthcoming war, Mr Mountney came home from work and told his wife and four children they were to go to Wales the next day. It was not to be the last time that Laura packed up and moved at less than twenty-four hours' notice.

2

Of Cheam and Chelsea

Although evacuation was entirely voluntary, thousands of families throughout Britain spent that first weekend in September packing into small cases their children's cherished possessions. Along with the best clothes and favourite toys went the new gas mask in its pristine case. Stations everywhere were crowded with stunned parents and dazed children, both weeping and wondering in whose house would they be billeted and would they ever see each other again? Train and bus crews worked overtime, many driving for thirty-six hours without a break, trying to shift Britain's juvenile population out of the danger areas as quickly as possible. Everybody's lives were turned upside down and no one knew what to expect.

Laura was one of the lucky ones. She, at least, was going with her mother to a house she already knew well. However, owing to the scramble to get to Wales, the Mountneys had to break their journey in Cardiff. It was a night Laura would never forget as Mrs Mountney insisted her children all slept in a cupboard to protect them, as she believed, from bombs. They arrived in Dowlais the next day unscathed. But this time Station Terrace was not as Laura had remembered it. Now there were ten people living in the terraced cottage: Mrs Mountney and her four children, Laura, Mary, Trevor and Francis; Uncle Trevor, who had by this time married a Carmarthen girl, Myfanwy, and their two children; and Grandma Wales. In a household ruled by women it was inevitable that three adult women in the house would result in frequent tension. And Uncle Trevor, now that he was married with his own children, could no longer make the two little London girls his sole focus of attention. At night, Laura and Mary were boarded out a few doors down the road at Aunt Ginny's. They shared a bed and often helped each other to fall asleep by singing hymns.

Number 31, however, contained one very special object; a radio. Grandma Wales was the first inhabitant of Station Terrace to have one, hired from Radio Rentals. At nine o'clock all the aunts, and occasionally other visitors, would gather in the front room to hear news from the front. 'Ooh!' they would groan at bad news. 'Bravo' they would applaud an advance. Uncle Trevor put up a map of Europe on the wall and stuck red pins in appropriate places. However, as many English schools were evacuated wholesale to the relative safety of Wales it was not as easy as the Mountneys had imagined for their daughters to attend the local secondary school. Dowlais itself was 'absolutely flooded' with children from Folkestone Grammar School. Laura was therefore sent to an 'establishment' in Aberdare, more of a secretarial college than a school; and so at fourteen her formal education was effectively over. The journey to Aberdare, only about ten miles away as the crow flies, was a long one over the mountains which required changing buses twice. But there was no choice. Almost all country schools suffered from too many pupils, too few books and too little equipment. As increasing numbers of teachers were called up educational standards inevitably dropped. Many fourteen and fifteen year olds absented themselves from school for a variety of reasons, ranging from the need to stand in food queues or tend baby siblings which their newly working mothers could no longer do, to having no shoes to wear. There were many stories of children with only one pair of shoes – due to war shortages more than poverty – and when these needed mending the children had to stay at home. The Aberdare school Laura attended was not a great success and she felt a keen sense of frustration at not being more involved in the war effort. Meanwhile her father, not yet old but in frail health, was finding life on his own in Wallington a struggle. In any case, after Christmas 1939 and in spite of the continuing dangers, many evacuated children started drifting back to city life. Fifteen-year-old Laura, having spent a year of disappointment in Wales, seized the opportunity to return and keep house for her father.

Her disillusionment at not finding the 'golden Wales' of her childhood memory served to strengthen her conviction that there had been such a golden age in the past and there would be more contentment to life if only that golden age could be recreated.

In her imagined memory, however, she skipped several generations by latching on to the Victorian era, of which she had no direct experience, as her idyll. 'I didn't set out to be Victorian but it was a time when people lived straightforward, basic lives, when everything was clear cut and respectable ... Respectability matters a lot to me.' How did Laura derive these visions of Victoriana? Reading the nineteenth-century classics fuelled her imaginative longing for a more perfect world; 'I think that one should attempt to be virtuous and improve oneself ... the way you live affects what you do,' she once told an American interviewer. She believed her aunts had grown up sheltered by the sort of close family life and calm ordered respectability she found in the novels of Jane Austen and Trollope, two of her favourite authors. But this culling of images from literature was selective and did not include the degradation, poverty and vice redolent of a Dickensian London slum. To her mind, the Victorian era symbolized gentle, gracious living, a time when standards, domestic and industrial, were at their highest and England at its best.

In 1940, however, these views were mere seeds which had yet to find their fertile ground. Once back in Wallington, Laura continued on a more mundane level with her secretarial training at Pitman's College in Croydon. This was in many ways a happy and maturing year; she discovered she loved housekeeping for a man who was both devoted to her and grateful. And it was not without significance that her first experience of domestic responsibility coincided with a period when so many goods were, officially at least, in short supply. This usually meant no supply at all. Making do with what there was developed in Laura an inventiveness as well as a natural cheerfulness in times of adversity. The house was peaceful now, with her younger siblings still in Wales and so she had plenty of time both for reflection and reading. She was still a rather solitary figure, preferring her own or her family's company to joining in activities with other girls. By the intelligent and thoughtful study of people she came to understand common human fears and needs to an extraordinary degree. Her preference for listening rather than for speaking helped her develop a deeper understanding of human motives than many of those who had enjoyed a formal training.

In 1941 Laura joined the newly formed GTC (Girls' Training Corps) and was promptly promoted to Sergeant. She was not tall, but had a trim figure which responded well to her navy-blue uniform and she liked the sense of purpose which she felt immediately she donned it. Her dark hair, brown eyes and small features were all perfectly set off by her delicate, pale skin. She had already acquired the gentle laugh, often a little giggle in conversation, which friends found so endearing. Her cheerfulness was reflected not only in this laugh but in her sweet smile with cheeks that slightly dimpled. At seventeen, Laura started her first job as a shorthand-typist in the Ministry of Health; an enviable position which her Uncle Ivor was instrumental in finding for his niece. Walking across the park to the station and travelling into town with such an attractive young lady was pure pleasure for him. For in spite of outward appearances which indicated a shy retiring girl, Laura was developing a confidence of purpose and certainty of direction in life. Those close to her recognized great strength of character beneath the soft and gentle exterior. 'If Laura had a fixation on something nothing would budge her. You knew you had to agree in the end or change the subject,' her sister recalled.

This small civil service taste of the outside world merely confirmed in her the growing self-knowledge that she could not be confined to suburbia and must find a way out as quickly as possible. Secretly, she applied to join the WRNS although on several occasions the women's branch of the Senior Service had announced that it was full and oversubscribed. While waiting for a decision on her application, she moved to a new typist's job, working for a man who ran an import-export leather business. Her uncle was bitterly disappointed at what he saw as a step down. But this was Laura's first strike for independence as it was a job she had found for herself. Evidently her boss thought highly of her as he presented her with an exquisite leather handbag at Christmas, which was the envy of her younger sister.

In 1943 Laura announced to the family that she had been accepted to join the WRNS and would be going away shortly to the training centre in north London. As the only one of the family actively involved in the war effort – the others were the wrong age – everyone was very proud of her. Uncle Ivor was sad that his accompanied trips into town had lasted so short a time. And she was leaving behind another man who took more than a passing interest in her. During her last year in Wallington, Laura had joined a youth club and went there some evenings for a dance, others for a game of table tennis but principally to meet boys. And there she encountered Bernard Ashley, who went principally to meet girls. A rumbustious, gangly but good-looking chap, Bernard was a year younger than Laura but equally driven. He was undisputed leader of his gang of friends. 'He always believed himself to be creative and different from the rest and expected us to recognize that,' one of the gang explained. Laura was fond of saying in later years 'The minute I set eyes on him I knew that this was the man I wanted to spend the rest of my life with.' But it was not so obvious to their friends that this pair of total opposites could possibly become an enduring partnership.

The Ashley family came originally from Bristol but, by the early part of the century, had dispersed throughout the country. Bernard's grandfather owned two small grocers shops, one in North London selling dry goods and wines, the other in Catford selling provisions and wines; both were called Ashley Stores. The next-door shop in Catford complemented their stock by selling dairy produce and game and was called John Sainsbury. Bernard's grandfather had a beautiful wife and two sons. But when his wife died at a young age, leaving him in charge of the boys, he sought the traditional solace of the alcohol he sold. Rarely a day passed when he did not consume excessively. As a consequence Bernard's father, Albert, was deeply ashamed of his own father and vowed total abstinence. In 1914 Albert volunteered for the Bicycle Regiment and served four years in France. He was involved in some of the bloodiest pushes for yet one more trench and was severely wounded four times. Amazingly, he survived and left the Army in 1918.

Almost immediately he met Bernard's mother, Hilda, at Peckham Tennis Club. Although her family was of Irish extraction they were living in Peckham where her father had a small engineering business which serviced the Royal Navy and therefore flourished. Bernard's grandmother toiled in the factory and, determined that no daughter of hers would work in service, enrolled young Hilda on a secretarial course. Albert saved what little he could of his soldier's pay, married Hilda in 1925, and, goaded by the aspirations of his ambitious new wife, severed all contact with his father and set up his own grocery store. It was above this shop in Beechdale Road, Brixton, that Bernard was born on 11 August 1926.

Bernard's mother, although small and terrier-like, could be amazonian in her ferocity. She was driven by ambition to leave Brixton and as soon as possible they opened a second shop in Wallington. She then despatched her husband to run the Brixton store while she, often single-handedly, undertook all the buying, selling, ordering and invoicing. The Wallington shop became home as there was a small parlour behind it and a tiny yard beyond that. The family lived above. Life for Albert and Hilda Ashley consisted of unremitting hard work which never allowed for holidays. Hilda had inherited her own mother's grim determination that the ladder to true happiness was social; her highest aspiration for Bernard was that he might become an insurance clerk but above all he must do better for himself than run a shop. To this end she made many sacrifices for his private education and, in addition, paid for elocution lessons. But in her struggle to rise in the world, to move away from Brixton and grocery shops, she devoted no time to her young son. She failed to understand him or ever to be aware of his interests. Friends remember how frequently she boxed him around the ears or threw out of the window intricate aeroplane models that he and his friends had spent hours constructing. Her aim was to make him something he would never be. Bernard resembled neither his mild and gentle father nor his strident, striving mother. True he was ambitious with a strong temper, but he was also a rebel who questioned the establishment, and a romantic who craved love and excitement. In Laura he found someone who would support him in whatever he wanted to do, would accept him the way he was for what he was (not for what he might become), love him unconditionally and nurture his hot-headed dreams.

In 1939, as Laura was moving away, the Ashley family moved in, able to take advantage of the slump in property prices. The Newlands, Wallington, was a wide, grass-verged road of large, detached suburban houses many of whose owners were selling up as quickly as possible through fear of bombing raids; it was about two miles away from Laura's family home. Bernard was then a pupil at Whitgift Middle, a minor public school which still exists under a different name, and not the more academic Whitgift Grammar to which his mother aspired. He boasted that he managed to get through his entire school career without passing a single exam. He excelled, however, in sports, captaining a rugger team amongst other achievements. When not at school he spent some time with his maternal grandfather, fascinated by his engineering business, and developed his own natural bent for anything mechanical. Otherwise he would endlessly take his bicycle to pieces only to reassemble it in order to race around Wallington with his friends, cocking a snook at authority wherever he found it. If ever one of them got into a scrape it was Bernard who was elected to talk them out of it. Not surprisingly girls were already attracted to this rather wild youth who did things other boys would not dare. One of his earliest childhood friends remembers well the day Bernard told him he was no longer allowed to play after school as his mother needed him to make deliveries for the shop. But Bernard suggested the friend could come with him. So the two boys set off on their bikes around the back streets of Wallington, Bernard knowing all the shortcuts and fast tracks, racing through people's back gardens if necessary and being utterly ruthless about the route he took. 'The point is that he made even a boring task like delivering groceries so totally enthralling that one would follow him regardless,' the friend remembered.

Other favourite high jinks were tipping a policeman's helmet in the river, his bicycle too if possible. When the gang found themselves jeered at by a more middle-class group of boy scouts, Bernard's response was to cut the guy ropes of their tents later that night. Once a cycling club with expensive equipment overtook the Wallington lads on their old jalopies. Bernard reacted by beating them at their own game. Summoning every ounce of energy, and without the proper kit, he peddled furiously uphill until, with sheer will, he had overtaken them. Stopping, one of the cycling club admired his skill and invited him to join. His real moment of glory was, of course, in refusing. 'He was a natural leader but he was also a rapscallion and devil. He made life exciting because he never did anything half-heartedly. We were all caught in his slipstream.'

Bernard and Laura met at an Air Cadets' dance at the youth club. Bernard and his friends thought they would liven up the proceedings by having a game of indoor rugger. Laura, terrified, spent the early part of the evening cowering behind a piano in the corner. But when someone enticed her out for a dance Bernard cut in. 'I was a bit of a yobbo,' Bernard confessed. 'But that, according to Laura, was the evening I got marked down.' Ever the strategist, she was apparently only dancing with someone else to make him notice her. Bernard took her home at five in the morning and later the next day they both went to morning service at Beddington Park Church, a visit that Bernard later claimed sealed his fate.

Both Bernard and Laura were of highly romantic age and disposition. Suddenly Bernard found himself in the company of a woman who was soft and admiring, receptive and sympathetic, all the qualities he found lacking at home. From that day, Laura never faltered in her love for him. Only eighteen, Bernard took longer to realize he was falling in love, but recognized that a profound change in his life was now possible. 'Laura never talked a lot, often she said nothing. But from the moment I first spoke to her she took me over and away from the hold my mother had on me,' he said years later. They dated a few times that autumn, often just getting together with the gang. 'Laura had a very winning personality and was good fun to be with but never silly or brash,' was how one friend described her at the time. She was one of the few girls accepted by the gang, many of whom felt she was much more at ease in male rather than female company. 'There were other girls brought along and we'd have to say "get rid of her" to whomever had brought her; but not Laura,' one friend of Bernard said. 'Other women were critical or bossy or felt themselves left out. Laura would simply laugh if one of the boys had had too much to drink or was driving too fast.' These recollections are, typically, men's talk. But it is interesting that Laura knew that to achieve what she really wanted in life, which was Bernard, she would willingly sacrifice much else which did not really interest her, such as independence. This was an instinctive feeling which she had yet to refine and articulate. She knew how to be pleasing to men and did not find it in the least degrading to flatter them or subserviently to boost their egos. On the contrary, she recognized that herein lay her path to true happiness. 'She treated me like a king, always. It was an extreme case of love,' said Bernard.

In later years she was fond of telling young girls who worked for her a story of how Bernard had once come to collect her for a dance, unexpectedly, on a motorbike. She had been to a hairdresser and was wearing a dress most unsuitable for a pillion passenger. But she acquiesced silently and uncomplainingly in his plans for the evening and never cared that her hairdo was ruined before arrival. Sometimes

Bernard was embarrassed by Laura's quirky style of dress. There was nothing remotely sophisticated nor sexy about her clothes and she always wore white ankle socks. All the other girls he had known would never be seen out with a boy unless their legs were stocking-clad. Notwithstanding her juvenile attire, Bernard was greatly impressed by her eleven months age advantage over him. 'I felt she was so mature, really much older than me, and I liked that.' Laura and Bernard spent the few months before they were both due to go off to the services endlessly discussing the future. Not in specific terms, such as marriage, but in general such as how they could harness their spirit of adventure to catapult them into the real world. According to Bernard: 'We were two suburban kids trying to break out of the Forties suburban mould. What we wanted was the whole world.'

On Christmas night 1943, Laura and Bernard talked and planned long into the small hours, a habit that was to continue for another forty years. They agreed to write to each other from wherever they were and, like millions of other couples, fervently prayed they would meet up again in a better world once the war was over. In spite of leaving school with no examination passes, Bernard applied for a commission and delighted his parents by being accepted first in the London Fusiliers and then sent almost immediately to India, attached to the First Gurkha Rifles. He asked his best friends to keep an eye on his girlfriend.

The next few months dragged on for Laura and she spent much of the time back in Dowlais. It was from Station Terrace that she bade farewell to her family on 8 March 1944, to begin her basic training with the WRNS. On arrival at the Mill Hill Training Depot all new recruits, called Pro-Wrens, were taken to a large requisitioned school. They were given an overall-type garment which they had to wear for the first few days while undergoing medical checks, including a search for head lice, about which Laura felt most indignant. She was not alone in being called upon to scrub and polish floors – or decks as they learnt to call them – on hands and knees at all hours. She learned not only to accept the discipline but the strange new world of custom and tradition dating back to Nelson's day. For two weeks Laura was put on a teleprinter course, learning how to send out a signal, short forms and quick ways of using words. It was here that she learned how to use a teleprinter switchboard and, also the most tedious, meaningless job-sending out messages in code. After various tests and examinations

Laura passed out and was given crossed flags to sew on her jacket. She was also given an injection and red ribbons to tie around her jacket to signal a very sore arm.

Now a trained Wren, ready for work, Laura and some of her friends were sent to Southsea, to another converted boarding school. This time there were mice in the cabins and although Laura had been allotted the bottom bunk she was so terrified that one of the little creatures might scurry into her bed that she preferred to share the narrow top bunk with her new friend, Margaret Boothroyd. Laura and Margaret enjoyed their waiting weeks at Southsea, visiting Portsmouth and, of course, HMS *Victory*. Finally, they saw their names on a list headed HMS *Dryad* ANCXF Although delighted to be together they had no idea where they were being sent; neither of the girls knew that the initials stood for Allied Naval Combined Expeditionary Force. They were soon taken to a magnificent country mansion where the D-Day landings were being planned. Here Admiral Ramsay addressed them: 'You have been picked for a very special job. Secrecy is critical and all letters will be censored. Your address will be Naval Party 1645.' But still they were given no clues as to what their job would entail.

The teleprinter room was in the cellar with a chute, down which the messages came from upstairs; there were direct lines to the Admiralty. Their living quarters, as they soon discovered, were still being built; long wooden huts with two-tier bunks near the house and about fifty girls to each long room. As they were all on different watches and with different jobs, there were always some sleeping while others were busily talking and changing shifts. Everyone soon learned to sleep through noise or else collapse as the work was arduous. Laura and Margaret, however, were always on the same watch and so they became the closest of friends. During the little free time they had they went out together and, occasionally, they took a liberty boat into Portsmouth. One night Laura and some friends went to Southsea Pier to hear Joe Loss; shortly afterwards the Pier closed and was used for landing the wounded from France until they were taken to hospital. Sometimes they played tennis, sunbathed or just went for walks. Occasionally they would go to a café with other friends and talk about life back home and boyfriends left behind. Laura often spoke of Bernard, her young man out in India, and her family, especially Aunt Elsie and Uncle Ivor. The correspondence between Laura and Bernard was erratic; Laura sent 'rather stiff, correct and formal little letters', as Bernard described them. Once she copied out the whole of 'Sea Fever', her favourite poem of the time, in a meticulously neat hand, to send to him.

It was a time of great socializing for Laura and she often found herself working alongside the daughters of aristocrats. During one walk she and Margaret met an American airman who turned out to be the pilot of General Eisenhower's personal plane. 'He wanted to take us up for a spin, but we daren't go – I wish we had now!' Margaret recalled years later. The girls were impressed by the many important faces they saw arriving at the country mansion. General Eisenhower and General Montgomery were often there meeting with Admiral Ramsay; King George VI and Winston Churchill also visited.

On 4 June 1944 everyone was addressed in the camp cinema and told that D-Day had had to be postponed because of bad weather. The following night Laura and Margaret were on duty watch when all the landing craft set sail. Before morning the field teleprinters were sending messages from the Normandy beaches; Operation Overlord, the allied invasion of France, had begun. During that day many of Britain's war cabinet visited the cellar where Laura was working to await the crucial first messages. 'We did not realize at the time we were making history.'

Further excitement was still to come. A few weeks later, as the allies pressed forward on the continent, volunteers were required to go to France. As she was under twenty-one, Laura needed her parents' permission for this. With growing pride in their daughter, they agreed. Saluted by the Navy as they left Portsmouth, Margaret and Laura were part of the first WRNS party to cross to the continent after D-Day. They were fully equipped with duffle coats, bell-bottom naval trousers and square rig as well as a navy-blue shirt and jersey – 'the capsule wardrobe', in Laura's later phraseology, that she believed every woman craved – also a green canvas bed, bucket, washbasin, bath and chair – all contained in a large green bag. Intoxicating indeed for a nineteen year old who had never before been abroad and Laura's principal emotion was elation, not fear. 'Our age, the job we had been called to do and the excitement all played a part in our being completely confident. The thought of going into the unknown, or death, never crossed our minds, we always thought we were on the winning side.' Both girls had fervent religious beliefs and frequently discussed how it was that their faith could sustain them through difficult times.

They docked on the Mulberry Harbour at Arromanches in Normandy and from there went by transport to Granville, a desolate old town where Laura and Margaret shared a room in a house in the old quarter. The field teleprinters were set up in a large factory nearby and the job started again. As they walked around the bomb-cratered town, the sight which shocked them most was women with shaven heads wearing headscarves. These women had fraternized with the Germans and 'in 1944 we were totally amazed that anyone could do such a thing'. From Normandy they went on to work near Paris, unbelievable luck they thought. Here they lived in a château, which had been German officers' quarters, and, as Laura and Margaret were among the first to arrive, one of their most enjoyable tasks was to tear down the many pictures of Hitler on every wall, making a large bonfire of them all. Margaret recalled those days: 'It was a fantastic time for us all, the French people were so very pleased we were there and nothing was too much trouble for us. The large hotels of Paris were open for dances, afternoon teas, hairdressing and manicure services at ridiculously low prices. All transport was free and whenever we were not on watch we made our way on the train to Paris or sometimes biked to Versailles.' The girls visited many French families, who invited them warmly to their homes, and they even managed a trip to the Paris Opera one night to see Samson. However, they had to leave before the end to catch a train or risk being late for their watch.

Not surprisingly, they were sad when the time came to leave Paris and move on to Brussels, which they found ordinary by comparison. Three of the girls lived in a garret of a house in Uccle, a Brussels suburb. They had fun decorating this themselves but were plagued with bombing raids which kept shattering their windows. At one point the Germans pushed ahead and rumours abounded that the Wrens might have to flee. But the Germans were driven back and the Wrens stayed on. The bombing never frightened Laura but when an interviewer asked her in later life if she wished she had been a man so she could have taken a more active role in the fighting she answered unequivocally, 'Oh no! I'm not like that. No, I don't think I could have coped with that.'

The spring and summer of 1945 were spent in Brussels and after VE Day the workload reduced and they had more free time. Among the many Belgian families who showed the young English girls the warmest possible welcome was one whom Bernard had urged Laura to meet.

Ever since Albert Ashley had been in Belgium during World War I, he had remained in contact with this family and now they welcomed Laura as if she were already an Ashley. Other families invited them to musical evenings in their *salons* or took them to the beach. For Laura, one of the most memorable aspects of her time in Brussels was joining the Church of England Choir of the Holy Trinity Church. This church, which today sits at the top of a road of night clubs, had naturally been without a choir throughout the war. But now there was no shortage of willing voices among the Wrens and some tenors and basses among English servicemen too. They met for rehearsals three times a week and were allowed to miss watch on Sunday mornings for church parades. Laura always responded to the formality of church services and the warmth of the emotion generated by the hymn singing sustained her.

After VJ Day the work was virtually over and the naval party moved on to Germany. But this time, Laura's father was unwilling to give permission for her to go. She did not question his decision. Probably he continued to look upon Germany as the source of his own injuries in World War I and would have been greatly pained by the thought of his daughter living there. Also Margaret, too, came home to England at that time as she was planning to marry and so the girls continued to work alongside each other for several more months in Chatham. In November 1945 Margaret wed and Laura was her bridesmaid.

Laura was demobbed in August 1946, in many ways a changed woman. Margaret had always considered her 'very mature' in coping with all the different situations in which they had found themselves. Another Wren remembered her as a 'dear sweet person [with] a shy habit of tilting her head to the side, a lovely quiet sense of humour – not given to hearty laughter and altogether oozing gentleness'. She adapted uncomplainingly to her new lacklustre life as an averages assessor in the City. She had a few boyfriends whom she saw occasionally, including a curate's son called Philip. But the focus of her life was waiting for Bernard to return from the Far East. Although he was back in England by 1947 he was not given his demobilization papers for several months; but Laura knew, even at twenty-two, that she was a patient person. They immediately rekindled their old friendship, even returning to Brussels one weekend as Laura wanted to share her wartime experiences with him. They revisited the family that had shown the British girls so much hospitality and Laura went to the piano and played it, as before. This upset Bernard; he was inexplicably jealous that a part of Laura from which he was excluded belonged to that house. She understood at once what had upset him and such was her faith in him that, in spite of all the music and singing in her childhood, from that day she never played the piano again. At the same time, he treated her to his highly generous and impulsive side; having saved up his mess money so that he had a grand total of £200, he now spent it all on Laura, 'to impress her'. Once back in England they continued to see each other most weekends, which became increasingly strained as their relationship developed. 'This weekend was very lonely and not very happy,' he wrote to her after a weekend spent at camp. '... All today I have been thinking about you and next weekend I think you had better wear a suit of armour.' Laura was happy to take her cue from Bernard: she could be passionately physical, romantically soft or gently maternal depending on his mood and needs. She never took it for granted that they were so much in love, but hoped the love affair would go on for ever.

When Bernard was finally given his release papers he was, like thousands of young men, desperately in need of work with no particular qualifications except military service. He had grown used both to command and to money, neither of which would he now willingly give up, and he had acquired some typical Gurkha attributes. Gurkhas are, according to a recent description, 'ferocious in attack, stubborn in defence and lovable at all times, except by those they are trying to kill'.* His natural scorn for excessive authority was, if anything, sharpened by his time in the army. Friends well remember the occasion when they left a pub at 10.30 pm and continued their revelling in the street. Some hapless reservist policeman approached them and requested their identity. Bernard, ever the natural leader, stepped forward and produced his papers, written entirely in Urdu, and communicated only in pidgin English.

His first job was as a clerk with a paint company. However, such was his boredom at counting pots of paint that he lasted only six months. Next, he found a post with an import-export agent, which lasted even less time, and then he was out of work. By now he and Laura were consorting regularly; he was briefly even supported by

* *The Economist*, 1988.

Laura whose earnings kept him in more than pipe tobacco. He had vague stirrings of an ambition to be an author and was thoroughly influenced by aggressively male writers such as Hemingway, Faulkner and Maugham. He started to keep a diary and a poetry book was always crammed into his pocket. But he needed a regular source of income and eventually found a job working for a small, family-run investment company in the City. He stayed there for four years and learned much about the need for money to make money.

Throughout those years Bernard and Laura continued to live at their respective parental homes. But if they considered suburbia before the war to be drab, by the late Forties it was far worse. Bernard was appalled by the spectacle of women who looked old at thirty, overcome by children and washing-up; many smoked forty Kensitas a day and were trapped in their homes of peeling wallpapers, de-stuffed sofas and utility furniture. He survived by going off camping as much as he could with his friends, but recognized how much more difficult it was for a girl to escape. He and Laura often met for lunch in the City and continued their endless talking and planning how things were going to be. He noticed that whenever he thrashed out a problem with Laura he always felt better about it afterwards. In a diary entry for September 1948 he wrote: 'I am confused about everything. Last night I told Laura about my feelings and how depressed I am. She told me – more or less – to use my guts about it. I spent all today thinking about this question – she is right.' Another day, after a City lunch with Laura, he wrote: 'After half an hour of getting nowhere we went into the church at Bishopsgate to pray. Afterwards everything was clear once more and it seemed so silly of me, having worried before.' Laura was exerting a more powerful influence over him than he could possibly ignore and was a rock-solid support for Bernard at that time. He was, according to his friends, highly restless and searching desperately for something which even he had not properly identified. He knew only that it entailed moving away from Wallington. He believed that in Laura he had found someone who would help in his search but, eleven months younger than she, he was not as certain as she was from the start.

By the end of 1948 they were both ready to get married, in spite of some opposition from his parents who thought it wrong to marry before you could afford to buy your own home, which they clearly could not. However, Laura was invited to the Ashleys' house where she underwent a trial by baking. This involved making a cake under Mrs Ashley's close supervision. As Laura survived this test Mrs Ashley then gave her some books to read, of which her own mother did not approve. The Mountneys, for their part, found Bernard rather wild and the family a little too English (as opposed to Welsh). The aggressive business woman that Mrs Ashley personified was an alien creature to Mrs Mountney. But they did not set any tests for their future son-in-law. In any case, Bernard was a dreamer who would never let mere parental disapproval interfere with his reveries; he was absolutely certain that Laura would help him fulfil them. 'My imagination running wild – into grandiose dream worlds to quiet firesides, to distant lands, was brought to a standstill as I turned the corner at the end of the green; for waiting there was Laura and in her my dreams seemed to crystallize and my imagination tucked itself away until I would leave her,' he wrote in his diary.

Bernard and Laura were married one freezing February day in 1949 at the Beddington Park Church where she had been confirmed. Bernard had spent the morning motorbiking on Tadworth Heath in an attempt to sober up after his stag party the night before. There were a few awkward moments during the wedding as the organist failed to arrive, but the shivering congregation sang lustily to no accompaniment 'Love Divine all Love's Excelling', Laura's favourite hymn. Bernard tried to avoid the photographer as he had just had some minor dental work carried out and Laura was concerned about a titled Wren friend she had invited who did not know any of the other hundred guests. They were entertained after the ceremony at The Grange, a large Victorian mock-Tudor mansion with huge grounds. For her going away outfit Laura chose a pale blue taffeta dress with an open neck showing three rows of choker pearls and a black straw hat perched on her head. But the couple did not 'go away' for very long. Although Bernard had requested cheques in lieu of wedding presents, three days in Seaford was all their meagre funds would cover. He had asked his parents if he might borrow their car for the honeymoon but the resounding 'No' was a clear pointer to the fact that Bernard and Laura were going to have to make their own way in the world. They moved into furnished rooms in Cheam at four pounds a week; but, with the unfaltering direction of homing pigeons, they knew exactly where they were aiming and, within a few weeks, had moved to an apartment in Drayton Gardens, Chelsea, furnished with elegant antiques and let to them by an elderly lady while she visited her son in Australia. Chelsea in the Fifties was decidedly and, as it turned out, decidingly different from Wallington in the Forties. Together, Bernard and Laura were ready to face the challenge of the post-war world. Separately, they were each a challenge for each other.

3

Children, Church and Countryside

The new Mrs Ashley had precisely formulated views on her role as housewife. Once the couple had settled into their third home together, an unfurnished flat in St George's Square, Pimlico, she handed in her notice at her City job to find work closer to home. More than a housewife, she was determined to be a 'husband-keeper' – Bernard's phrase – and for this reason she considered it essential that any job she might undertake would involve her leaving home after her husband, and returning before him. This was not only so that the domestic chores could be achieved, apparently without effort, and the evening meal prepared by the time Bernard returned, but so that he need never be aware that his wife was involved in work at all; something which always antagonized him. Already discernible were Bernard's incurably romantic notions of a wife's role in which Laura, the realist, willingly acquiesced.

The Headquarters of the National Federation of Women's Institutes was at Eccleston Street, Victoria, within walking distance from their flat. There Laura was offered a secretarial job in the handicrafts department. She was the perfect secretary; highly efficient, organized and calm and now she always looked immaculate. She made almost all her own clothes in those years and, by cleverly changing accessories, could transform just a few basic outfits. Everyone considered her attractive and well-groomed with hardly any make-up except a little eye shadow and lipstick. Friends recall that she was 'either knitting madly or had a dressmaking pattern spread out on the floor at home and she was a wonderful cook as well ... We talked about girlish things such as the best type of cleansing cream, but nothing very deep such as her ambitions in life or any worries. She was a very private sort of person.'

If Laura had worries at this time she did not betray them to anyone. She might have been worried about her failure to get pregnant; her mother had been twenty when Laura was born, yet by twenty-eight Laura was finding it difficult to conceive. She had intended to have babies as soon as she married and therefore never believed in the need for contraception – a view which she later had trouble in reconciling as her children and her work brought her into contact with a new generation of morals. But she never for a moment imagined that she would not one day successfully conceive. As she explained to her daughter years later, 'Falling in love is for having children, at least to me that is the only sense in the world because if you love someone that much of course you will want to have their child as a creative expression and, instinctively, one is attracted to a man who is strong enough to be able to share your protection of that child.'

She might also have been concerned about how to harness the energies of her increasingly restless husband. He was writing by night; short stories, magazine articles, and small sketches about people he met during his working week. But the rejection slips were becoming all too familiar. Creating excitement in life was far more of a spur to him than making money. Although he was not so foolish as to imagine that money had no importance, his greater fear was being forced to lead a boring life. After a visit to a London theatre one day he wrote in his diary that it must be as boring for the rich to 'live like they do as for a poor clerk living in a dull suburb. For if neither has the intelligence to avoid boredom it makes no difference to have money.' For the first few years of his marriage Bernard was convinced that in writing lay the key to his creating an exciting life. Sometimes he would take Laura on a pilgrimage to favourite literary haunts, such as Somerset Maugham's house in Vincent Square. 'The house was dingy and rather sordid. When I saw it I wondered how a man who has risen to such a position in the world of letters could have stuck it out for so long.' So important was it for Bernard to have the right atmosphere for writing that when he could not force his basement neighbours to keep quiet he decided that he and Laura must move. The alternative was an attic flat on the fifth floor of the same building. It was ninety-nine steps up with no lift, and consisted of three tiny rooms plus kitchen and bathroom.

Pimlico in the Fifties was, by Bernard's own description, 'full of streets that are almost slums, others are just sordid and now and then there is a square and some green and some trees and it's not so bad ... The pavements are fairly well covered by prostitutes who look as if they have been relegated there from the West End ... There are a number of artists living near the Thames and on the whole it is a jolly place.' They would have lived in Chelsea if they could have afforded it. But Pimlico had to do. It was as near as they could get to the centre of things. By day Bernard's work for the investment trust was giving him valuable insight into the workings of the City and a permanent view of the City 'type'. It taught him that he could never expect a place on the board and that he was temperamentally unsuited to working for someone else. Friends who visited them in their Pimlico days remember that there was almost always a new scheme being talked about and an unswerving determination that one day they would be 'doing their own thing'. Bernard adored jazz, would listen to Acker Bilk endlessly and wanted to try and run a chain of jazz clubs. Another idea was to sell tweeds to America.

After a few years, Laura changed jobs and was now secretary to the First Secretary at the Pakistan High Commission. But she continued to attend courses run by the Women's Institutes and never lost a deep-seated feeling of warmth for the organization. 'To hear 5,000 members singing "Jerusalem" in the Albert Hall is to render me personally quite helpless and one of those moments when God's presence feels very near,' she wrote. The WI woman remained forever Laura's *alter ego*. Sometimes she would attend evening classes and lectures while Bernard closeted himself away in the small back room writing. Although these were never intended by her to be vocational, they were crucial for developing and defining her quiet, native good taste.

In March 1952 the Women's Institute organized a major display of traditional handicrafts at the Victoria and Albert Museum. The work on show included embroidery, hand-printed fabric, hand-woven material, patchwork and quilts. Although she had already been exposed to the high calibre of women's domestic work through her job as secretary to the examinations organizer, she was now captivated by the discovery that crafts produced by home-based women like herself were of 'museum standard'. This time she was goaded into action and wanted to make some of the exquisite patchworks herself which she had watched her aunts in Wales painstakingly assemble. She started to search the shops for fabrics with small prints, diminutive stripes or flowers in one colour which would be suitable for patchwork, but was dismayed to find they did not exist. She let the idea drift for almost a year until, in the spring of 1953, after a visit to a gynaecologist who corrected a minor problem, she finally established a stable pregnancy. As she was advised to rest as much as she could, sewing was an obvious way to pass the waiting days and weeks. Now, for the first time, she even contemplated how she might be able to print some of her own fabrics that would be suitable for the patchworks.

According to some later versions of the story, this was when Laura Ashley started printing with potato or lino cuts; yet although the facts do not bear this out, in a sense the myth need not be destroyed. She might well have experimented with such simple methods since she had absolutely no other knowledge of how to set about printing. But, at another level, it is significant that the Ashleys' subsequent huge success was not built merely on child's play. Although in 1953 they had no clue about the methods of transferring colour on to fabric, they always knew, much more importantly, how to acquire knowledge. Laura borrowed several library books from which she gleaned that the essential prerequisite was the ability to build a silk screen. And here at last was something for which Bernard's childhood interest in engineering had prepared him. Desperately eager to work with his hands, he snatched the book from his wife and within a month had constructed their first textile printing screen stencil. At the same time he made contact with a teacher from Chelsea Art College and devoured everything he could about printing methods. All this was, of course, in the evenings; it was still far too premature to consider giving up his job.

It was a lucky coincidence that, just at this time, Bernard's younger brother Geoff, had left school and, now waiting for his army papers to be processed, had come to live with Laura and Bernard, sleeping on a sofa. As Laura became increasingly immobilized by her advancing pregnancy, he provided a valuable extra pair of hands. He too was caught up not only in the numerous discussions, intensified by the knowledge of Laura and Bernard's impending parenthood, as to exactly what they could do to make a success of their lives, but in his older brother's surge of enthusiasm which made even the most tedious work seem pure fun.

The spring and summer of 1953 was the most exciting time of their lives. There was office work all day, with experimenting, planning and building all night. As neither of them could draw, the first designs were basic polka dots, stripes and noughts and crosses grids. Bernard adapted the now famous kitchen table as a printing base by covering its scrubbed, wooden top with a felt blanket and a plasticized cover to hold the material securely in place. Once they had bought their first roll of cloth, which Bernard ordered from a supplier in Lancashire while he was still working in the City, and the dyestuffs from Skilbecks in Upper Thames Street, London, they were ready to start printing on his handmade screen. Bernard had spread wires all around the attic dining room to hang the squares for drying and had also made a rack with wires to fit in their small kitchen oven. The squares would be attached to the rack in order to fix the dyes by baking them in the oven. A cupboard was turned into a darkroom and Bernard had by now taught himself all he needed to know about developing and printing. When they were utterly exhausted they would revive themselves by going to Dolphin Square for a midnight game of squash or a swim; Laura would often stay behind reading. A few months previously they had entertained the Pakistani High Commissioner for dinner in their sparsely furnished flat. But there was neither time nor space for any kind of social life now. They often went to the cinema and the film *Dillinger* impressed itself above all others with the eponymous hero temporarily becoming Bernard's glorified role model. It was in this buoyant mood that they decided to go to Italy for a holiday before the birth of their first child. Italy in 1953 was a typically adventurous choice. Their lifestyle had advanced a long way in the four years since Wallington.

This holiday was to have important repercussions because it coincided with Audrey Hepburn's rise to fame in the film, *Roman Holiday*. Young Italian girls everywhere sported the simple little sweater scarves that she had knotted around her neck in the film. Laura and Bernard brought a few of these home and, since they had already set up the equipment for printing, but had not thought of scarves, they returned to their small flat with renewed vigour. As the table's width limited the length of the screen used, fabric had to be cut into single squares, and as there was no means of continuous printing, each square formed a single design. Table mats and scarves, both conveniently sized small items, were cut, hemmed first and then printed. Laura's original idea of small stripes and miniature flowers proved far too intricate for Bernard's silk screen and had to be abandoned in favour of bold geometric shapes in bright colours. But, as Laura said with typical modesty years later, 'They just happened to be what the market wanted at the time.' A week after production had begun Bernard sold six linen table mats with a two-colour African print to a handicraft shop in Ludgate Circus. The order was worth one pound. The enterprise was underway. The original investment in the business was ten pounds spent on wood for the screen frame, dyes and a few yards of linen. As yet, they could only afford to order one roll of each fabric at a time but cotton and silk were added shortly afterwards as this fabric was needed to make the twenty-one-inch women's headsquares. Thus the decision to use only natural fabrics was as old as the business itself.

Far from giving up work in order to await the birth of her first baby quietly, in these few months Laura was charging around more busily than ever. She undertook hemming the squares, attaching the small label 'Ashley', packing and invoicing as well as any other administrative tasks that were necessary. She was also called upon to do some selling, the very idea of which she viewed with horror. One morning after Bernard went off to work, Laura took the bus to John Lewis, in Oxford Street. It was the biggest department store in London and had a newly-opened boutique on the third floor. 'I was rather nervous so I went into the furniture department first and walked around to get some strength and pluck up courage. While I was there an assistant came over and asked if I needed any help. When I explained what I was doing she said "Oh! but these are absolutely charming," and picked up the telephone to ask for the boutique buyer. She described me as a charming young art student with some absolutely delightful scarves to sell. Although I had arrived with no appointment; the appointment was made for me.' To Laura's immense relief the buyer agreed to take two dozen on a sale or return basis without Laura having to say a single word. Within hours of Laura returning home these had sold and the buyer immediately ordered seventy-two more, an enormous amount for a fledgling company. Indeed it was the limit of their capacity for one evening. When Bernard came home they immediately set to making the scarves for the next day. The three of them were up all night but the order was fulfilled. Bernard delivered them on his motorcycle on his way into work. Twenty-four hours later it was repeated.

In September Bernard decided to leave his job in the City in time for the Christmas season. Over the next few weeks production rose along with their confidence and they sold to other shops. Many were the scorched squares that had caught in the corner at the back of the oven; if they were not too badly burned, they could usually be sold cheaply in the little shops in the City where they quickly became high fashion for secretaries. The best ones were sold at John Lewis, Peter Jones, Heals and Woollands, priced at three shillings each.

Later that month, Laura was summoned into St Thomas's Hospital where she had to remain for two weeks with high blood pressure. Bernard and Laura's first child, Laura Jane, was born on 1 October 1953, after a difficult birth which left the mother exhausted, and, for the first time in her life, depressed. When she returned home it was to find her flat transformed into a factory. The dining room was now the print works where dyestuffs were weighed and mixed, the table remained as the printing surface and ever more wires around the room acted as drying lines. The living room had become an office, studio, warehouse and canteen and the kitchen was used for curing and finishing. The bedroom was the only more or less comfortable room in the flat with the landing doubling up as dining room and Geoff's sleeping area. Laura went out as little as possible because she dreaded having to trudge up the ninety-nine steps home with baby and shopping, and she felt some misgivings that her idea had ended up with so much disruption to their lives, whereas hitherto all their dreams had centred on Bernard's writing. However, between April 1953 and Christmas that year sales amounted to almost £1,500. Early in 1954 Geoff left to join the Army and so several of Laura's girlfriends, as well as her sister Mary, were occasionally cajoled into helping tide them over busy periods. Once Jane began crawling, she participated too by tasting the dyes; and friends remember her with splodges of paint spilling out of her mouth on to her clothes. The attractions of remaining in the flat were obvious as overheads could be kept to a minimum – the major cost was heating the oven for long periods.

But early in 1954 Laura was pregnant again and Bernard realized it was therefore imperative to find larger printing premises. A few blocks away, he discovered a large basement in Cambridge Street, SW1, for three pounds a week. It consisted of a large back room and a smaller front room and it was here at last that he was able to put some of his engineering ideas into practice. On 19 March 1954, Laura and Bernard formed the Ashley Mountney Company – a name which indicated it was to be a true partnership. The company had a capital of £500. In registering the company it was stated that its purpose was: 'to carry on all or any of the businesses of manufacturers and dealers in textile and fibrous fabrics and substances of all kinds', a description that indicated they were not prepared to limit their horizons at this juncture.

In April, the couple bought their first car, a battered old van costing thirty pounds. It was, Laura said, 'the only thing taxis would make way for'. Bernard spent from May to September building machinery for Cambridge Street at his grandfather's engineering factory, aiming to develop his own continuous printing machine. There was an office-cum-design studio in the small room while dyes were mixed in an adjacent alcove. Bernard now expanded these to a range of some twenty colours, including not only the bright primaries but the more sludgy blues and browns which were to become a 'Laura Ashley' hallmark. More significantly, within a few months he had designed a massive machine which took up almost the entire space in the large room and which could print cloth continuously. The cloth was drawn from a feed roller across a table bed where it was printed, then drawn under drying lamps and afterwards rolled up. At first he did not have a suitable curing and fixing oven so he used to take the fabrics to a commercial oven. But soon he had constructed his own electric curing oven. As he also mixed his own dyestuffs, with variable results, the capital outlay was still minimal. These machines left barely enough space for people to squeeze past and operate them but having a continuous printer in operation represented a huge breakthrough. Without the cash to buy such a machine Ashley Mountney would probably have atrophied; only Bernard's application and engineering skills drove them on to the next stage.

In November 1954 David was born at home in the attic flat. Although it was a much more straightforward birth, with two children under two Laura was hardly able to help with the business. In any case, the company was slowly moving in a different direction. With Bernard's new continuous printer, weekly production could now average almost 300 metres per week. And he was designing some of his own furnishing fabrics for hotels, institutions and cruise ships. These sold as Bernard Ashley Fabrics and could not have been further removed from Laura's original conception of tiny prints. For the first time the company now began hiring staff; two local artist friends helped with the printing on an occasional basis but a graphics graduate from Camberwell Art College was soon employed on a full-time basis. She had to help with the artwork, prepare silkscreens and take care of the office work. Among early customers for Bernard Ashley Designs were the P & O shipping line, which required vast quantities for decorating ballrooms and dining rooms on their cruise ships, and Terence Conran, one of the brightest new names in furniture design. The fabrics Bernard produced for these customers were brash, modern, bright abstracts which required little artistic skills. But after so much drabness and post-war austerity they were seized upon as conveying an optimistically bright mood for the future. A black and white jazz fabric was a good example of Bernard combining his two interests of jazz and photography; it contained details such as a keyboard, drum unit, fingers on the fret of a guitar or on the valves of a trumpet – all transposed from photographs. The commission from P & O was, of course, of major significance for a new company but it was never enough for Bernard. He was constantly stretching himself, looking for new markets into which to sell his products or for refinements to his machinery.

In some ways, that such a young company could win such significant orders begs belief. But the climate in the early Fifties, in the aftermath of the Festival of Britain, was highly receptive to new ideas from designers and architects. It did not seem to matter that there was a paucity of retail spending money; suddenly there was an awareness of design at the wholesale level. 'The post-war shortages created an enormous need,' Terence Conran explained, 'therefore anything that came into the shops could sell and the retailers almost did not have to try. But in the late Fifties, early Sixties, as needs turned to wants, then the designers could flourish because they had a solid base to build on.' In addition to the optimistic mood of the moment (1955 saw the opening of Mary Quant's trendsetting 'Bazaar' with a shop front in Knightsbridge Green designed by Terence Conran), there was the personality of Bernard himself, which was crucial at this stage to the company's development. Bernard was a salesman with an extremely high profile who made sure he got himself known. 'Bernard was always there,' reminisced Terence Conran. 'When I started The Soup Kitchen in Chelsea in 1954, there was Bernard, a most unlikely figure because of his military tendencies and bearing in a world of creativity. We always thought he was a bit of a joker at that time. He was very ambitious with grand plans but we wondered what there was behind it. He already behaved as if he were bigger than the Courtauld Group.'

Another friend who met him through The Soup Kitchen was equally impressed by Bernard's vision. 'If only I could run the machine for three or four hours continuously I know I'd be a millionaire,' he would say to furniture designer, Peter Brunn. While other designers were happy just to do something that they enjoyed, Bernard was always looking for something more; better ways to print as well as producing more cloth. 'I had a lot of design friends at that time and Bernard stood out head and shoulders above them all,' commented Brunn. 'He combined so many different qualities. He had an astute business brain developed by his city training; he was always very dedicated and worked like stink and on the technical side he did things very cleverly because he was not shackled by a training. If he had been 100 per cent engineer he might have been daunted by the difficulties of what he was trying to achieve.' He was constantly throwing out new ideas and projects, for example he wanted to use sprays instead of screens to print, passing the fabric under the spray for a random design. Brunn remembers the tremendous sense of achievement when Bernard invented a machine, mounted on Dexion, with a motor and sensors to monitor the movement of fabric. 'He was an inspiration to me because of his positive outlook, he never considered the possibility of failure.' As early as the mid-Fifties, Bernard and Peter contemplated a joint venture selling wallpaper. They saw a gap in the market and even went as far as producing a sample book of very modern designs. But although they had a warm response from many of the Chelsea and Knightsbridge decorator showrooms, none was prepared to hold stock and so the idea died.

It was almost as if the throbbing production at Cambridge Street ran on nervous energy. But despite the constant activity it was not without its problems. There was an appalling smell of chemicals, in the street as well as in the rest of the building, and other tenants complained.

One day Bernard visited an officer in the Royal Army Medical Corps, which had its offices on the floor above, and could hardly see the man through the fumes which had risen from his own workshop. They might nonetheless have avoided the attentions of the police completely had it not been for the heat emitted by the ovens and machinery. This made it a favourable waiting place at night for prostitutes, who regularly stood on the glass panes embedded in the pavement waiting for customers. But Bernard was able to talk himself out of every corner and production continued.

Laura would have been the first to admit that for the two years when she lived in London with two babies she could have little practical involvement in the business. After her one success at John Lewis she never undertook selling again. But she did not need to. Bernard was enjoying a small success with the fashion industry, mostly printing headscarves. Even so, it appeared as if the company's future at this juncture lay in contract printing of furnishing fabrics. And then the Ashleys started printing the first linen tea towels with Victorian themes, which were an immediate, huge success.

'No one can now recall why we first printed Victorian subjects,' Laura once wrote in an attempt at producing a company memoir. But then she crossed this out and, according to the new version, said it was Bernard who caught sight of an old theatre playbill from the turn of the century and, because it was the right shape and he liked the old typeface, decided to print it. This started them on a run of Victorian subjects, which Laura was deputed to research. She found she enjoyed her increasingly regular visits to old booksellers in the Charing Cross Road and usually knew exactly what she wanted before she arrived. This marked the beginning of her ability to translate into her products her feelings about life. But although the orders were impressive, the Ashleys allowed themselves virtually no spending money. Any extra cash they made went back into the business with Bernard already dreaming of one day being able to buy a Buser printing machine.

Then an advertisement in *The Sunday Times* transformed Laura's life. A small cottage on the Kent/Surrey borders was available for rent at only thirty shillings a week. It was part of Trevereux Manor Estate and Laura thought it would provide a peaceful home for her and the children yet be close enough for Bernard to commute into London. Set at the foot of a gentle escarpment of woods and fields just south of

Limpsfield Chart and attached to an arable farm, the tied cottage was a dramatic change from Pimlico. It was built of locally quarried stone, with wooden beams and leaded light windows. It was small and in a poor state of repair with damp patches and peeling wallpaper which the Ashleys never had any money to repair. But the surroundings were idyllic as the house boasted its own orchard and kitchen garden and afforded breathtaking views of fields and parkland from all directions.

Since the fourteenth century, Limpsfield Common has provided grazing for villagers' animals, as well as gorse turves and dead wood for cottage fires, and bracken and heather for animal bedding. Stone could be quarried and timber cut for repairing the cottages and fences. The common is bordered by the densely wooded High Chart, so-called because the villagers have long-standing wooding rights there. Although by the twentieth century Limpsfield had undergone certain modifications to accommodate modern life, the village retained much of its old-fashioned identity and character thanks largely to the un-changing nature of the surrounding commons, woods and farms. 'The cottage,' wrote Bernard, 'was as much a birthplace for Laura's philo-sophy on design and living as my Pimlico basement was for my ideas on machines. Although her childhood was largely spent walking over the mountains behind Merthyr Tydfil ... it was the ... hedgerows and small fields of rural Surrey that began to shape her ideas more fully.'

For a young mother with two babies, living at East Cottage could have become a nightmare of isolation and loneliness. But Laura thrived on her own company and one of her closest girlfriends, Jeanne Watters, came to stay regularly at weekends. 'Aunty Jeanne' as the children called her, often helped by looking after Jane and David so that Laura was again free to see to business and other administrative tasks. 'Laura worked so hard,' Jeanne recalled, 'that finding time to be with the children was the most difficult thing for her. They were both very wrapped up in the business by now.' Laura's sister, Mary, who had married one of Bernard's childhood friends, David Coates, but who did not have children of her own, and her mother, Mrs Mountney, both came regularly to help out. Occasionally Laura took advantage of their visits to attend a local WI meeting.

Living in the countryside seemed to release Laura's natural interest in all forms of rural life; she would spend hours roaming in the fields picking wildflowers, inventing names for them and always had dozens of books on gardening and flowers to hand. 'Everything I know I've learnt from books,' she would tell Jeanne, who considered that there was a fundamental depth to Laura which ripened and matured in these wild surroundings. She was utterly unflappable and calm with her husband, children and business no matter what the crisis. She kept goats in the orchard, which she milked at six every morning (learning the technique from a book, as ever), collected fuel from the woods as villagers had done for centuries, and grew a healthy crop of potatoes and other vegetables. She longed to be self-sufficient, considering it a real challenge to manage on thirty shillings housekeeping per week. Friends would often arrive to find Laura sitting on the doorstep preparing vegetables she had grown herself. Although she always wore a skirt and twinset, hardly ever trousers, she would cover her clothes with a smock for work.

To label East Cottage simple and unpretentious, while explaining its rustic charm, is to undervalue Laura's struggle there. Today a family living in such conditions would be considered to be existing below the poverty line. The Ashleys drank out of jam-jars and the children, as well as Laura herself, sometimes wandered around without shoes. The latter caused quite a stir in the village, where some of the old-established residents felt that this gypsy-like family should be made to tend their children better. None of this worried Laura. Her life in Limpsfield was greatly enriched by her close involvement with the local church, and its forward-thinking young vicar, Father Reg Fletcher. Very soon Laura was put in charge of the youngest class at Sunday School, an experience which, once she overcame her initial nervousness, she enjoyed very much. Other mothers remember how talented she was at suggesting new models to make with the children, such as boats out of balsa wood, which they all considered most original. Sunday was a high point in her week 'until one day the rector telephoned to say that he had gone down with influenza and would I take the service. Imagining that I could pass this task on to Bernard I said "Yes, do go back to bed." But Bernard said "No, you have to do it yourself."' Of course, Laura managed it admirably.

Although life was austere Laura managed with a cheerfulness that her friends still remark upon. 'We were all terribly hard up; there were no frills like books, records, holidays or cinemas but she was a very non-materialistic person and so the lack of money didn't worry her at all.'

Her own children attended the local Church of England primary school which required them to undertake a rigorous walk to the top of the hill and then catch a bus. This was quite a hike, which she and the children managed uncomplainingly. She was noticed for her unusual clothes. At a time when women went to church in their smart, if rather severe Sunday best, Laura would arrive in ankle length, flowing jumble sale-ish outfits, with her long wispy hair piled up in a 'beehive'. 'She was just very natural, and, we all thought, ahead of her time in many of her ideas.' One of these was her belief that children from the new council estates (several of which were built around Limpsfield in the mid-Fifties to help those finding their feet as they emerged from the forces), should be mixed in the same Sunday School classes as those from a traditional, aristocratic or landed gentry background. This was greeted as a radical proposal but the idea eventually won through after considerable argument.

Within a year of moving to the country, she was again pregnant. David and Jane were, of necessity, given considerable independence and life for them at East Cottage was, in many ways, a child's paradise. They were allowed to roam free with the animals and were expected to entertain themselves with whatever nature had to offer. Laura would do all the business and administrative work that was required of her in the evenings. From about 4.30 pm onwards if it was light, she would dig potatoes and milk the goats and then settle down to type invoices, pack goods, inspect or hem tea towels as she firmly believed a mother should not work while her children were around. Thus the children were sent to bed at 4.30 pm, in summer and winter alike and told simply that it was night time. Once David was old enough to tell the time he realized they were being sent to bed in the middle of the afternoon and were expected to lie quietly until morning even if they could not actually sleep. But they never rebelled. 'You didn't dare; if you had a father like mine sleeping next door you'd sleep through the night,' David jokes today. The children believe their father treated them like an army of mini-Gurkhas, who must at all times do as ordered and then everything would be fine.

Laura would always stand united with her husband but was the first to defend her children if she thought they were being threatened by outsiders. David recalled: 'My mother badly wanted me to be a typical Welsh schoolboy of the Thirties, not a rough English Fifties school child. So she made me wear a cap to school in Kent, although the school did not make this compulsory, and she insisted that I raised it to adults or older boys who passed by.' Inevitably David was teased cruelly and often his cap was taken from him and thrown high up into the trees. At first Laura, clinging to the symbols of a disappearing age, told him to persevere but when she saw for herself how her son was being bullied she complained to the school and David never had to wear a cap again.

If the core of Laura's life in the Fifties was church, children and countryside, embracing all these concerns was the family's expanding textile printing business. The month that they moved to the country, *House and Garden,* like everyone else hungry for new ideas, gave the young company its first taste of publicity. An article entitled 'Good Mixers', featured Bernard Ashley's cotton 'Plaza' design in which the charcoal coloured jigsaw shapes were silhouetted against a white background and the thirty-six-inch wide fabric sold for fifteen shillings a yard at Woollands. *House and Garden* continued to give Bernard Ashley Fabrics regular coverage for the next few issues. In October an editorial praised Ashley Mountney tablemats and household linens; a tablecloth designed with thick black irregular lines on white linen and costing six shillings and eleven pence, was one of the gifts chosen for good looks and good quality. The publicity was of enormous value and, by the end of 1955, a collection of about 200 accounts had been built up, together with frequent enquiries from overseas. Laura and Bernard decided therefore to take a showroom in Old Burlington Street, at the heart of London's wholesale textile trade. This was a comfortable suite of rooms which Bernard converted to look very impressive and he hired a secretary. One of the first visitors was a buyer from San Francisco who ordered the complete collection of Victorian tea towels for shipment on a continuous basis. Bernard travelled the country at this stage, trying to build up the number of wholesale outlets; it was a time when dozens of kitchen and craft shops were opening, all with rapacious appetites for new, original products. The Ashleys supplied them with their scarves and tea towels and soon found themselves being asked for various other household items.

The timing could not have been better. The Fifties housewife was being targeted from a number of angles. In the contemporary, servantless household more and more women had to undertake many domestic chores which would have been inconceivable to an earlier generation. The woman's role at home was being glorified, partly to prevent her from flooding the workplace, and yet no one could escape the fact that the tasks she was being expected to do were achingly boring. Increasing prosperity gave a handle to advertisers to make products more attractive and at the same time there was a relentless drive for higher standards. Thus in 1956 the Ashleys began printing cotton drill and making it up into aprons and oven gloves. 'Our favourite cotton drill (the same fabric used extensively by the British Army for a great many years) ... was to be very important to us from then on,' Laura wrote.

However, 1956 was also the year of the Suez crisis and ensuing petrol shortages, which made not only daily commuting to London from Kent impossible, but also severely threatened Bernard's ability to sell. He knew he had to find new premises nearby as quickly as possible and, in any case, the steady expansion of the company meant that the Pimlico works had been outgrown. Three important events occurred in January 1957: Bernard bought a motor cycle at Pride and Clarke in Clapham, their second son Nick, called after a favourite character in a Hemingway book, was born on 15 January, and new premises were found in an old coach house at Brasted, four miles from Limpsfield on the banks of the River Darent. The coach house with its cobbled floor and arched ceiling offered approximately 3,000 sq. ft. of space, ample room to accommodate the various stages of fabrication for the different products, as well as the much larger printing machine Bernard was busy building at the workshop next door to East Cottage. They now employed two school leavers who were expected to learn all aspects of the business as quickly as possible to leave Bernard free for selling and engineering. At the same time three or four women outworkers were found by Laura to help with the sewing. These local women were, like her, married with families and she saw it as a way of providing them with extra income without taking them away from their families, which she believed was morally wrong.

Laura cared deeply about the home circumstances of people she employed and always believed that those years, when they had to begin employing others, 'changed our lives more than almost anything else had because we were now responsible for the working conditions of others'. Laura wrote later, 'One of the things to admire about my husband is that he has truly put his employees' welfare first, as any modern employer must, and so has created a good company of people – more like a family. He still turns to The Bible when in doubt about acting fairly.'

Although Bernard was constantly refining his printer so that production could be stepped up, technical problems remained with the finish on the furnishing fabrics. The flatbed printer had difficulty in registering individual repeats and this often led to flaws and inconsistencies in continuous patterns. It was still possible to produce furnishing fabrics, but the quantities were limited by the problem with the repeat. This was a nuisance. But Bernard was determined to resolve it and, in the meantime, concentrated on products which could be produced on a continuous roll of cloth but which would consist of a single panel. The tea towels were extraordinarily popular, they could never build up a stock but sold everything they could produce and any printing flaws on them merely added to their authenticity. Most of the Victorian images Laura discovered from books, posters and other ephemera were mildly humorous. One best-selling style was a theatre bill announcing the commencement of a new season at the Adelphi Theatre on 7 October 1822 'when will be reproduced the Burletta "Tom and Jerry" or life in London, of which so many distorted shadows have appeared'. Another, Edwardian in flavour, showed a group of respectable gentlemen with the words 'Anyone for washing up', below. These tea towels, used as much for display as for drying up, were soon selling in major department stores worldwide including Myers in Sydney, Metz and Co in Amsterdam, Globus in Zurich, Galerie Lafayette in Paris and Macy's in New York. Ashley Mountney bar towels, as they were called, won a gold medal for good design at the Sacramento Trade Fair. In the UK the cloths cost between two shillings and sixpence and four shillings and eleven pence, depending on whether they were cotton or linen. They were almost all black on white but some experimentation was being done with black writing on a coloured background. A few stores such as Harrods and Fortnum and Mason soon asked the company to print 'specials' with their own company names or images. Although several thousand were printed each week Bernard still looked on them as a sideline while he rectified the problem with the repeat. Such a domestic product had better carry a woman's signature, pronounced Bernard, never one to rush for the washing-up brush or drying-up towel himself. Thus was his fate sealed. On some of the towels a printed copy of Laura Ashley's signature even formed part of the design. Bernard hoped and expected it would not be long before Bernard Ashley Designs again took over as the core of the business.

In 1958 there was an enormous storm and the River Darent overflowed. The next morning when Bernard arrived at the Coach House everything was floating in water; silkscreens, dyestuffs, fabrics – and the machinery was almost ruined as well. Just as the company was settling into a period of expansion, such a major setback put its entire survival in jeopardy.

4

The Promised Land

'Looking back to the three years which followed we seem to have been in a holding position, with no great increase in turnover.' Laura wrote, flatly and unemotionally, at the time after the flood. There never was any question of giving up, or starting something else. The immediate problem was how to rebuild the production room at the Coach House to prevent a similar occurrence. They had, in any case, been running out of space there before the flood. The solution, to add a mezzanine floor, meant that dyestuffs, frames and fabrics could now be stored out of reach of future flooding with enough space for Laura to have her own small office. The alterations were soon carried out by Bernard, using his favourite steel racking.

Simultaneously, the London showroom in Old Burlington Street was being pulled down in order to make way for a multi-storey car park. However, they soon found a first floor studio in Lower John Street, Soho, and were able to use some of the insurance proceeds to pay for this. A bigger London office had, in any case, become increasingly important for negotiating sales with the many foreign buyers interested in Ashley Mountney goods and so, for the first time, the company actually had more space than it needed. The product range, after several static years, began expanding, partly in response to demand but also because Bernard had, to his intense annoyance, not yet rectified the problem with the repeat. He developed some unusual single panel hangings, such as one entitled 'Carts', a printed reproduction of a black and white photograph with a hazy, speckled appearance; two widths of this were often enough for a pair of curtains. But it was the simplest items which brought them the greatest success. For example, the gardening apron led to a gardening overall or smock which was, quite simply, an identical back and front sewn together with three large patch pockets to the front. This took ten minutes to sew, and when made out of cotton drill printed with wide stripes in two primary colours, the effect was striking. The wastage from the scooped neck provided enough fabric for oven gloves, which gratified Laura's 'never waste' philosophy.

Thus stealthily, unintentionally, did Laura and Bernard enter the fashion industry. The ten-minute gardening garment sold so many thousands that it was followed, 'quite naturally', by what they described as a 'Basic Dress' or 'BD'. This was constructed on a similar principle (one size fits all; no pattern necessary) and was also sleeveless and knee-length. It was almost a joke, since neither of them could draw at all. But that was of no consequence as the dress proved ideal for maternity wear, a market hardly catered for hitherto. The 'BD', like the smock, was so cheap to make that the Ashleys were able to include a sun hat and still sell it for twenty-nine shillings and sixpence. 'We were cheap but never nasty,' Laura declared.

In Laura's subsequent descriptions of the development of the company everything happened 'very naturally'; a 'basic' shirt followed in cotton lawn and, for the first time, they began to use very small prints for these. 'Because of our Victorian tea towel prints it was natural to use small Victorian prints on the cotton lawn.' Nevertheless, the first floral motif used by the company was not so small, a simple daisy with four petals printed in two bright primary tones. The immediate warm reaction resulted in other, more adventurous floral prints. Laura was always amazed by the success of her ideas and her company, because so much happened without forward planning. The implication that it also happened effortlessly was, however, far from the truth. Others remember those years in Kent at the end of the Fifties before the full force of the Sixties unleashed itself, as difficult and traumatic in many ways.

In the first place Bernard was travelling regularly in the British Isles and overseas, to sell the products. This left Laura at home looking after both children and business for extended periods. Increasingly, the sixteen-year-old school leaver, Antony Sheppard, took over production but Laura had to supervise as well as maintain the administration. Although Antony was soon left in sole charge he remembers many a potentially dramatic fire just smothered in time. 'If we all went out for a quick drink and forgot about the leader cloth this would drop to the bottom of the oven and burn, filling the whole place with smoke.'

It was not difficult to recognize Bernard's frustration at not being able to raise more working capital in order to expand; every penny of profit was reinvested into materials and supplies. And he was exposed, for the first time, to the twin horrors, as he saw them, of tax inspectors and bank clerks. This double-pronged attack, on the one hand from officials wanting more money and more information, on the other from bureaucrats not prepared to lend any money until there was evidence of sustained profitability, began to consume Bernard with rage. One short-lived venture which he hoped might bring in some much needed cash was his involvement with a friend in chicken farming. Charles Morton had lived in Limpsfield for many years and both men believed that broiler chickens might be a major product of the Sixties. However, the venture did not work out for many reasons, not least of which was that the product bored them. But sometimes, as he viewed a company that was becoming increasingly feminine and domestic, where almost all the items now bore his wife's name, he wondered if he might not have more success running an engineering business.

In retrospect, it is easy to see the company, as Laura liked to later, as if on a permanent climb from 1955 onwards. Sales from that year until 1960 grew from £2,000 to £8,000 per annum. The number of accounts and the product range was expanding with similar gusto. But the reality behind the figures was less straightforward. Laura was living under cramped conditions in a tiny cottage with three highly active children, under six, almost no money and a husband who was regularly absent. Those who knew them well recognized that it was a time of extreme tension for both, yet Bernard's pride made it difficult for Laura to confide her worries to anyone. There were often acrimonious verbal explosions between them, usually over nothing more serious than minor inaccuracies to do with the business. 'Watching them both was like lighting a fuse; she'd soak it up and then he would go off in a rage, slamming doors and shouting around the car park. But when he came back, that would be that and it would be all over,' recalls a colleague from those days. Laura understood that he had a temper which easily flared and was quickly doused; her own reaction was to brood, silently, and then her inner hurt and embarrassment would take even longer to heal.

One long-standing friend who had not seen them for some years, felt they were living in 'grinding, almost Dickensian poverty, yet somehow there was an idealistic edge to it. They were so absolutely skint I thought they would drop through the bottom. Sometimes they used no electric light – it was almost as if they used only fresh air to live on.' Even in times of acute financial difficulty it was, however, a matter of principle that no employee went unpaid. But, whenever the telephone was cut off, she would dread that their friends would learn. In spite of the surface turbulence between them, in public Laura would always give her husband right and credited any temper less to him but rather to some third party, such as an uncooperative bank manager, inquisitorial tax official or recalcitrant wholesaler.

In the midst of this difficult year Bernard's brother Geoff returned from the Far East and toyed with the idea of joining Ashley Mountney on a more permanent basis, wanting to become more involved with the business. But the partnership did not work out and Geoff remained for less than a season. As the lease on East Cottage neared its end, and the landlords did not want to renew it, Bernard decided he had had enough of Surrey's 'gin and jag belt', different, but no more appealing, than Wallington suburbia. He felt an outsider and had no desire to become an insider. He and Laura wanted to buy their own house but were meeting with repeated resistance from building societies and bank managers; they were self-employed and the company did not seem stable enough on which to base a mortgage. In addition, he was spending money on surveys for houses which he then could not buy. It was the lowest point in their relationship. Bernard had friends who were cheerfully borrowing thousands of pounds for property developments. Yet the banks steadfastly refused to lend to him. Bernard grew angrier after each rejection until Laura finally resolved the future of the family and the business. Aged thirty-five, after eleven years of marriage, and with three children, she walked out.

It was a bold step but in both the Ashley and Mountney households domestic decisions had been taken by women. It was also typical of

Laura's future business style to achieve what she wanted by non-confrontational means. She desperately wanted the business to succeed. She knew that printing could be carried on anywhere but harmony at home was an essential prerequisite and it was currently absent. She knew that Bernard would follow, but not when. She knew that she would find somewhere they could both live and work, but not where. Laura always maintained that she felt utterly secure about their relationship. As she joked years later with her children, 'No one else would have him, no one else would put up with him, no one else would understand him.' Equally her own existence would have no meaning without him. 'He is larger than life, I could never escape his shadow,' she once confided to a close friend. The family had few possessions and, once the decision to leave was taken, Laura packed in an hour. She put some old tents, sleeping bags, odds and ends and three children into her battered Morris Minor and drove away. 'We never even said goodbye to our schoolfriends or teachers, and we never understood why,' Jane recalled. First they went south, to Eastbourne; it was an area she knew and camping on the coast in early summer had some appeal. The children were exhilarated by the whole project, but the place did not have the right feel and she soon packed up and set off again. North-west this time, to Wales.

She and Bernard had periodically discussed the possibility of moving to Wales once it became clear to them not only that houses in the South were beyond their reach but that the possibilities for factory development were slight. Rather than let the constant turn-downs sap Bernard's energy, Laura decided that a clean break in a new place was essential. The move can certainly be viewed as a return to the country of her birth, as a romantic choice. But Laura was too pragmatic for this alone to have swayed her and she did not settle in South Wales, where she was born. This time she went beyond the Brecon Beacon barrier, to mid-Wales, where she had no family, no connections, no roots. But this difficult and beautiful country, with its annual rainfall of over sixty inches, its fragmented valley settlements forced apart from each other by stoney hills or mountains of coarse grass, was in her blood.

There were, of course, more practical considerations. In was an area desperate to attract industrial development, in an attempt to stem years of serious depopulation and the recently constructed M1 motorway made for excellent connections with London and the South-East. But perhaps the best reason had to do with Laura's canny knowledge of her husband's nature. She knew that in Wales there would be no distractions, 'nothing else for me to do but work,' explains Bernard. At all events the summer of 1961 found Laura and her three children encamped on the banks of Mawddach Estuary near Dolgellau, right in the centre of Wales. They had two tents, both army surplus, one for cooking and eating and the other for sleeping. Laura, summoning all her remaining girl guide knowledge, tried to put them up as best she could but they sagged miserably and, one night after a torrential storm, all but collapsed. The next day, most of the families went home, in disgust at the weather. But a few of the men left on the campsite, in sympathy for this struggling mother, came to help her re-erect the tents. Laura was dogged in her determination to stick it out. What else could she do? The children, meanwhile, found life idyllic; no one here commented if they did not wear shoes, they swam in the river where Laura washed their clothes, had playmates at all times of day and wished this life could go on forever.

As a natural 'hippy' (but years before the phrase was in vogue) Laura proved to herself not only that she could manage on her own but without material possessions as well. After three weeks, as Laura knew he would, Bernard arrived. David remembers the stir his arrival caused at the campsite, when suddenly his white Lotus Elite, that he had bought in kit form for £500 and built himself, came roaring in. 'Nick and I went running over to see what it was. Dad said "Okay! Off with your boots and I'll take you for a ride!" It was such a thrill and we had such confidence in him. He overtook six cars at once and we thought it was great.' For that matter, so did Laura; she gloried in his dynamic power, which in turn fed him. Bernard stayed a day or two, taking Laura away to the local pub for the weekend (while Jane, aged eight, babysat), and then disappeared back to Kent, where production was still flowing at the Coach House. 'The other families at the campsite used to ask us if our parents were actually married. They assumed this was just some glamorous playboy up for a wild weekend or two.'

After six weeks Laura found a small house of great charm in the historic market town of Machynlleth. One of the planned towns of the thirteenth century, Machynlleth stands at the head of the Dyfi Estuary with the Snowdonia National Park to the north and the Cardigan Bay coast to the west. For more than six hundred years it has held a weekly market and twice yearly fair, but the town's chief claims to historical importance came in 1404 when Owain Glyndwr, the Welsh rebel prince, called an assembly of his supporters there. The Parliament House is in Maengwyn Street, just a stone's throw away from Gwalia House, which was to be the Ashley's new home. In 1961 Machynlleth was a small town of less than 2,000 inhabitants which attracted tourists, fishermen and gossip. It boasted sixteen chapels and sixteen pubs. But if convention had not worried the Ashleys in Surrey, still less did it in Machynlleth. Here too the couple was quickly noticed and commented about. Laura and Bernard were now together again, but Bernard's stays were punctuated by trips abroad as well as commuting to Brasted. Locals described them as both 'wild and weird'; one of their most remarked upon habits was that they were known to eat raw vegetables. Even their occupation, printing tea towels, was considered 'quite exotic for the area'.

The house was an amalgam of three tiny fifteenth-century cottages for which the Ashleys paid £1,500, the last of the funds remaining from the insurance claim. One of the cottages still had a tenant, an old lady who continued to live there after the Ashleys moved in, and another part had once been a tailor's establishment and retained its old-fashioned bay window giving on to the street. There was 600 sq. ft. of shop space in the new Ashley home. The remaining living area was a maze of sloping, beamed ceilings and winding staircases. Spread across three floors were four bedrooms, a sitting room above the shop, and a breakfast room. Bernard himself built on a bathroom. The kitchen, with its large grate on one side (which Laura loved to blacken), dark oak beams and Welsh slate floor, was very much part of the shop. The atmosphere was complete once they had bought a few pieces of Welsh oak furniture. It was their first attempt to create an interior that harmonized with its surroundings.

Laura had often thought how perfect it would be to have a shop selling their own products; Bernard had demurred, more interested in the mechanics of quantity printing than producing small domestic items. In any case a shop was too reminiscent of the background from which he wanted to escape. As the company was not making enough products to fill an entire shop, Laura decided to stock local honey, walking sticks and goods made of Welsh flannel, all of which attracted tourist traffic, as well as some Ashley Mountney household items, mostly seconds or samples. Soon, Gwalia House became much more than just a shop. It acquired a reputation for its informal, friendly atmosphere as customers would come in to sit by the fire and chat. On Saturdays, Laura occasionally found herself serving some twenty customers, as well as her family, with lunch. Some of these customers became long-lasting friends and they remember meals at Gwalia House as 'a time when you might take along a piece of old lace or an old print and discuss its origins and its possibilities. Laura was always full of charm and full of interest for your suggestions and full of ideas. The con-versation was almost entirely about fabric, printing and design.' On other days customers might wait while a special outfit was being made. Laura would try, with her easy charm and desire to please, to make anything that was asked for. At the back of the first floor was a small cubicle with just enough space for a seamstress to sit with a sewing machine. This meant that while tea towels and oven gloves could still be printed and made up at Brasted, sample clothes could also be tested in the shop at Machynlleth. Within weeks therefore the Ashleys needed to hire staff and found a ready pool of young girls with farming backgrounds and few other opportunities.

Ceinwen Edwards, then seventeen, had done her apprenticeship in a ladies' underwear factory but knew it would be difficult to find work locally. She was thrilled to be offered a job with the Ashleys. 'I loved working for them – they were fantastic people. I was very influenced by Mrs Ashley's peasanty sort of style and tried to do my hair in the same sort of way; in fact, lots of people in Machynlleth copied her,' remembers Ceinwen. The hours were long, from 7.30 am until, occasionally, 11.30 pm and the work – including anything from making up samples to selling in the shop or minding the children – was hard. 'But I didn't mind, it was such a team effort and everything I did was appreciated.'

When Ceinwen began neither she nor Laura had much idea of how to sew beyond following and adapting a commercial pattern. 'Laura was very fussy and everything had to be just so,' Ceinwen recalls. 'If I left a thread sticking out after hemming a tea towel she would get very upset unless it was finished off correctly.' One of the most popular items sold in the shop was a 'Grandad' shirt made out of Welsh flannel. This was Laura's idea, adapted from a pattern Laura and Ceinwen had made together. 'The students from Aberystwyth University flocked to us to buy these shirts, sometimes taking several at a time and usually putting belts round them. They looked terrific.' In spite of the long hours, Ceinwen was treated as one of the family, and this meant eating what Laura considered sensible food. 'Every lunch time I would eat with them and not just a sandwich, it was often steak and wine and such strange vegetables. I don't know where she bought some of them from.' Among the 'strange' Ashley ingredients was garlic, so unusual Ceinwen and others in the town had never even heard of it.

After Ceinwen's arrival, Laura could take a much more varied role in the business. She was involved in developing and designing new products, running the shop, organizing the window displays, seeing to all the administrative chores as well as researching new designs in London and, of course, looking after the children. She hoped to have a bigger family, but suffered at least two further miscarriages at this time. 'Bernard always gets so cross with me,' she joked 'whenever I tell him I'm pregnant.' He did, but having babies was an area where Laura took the decisions.

After eighteen months in Machynlleth, as the Ashleys were no nearer to locating a potential factory building near them, Bernard was still spending much of his working week in Brasted, as well as travelling to Bermuda, Switzerland and many other places where their products – considered original, good quality and cheap – were now in increasing demand. If they were to satisfy this demand, building their own factory near Machynlleth was now an urgent priority and as there was no industrial land available in Machynlleth itself, they had identified a 3,000 sq. ft. site at Felingerrig which they thought would be suitable. However, in July 1963 the local authorities refused them planning permission. Bernard and Laura had been in Wales for almost two years and this first bureaucratic blow meant that Bernard would have to continue commuting from Kent.

However, two months later the Chief Officer of the then mid-Wales Industrial Development Association, an organization dedicated to increasing the provision of jobs in the area, informed Bernard that there was an existing building a few miles down the road which he might be able to convert for his use. It was a Sunday when Peter Garbett Edwards first took Bernard to view the disused social club at Tybrith. The obscure licensing laws in Wales at the time had resulted in a number of so-called social clubs springing up. But this one had been closed down after a police raid had discovered drinking taking place in the small hours. It was now vacant. 'I've never met anyone with a greater, more burning desire to succeed than Bernard Ashley,' recalled Garbett Edwards. The building on offer was a long, low, dark 3,000 sq. ft. single room with a reputation for raucous excess. Although not what they had originally anticipated, and quite unprepossessing in appearance, Bernard and Laura thought it was adequate. Laura particularly liked it as it faced Pentre Felin, the site of a nineteenth-century weaving factory.

Bernard stripped out the inside and fitted it with rows of Dexion as floors, dividers, shelves – even the printing table was made of it. 'Bernard and Dexion was like a boy with his Meccano,' recalled Antony Sheppard, who decided at this point not to go to college but to come up to Wales and continue working for the Ashleys. After two years of limbo-like existence, Bernard wasted not another day. Unbolting the boilers and taking the machines apart in order to bring them from Surrey to Wales provided hours of hard work for him. He enjoyed it, but found dealing with the financial aspects of the move intolerable. Dressed in his dirty boilersuit he would walk into one bank after another trying to raise an overdraft to finance the planned expansion, but was constantly met with rebuffs, or was offered to see an assistant but never the manager himself. This treatment left a lasting bitterness. There was still enough of the prankster left in Bernard to guess that he must actually have relished walking into a bank dressed as an operative but playing the entrepreneur. Both parts were his. The day he hired a van to bring up their remaining possessions from Kent he felt a symbolic severance from English life.

For almost two months, until the machinery was working again, the Ashley family was virtually without income. But it was not long before outstanding orders were met and as new orders advanced, more staff were taken on at the factory. One of the first was Rosina Corfield, fresh from her training with a Marks and Spencer supplier, who welcomed the opportunity of a local job. 'They were really happy days, everyone just got on with their work without being asked, but we used to go home black as heck because the print came off. We sat all day on upturned bins of paint as there weren't any chairs.' Laura was in charge of quality control and Rosina, like Ceinwen, recognized immediately that although their boss was always calmly quiet and nothing ever upset or shocked her, her standards were extremely high. The inadequate machinery often made life difficult; for example, with no overlocker the slightest tug could rip seams apart. There was no button-holing machine and so they could only make garments that could be put on over the head. Quality control in 1963 was still very rudimentary and included instructions about how to tackle bias binding, making sure that zip-facing actually covered zips and that side seams and darts were pressed in the right direction. Often it was simply a question of getting seams straight.

Within months, Rosina was joined in the factory by her sister but it was the hiring of a secretary which suddenly freed Laura to pursue a more creative rôle. The first designer the Ashleys engaged lived in Cornwall and visited Wales four times a year, staying a week or two at a time, rather like a nineteenth-century travelling seamstress. She and Laura worked together and using a mixture of magazines, imagination and commercial patterns, increased the range of garments now being made because Laura saw clearly this was where demand was greatest. 'Whatever else a girl can find a penny for she can always find it for a dress,' was one of her favourite maxims. The Cornish designer (who was a sailing instructor for the rest of the year) dreamed up a shirt-dress which sold for years, gave a more professional finish to many of the existing shirt designs and, most significantly, created the first Victorian nightdress for 'Laura Ashley'. The wholesalers soon started to expect different clothes each season.

Almost immediately, the health of the young company became inextricably linked to the area of Wales where Laura's old Morris had brought them. The mid-Wales that welcomed the Ashleys in 1961 was one which had witnessed a spectacular and constant decrease in population. The 'never-had-it-so-good' boom in prosperity enjoyed by the rest of England had largely by-passed this part of Wales which, by contrast, had been sucked into the downward spiral of a drift away from the countryside and an exodus of the young and better educated from their roots, which no community, urban or rural, could experience without damage. By the early Sixties, the proportion of inhabitants over the age of sixty-five was 25 per cent, higher than in the remainder of the country. The outlook was particularly bleak as even the prospects of employment in agriculture were dramatically decreasing through the mechanization of farming and the amalgamation of smallholdings into larger units. With the high preponderance of elderly people and the scarcity of opportunity for women to earn money, the income of most families was severely stretched. The problem was self-perpetuating; for example, small village schools were closing, train lines were being cut and stations left to ruin, mobile libraries were visiting less regularly and the resources of local authorities, whose basic services had to cover such a wide area, were strained to the limit. In 1962, between 20 and 30 per cent of houses in mid-Wales were without piped water supply. Nearly 3,000 farms were without electricity. Emlyn Hooson, the new Liberal Member of Parliament elected to represent Montgomery, argued in 1965: 'No one can expect young people to remain in the perpetual twilight of a farm kitchen lit by paraffin lamps or bottled gas.'* Hooson, a former barrister then aged thirty-seven, reflected the problem clearly enough. 'In the country, as in the towns, remunerative work is the foundation upon which the rest of life is built. Without work there can be no facilities for civilized living, neither can there be an expression of culture.' He knew it was not enough that Wales, being an area of great natural beauty, was attracting tourists or second-home owners. 'The drift from the land had to be stopped and a livelihood provided for young people so that they could remain in the community if they wished.'

Emlyn, now Lord, Hooson, remembers Bernard attending one of his early political meetings when he was vigorously propounding such views. Many of the villages were at the time entirely Welsh-speaking and political meetings were often conducted with no English spoken. 'Suddenly I noticed this tall, lanky Englishman asking questions, and then he started writing letters to me.' The Hoosons struck up a friendship with the Ashleys which was beneficial not merely for the two families concerned. Lord Hooson accepts that, if the Ashleys had not come to mid-Wales, another firm might have been attracted to the area. But he is nonetheless convinced that it was their peculiar blend of paternalism (obliquely following the tradition of the eighteenth-century industrial reformer, Robert Owen of Newtown) mixed with their sensitivity to all things Welsh, which ensured that their then

---

* '*The Heartland – a Plan for mid-Wales*' by Emlyn Hooson and Geraint Jenkins. Published by the Liberal Publication Department.

moderate livelihood was transformed into one of the major international success stories of the late twentieth century. Everyone knew they were from England, but they melded into the local lifestyle and never stood aloof. The Ashleys could not possibly have grown so fast without the farmers' wives and daughters willing them to succeed. These women wanted to stay at home – perhaps a home that had been theirs for generations – but could not have afforded to without the outwork fed to them. It was crucial that they won over all locals, male and female, and they did so, as Laura would say 'quite naturally', because she drew on her own sense of Welsh roots to identify with the small community and to understand their needs. She deliberately employed mothers with young children as part-time workers and instituted a half-day on Friday (to this day regular practice in 'Laura Ashley' factories) because she knew that the women would not be, nor want to be, released from any of their weekend chores merely by also working in the factory. Wages at Ashley Mountney were considered excellent in the area, with a basic five pounds per week for the factory workers. Although there was no room for a canteen at Tybrith the Ashleys paid for staff to have lunch at the local pub. This sense of belonging, being part of the community, was one of Laura' special gifts. She combined it with a longing and nostalgia, a sort of homesickness for the past as it might have been lived in that village, '*hiraeth*' in Welsh, so that her employees could not fail to be aware of the passion in her commitment.

The printing routine at Tybrith was identical to that at Brasted. Apart from the outworkers, every stage in making up was carried out under one roof and the room quickly became crowded and hectic. The procedures were still unsophisticated: cloth was printed and baked in a custom-made oven, then washed out to remove excess dye with winch washers and finally dried over cans or cylinders filled with steam. Fabric was then passed through a shrinking machine and was ready for cutting into garments. At the rear of the floor, dyeing and mixing was carried out by hand while a second section of the building, partitioned off with slotted angle Dexion, formed a sewing room, later an office. Owing to shortage of funds for new equipment, female staff collected together old nylon stockings and used these as a more or less effective means of straining dye solutions; colour matching under these conditions was, of course, unthinkable. But that was all part of the charm. Bernard was perpetually working on improvements to his flatbed printer so that it could produce 5,000 metres of cloth per week; his goal, as ever, increased efficiency. 'We're here to sell fabric, that's the main thing,' he would exhort.

Within two years, the factory had become an established and profitable, indigenous enterprise nestling within the farming community. The staff had nearly doubled to include a manager, secretary, two printers, seven machinists and five outworkers, as well as Ceinwen, Laura and Bernard. Laura, simultaneously, was keener to develop image rather than quantity. She loved to be asked to make up traditional Welsh flannel costumes with shawls and pointed black hats for little girls. These were hardly lucrative but built up a huge store of goodwill. 'The combined effect of the romantic old house, the mountains and the Victorian prints we were producing naturally led us into costume dresses. Two old ladies came into the shop one day and presented me with a magnificent eighteenth-century ball dress heirloom, simply because they felt ours was a good home. I displayed it in the Machynlleth shop for about a year and it just had to have companions so we made full-length dresses and they were immediately bought for all kinds of uses; brides, beach cover-ups or just to be comfortable at home by the fire in the evening.' Ceinwen had learned to make up samples in record time and reaction to them was almost as fast. Machynlleth, with its mixture of students, tourists and country locals, was a perfect base from which to experiment. It was clear that clothes were the demand of the hour and that these unusual originals in natural cotton filled an unsatisfied demand. Laura, because she made this discovery for herself, through the shop, was quite certain what young women were longing to dress themselves in, if only she could supply them.

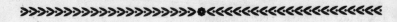

5

Sex and the Sixties

The Sixties gave sex a bad name. They gave it other names as well, some of them in public, which many feared signalled the collapse of the nation. Others believed that the new pop culture was the outward symbol of a genuine opportunity for a freer, more egalitarian society in which hypocrisy and privilege would cease to count. Throughout the decade it is possible to identify conflicting strands of thoughts and ideas which were not necessarily mutually exclusive. The prolonged war of attrition was not fought simply between one generation and another or only on the battlefield of sex, although sexual liberation and equality between the sexes were certainly two of the loudest battle cries and there were not many fifty-year-old hippies shouting.

From about 1963, with the departure of Harold Macmillan, the aspirations of Jack Kennedy and the publication of Betty Friedan's *The Feminine Mystique*, the Sixties began to 'swing', with the young undercutting as many, or all traditional bulwarks of authority, as they could, ranging from the family and religion to the economic system, the monarchy, literature and the arts.

On the one hand, there were those who seemed obsessed by the need for absolute freedom in all things artistic. A feeling that the time had at last arrived when nothing was sacred led the drama critic, Kenneth Tynan, to comment on live television that he doubted there were 'very many rational people in this world to whom the word "fuck" is particularly diabolical or revolting or totally forbidden'. But ranged against such views were equally strident voices. Malcolm Muggeridge, the veteran journalist, in a stinging attack on the permissive nature of the decade, forecast the culmination of current liberality as a time when 'birth pills are handed out free with orange juice and consenting adults wear special ties and blazers and abortion and divorce – those two contemporary panaceas for all matrimonial ills – are freely available on the public health, then at last with the suicide rate up to Scandinavian proportions and the psychiatric wards bursting at the seams it will be realized that this path, even from the shallow point of view of the pursuit of happiness, is a disastrous cul-de-sac.'

But in spite of many a persuasive declaration in favour of relinquishing values which no longer seemed necessary, there was no certainty as to what the new generation should grasp instead. The sheer size of this new generation, the post-war baby boomers, ensured that its needs, wants and beliefs were taken seriously.* Not only was it numerically powerful, it had spending power as never before, which enabled it to evolve a culture of its own, of which blue jeans and beefburgers were the most obvious manifestation of the new mass production. And this, naturally, led to a desire for shops of its own, where parents did not, would not, want to go.

The youth of the Sixties also laid claim to another power: flower power. This appeared to mean long hair, free love, peace and goodwill to all men – except parents, as they would be abandoned now. The Fifties and early Sixties were prosperous years, offering new comforts and social affluence. Thus cushioned, the young felt able to indulge in protest movements and endorse the sexual revolution without being quite sure of what they wanted instead. It was enough, for some, to feel that they exerted power to shape their own lives, away from their parents' values. Yet the teenage restlessness was echoed, if not exacerbated, by uncertainty voiced by their parents who eagerly turned to Dr Spock to enquire if they were 'doing all right?' This domestic questioning was matched in Britain at large by national self-doubt. 'What's wrong with Britain?' asked more than one newspaper editor more than once. With all this confusion in the minds of the young,

---

* In 1965 there were just over 7 million teenagers in England and Wales compared with 5.9 million for 1955.

whom could they find offering a rigorous set of rules for such a rapidly changing scene? Enter, stage centre, the Beatles.

'Why would she treat us so thoughtlessly?' sang the Liverpool Four of the girl leaving home. 'We gave her most of our lives, we never thought of ourselves, what did we do that was wrong?' Throughout England thousands of teenagers were leaving home, be it for fun, for freedom or to meet a man from the motor trade, and most were converging on London. The Beatles' hauntingly poignant songs were mostly about love; but sex was, lyrically speaking, understood. The liberated girl in 'Norwegian Wood' (1965) epitomized the new morality; as Malcolm Muggeridge had insisted, Scandinavian in origin. She lives on her own and is not frightened to invite men to stay the night. 'The girl who came to stay' was a similar type. 'She's the kind of girl you want so much it makes you sorry . . . But when you say she's looking good she acts as if it's understood.' As inhibitions crumbled, the Beatles acquired a reputation as standard bearers for the brave, new, taboo-free world. But towards the end of the decade their implicit endorsement of the drug culture led many to worry that morals, if not life itself, were being crushed in the stampede. How many young people might be tempted to discover their very own 'Lucy in the Sky with Diamonds', or 'Tangerine trees with marmalade skies . . . with only a little help from their friends?'

The Beatles, of course, did not create the rampant iconoclasm. But, just as Noël Coward and Cole Porter reflected the louche, carefree attitude of the Twenties, so did the Beatles' music capture the rhythm of breaking free experienced by an entire generation of young people growing up in the Sixties. Yet even Lennon *et al* clearly had not discovered any certainties on the road to riches. They were publicly searching and, at times, it seemed desperately, for an inner meaning to life.

The Sixties' culture was all-embracing. Soon, not just music, art and beliefs but food, clothes, language, and make-up were hijacked by the young and re-directed. Everyone wanted to look and sound alike. Girls highlighted their cheekbones, blackened their eyes and whitened their lips, enviously aping the lanky models, Jean Shrimpton and Grace Coddington. Or else they ironed (and often singed) their curls, copying the rigidly straight black hair and overlong fringes of Sandie Shaw or Cathy MacGowan. Talking cockney was a great asset as the skeletal waifishness of Twiggy demonstrated while Rita Tushingham had her own brand of Liverpudlian charm. Clothes, now called 'gear', were either 'groovy' or 'way out', and girls, called 'dolly birds', were prepared to queue for hours for anything that was 'with it', however badly made and skimpy, as nothing was intended to last. The important thing was to look like everyone else. One of the most potent symbols of Sixties daring, brashness and vulgarity was London's Carnaby Street. Here one could buy all the worst products that British (or Far Eastern) factories were churning out from tin mugs to indecent mini-skirts and knickers with union jacks emblazoned across them.

But alongside all that was new, modern and pop, there was also a retrospection. Sanderson, the wallpaper manufacturers, began in 1965 to print coordinating William Morris designs on fabrics and wallpapers. The fabric was heavily in demand. Shirts and ties made in nineteenth-century paisley patterns suddenly epitomized fashionable manhood and the tin or enamel mugs, without which no self-respecting tourist could leave Britain, were closely modelled on a workers' style mug of Victorian days. Even the kitchen equipment selling so rapidly in the ultra-modern shop called Habitat had more than an echo of low-Victorian style. There were other examples of the schizoid nature of Sixties Britain: Biba, the quintessential Sixties boutique where anyone older than twenty-five felt wrinkled, was one of the first shops to provide cheap, original clothes with a well-defined youthful and slightly rebellious image, as well as an atmosphere which reeked of sex. The interior of the shop was designed to look like a bordello with its scarlet, black and gold plush fitments, but, interestingly, it implied an old-fashioned, Edwardian style of forbidden sex with its feather boas, potted palms, bentwood coat racks and dark lighting.

In the theatre the shock waves came from such revealing musicals as *Hair* or *Oh Calcutta!* while on television, the anti-establishment satire, *That Was The Week That Was* managed to shake most viewers out of their complacency on a regular basis. At the same time, however, an estimated twenty million viewers were enraptured by the BBC's black and white twenty-six-episode retelling of John Galsworthy's classic, *The Forsyte Saga*. Here was the unassailable proof of the nation's deep-seated craving for romantic escapism, its need to believe that, in spite of the widening competitiveness of an opening society, old-fashioned values and the continuity of English life would prevail. Even at the end of the decade it was not clear which path the nation might opt for; the choice between 'Old' and 'New' seemed so stark. There was much in modernism that was appealing to a new society of shifting and complex relationships. Yet for an ancient nation that had lost its burden of Empire and world role it was comforting, to say the least, to return down the old familiar road.

What emerged ultimately: compromise, or the typically British, refreshingly doctrine-free, consensus. Authoritarianism may have vanished, but authority, based on public opinion, nonetheless prevailed. State schools and the National Health Service expanded, but public schools and private medicine flourished alongside. There are those who believe that in politics as in art and design, a great opportunity was offered and lost; the sparks of originality were extinguished by a public fire bucket filled with nostalgia and respectability which had, in fact, never been far from hand. A new vogue word, conservation, slowly came into play as well. Hundreds of thousands of terraced houses, no great architectural gems but prettier and more spacious than anything builders of the Fifties and Sixties had to offer, were now being gutted and refitted, where a decade ago they would have been bulldozed. This was compromise in action.

Compromise alone can never confer a sense of vision or direction; qualities that Laura Ashley had formulated by the Sixties. She believed that people in London were 'going crazy', that hot pants and mini-skirts were 'dreadful' and that 'I had to do something that was completely different ... because I knew in my heart that was not what most people wanted ... I sensed that most people wanted to raise families, have gardens and live life as nicely as they can. They don't want to go out to night-clubs every night and get absolutely blotto.'

Nonetheless, within herself Laura contained many of the conflicting strands of Sixties' thinking, some of which she took and used as her own, others she determinedly discarded. She was young and sensitive enough to be in touch with new trends, but old enough to feel the weight of experience and responsibility. She was not tied to possessions, nor did she hanker after material comforts and her instinctive, religious sense of justice coincided with the egalitarian mood of the moment. Yet she was never a believer in so-called women's liberation: she did not accept that women wanted to be liberated from the home as this was, on the contrary, where they found true fulfilment. And she did not believe in free love, divorce or any other influence which might weaken family ties. Keeping the family together was her most cherished ideal. Above all she was authoritarian; she believed this was the only way to run a successful business and that it should in no way detract from the unstinting care and concern for her workforce, which was their due. Symbolically, she decided now that none of her staff should ever refer to her by her first name. They could call her Mrs Ashley but she preferred to be known as LA (and Bernard as BA). It was both more and less formal, as the occasion demanded. No one she worked with was exempt.

Her own children were now almost teenage – keen to explore life – and thus Laura was not to be spared many of the excesses of the decade. But the realization that she found deeply repellent many of the new attitudes espoused by her children's friends, if not her own children, was to prove one of her most secure creative mainsprings. 'In a way,' she wrote years later, 'we exaggerated our own ideas and reacted against the harshness of the London scene in the Sixties. It was not merely the mini-skirts, but the whole style of living which didn't appeal to me ... we had nothing in common with this.'

The circumstances of her work constantly forced her to define and redefine her philosophy of life and, as she did this, she found increasingly that the values which she believed mattered were those she had gleaned from an earlier, though not necessarily Victorian, age. She was trying to create clothes that reflected a purer life, lived according to the stricter standards of a century earlier, that knew nothing of the lax morals which had appeared in the meanwhile to destroy their wholesomeness. A search akin to a winegrower's bid to produce a pre-phylloxera wine.

One of the first decisions Laura had to make immediately after moving to Wales was where the children should go to school. 'Schooling, feeding and clothing of us children were all her department; my father did not take any interest in them,' Nick explained later. Yet there were not, in fact, any decisions taken at all and Jane and David were duly enrolled at the nearest school, Machynlleth Junior. Neither Laura nor Bernard were ever academically ambitious for their children; they believed that experiencing life or, as Bernard put it, 'having the rough edges knocked off them', was always better than anything any educational establishment could provide. They believed that if they had managed without conventional academic achievements, then so would their children.

Increasingly they concluded that the formal qualifications of the people they employed bore no relation to their ability to perform a useful role within the company. In fact so strong was this feeling that, for many years, they deliberately avoided hiring graduates under the impression that formal training merely fixed limitations on what was possible and might prevent original thought. They resorted to informal handwriting analysis to assess potential employees. In addition, they believed it was healthier for the children of the employer to grow up alongside those who might ultimately be working for them on the factory floor.

However, all these theories were severely dented when Laura saw her own children become miserable from bullying and teasing. Machynlleth Junior was a fervently Welsh-speaking school and the new English children, who scarcely understood a word of Welsh, were badly teased for having posh parents. This pained Laura greatly, but worse was to come when she discovered that David's teacher had tied his left hand behind his back to force him to write with his right and told him that only children with Satan in them were left-handed. As a left-hander herself she understood his difficulties only too well. She wanted to take David away, but there was no money to spare for private schooling, nor was there the will. It is inconceivable that, if Laura had seriously believed she was disadvantaging her children by sending them to the nearest state primary, she would not have removed them. She would have been genuinely horrified if her friends had spoken their opinions to her face concerning her failure to choose schools which suited her children's needs. Nor would she have believed them if they had told her that her unwillingness to make them stick to places or courses they did not like, was fundamentally limiting their horizons, self-respect and, ultimately, independence. Nonetheless, Laura would have considered time spent investigating different schools, talking to teachers or poring over the children's homework with them, as a middle-class profligacy.

The children themselves were under no illusions that the business came first. They recognized their parents' lack of concern if they were put in the bottom set and were never challenged to rise above it. It was not long before they realized their ability to take advantage of this attitude so that Nick managed to sample a total of some thirteen schools from Machynlleth to Caersws and Aberhavesp, with David and Jane attending only slightly fewer. 'My mother was an absolute pushover; she just wanted me to be happy. If she didn't like my teachers she'd let me change,' Nick believes. 'My parents were wrapped up in the business and themselves during those years,' according to David. The immediate difficulties with Machynlleth School were resolved by the family moving house. But it was only a temporary lull. The problem of educating her children was one which found Laura lacking in her customary sense of vision; she succumbed to the Sixties' disease of self-doubt in the face of her children's growing quest for independence. If Laura had a weakness, it was indulgence of her children. Bernard, self-confessedly jealous of time Laura devoted to her offspring, knew it and made his own demands irresistible.

There never was a time when Bernard, constantly seeking new adventures, was not planning a move to a bigger home or factory. In 1964 it was both. Laura, eager as ever to fall in with his exciting schemes, was simultaneously pushing for a bigger retail outlet than the single small shop at Machynlleth. They found the thirty-mile drive from Machynlleth to the factory on narrow mountain roads too tiring and time-consuming, although Bernard adored driving at high speed without traffic, a habit Laura encouraged – to please him. One of his favourite antics while driving fast was to drop his head and pretend to be asleep at the wheel. Laura would giggle girlishly, 'Oh Bernard, you are naughty!' which both knew meant she thought he was quite wonderful. But the most pressing reason for a move was that Laura, then in her fortieth year, was pregnant again and their eccentric little house would no longer be big enough. She had had further miscarriages recently, one of which was quite serious, and she desperately hoped she would not lose this baby.

They discovered a new house, or rather, a new way of life, more easily than a new factory. Clogau was an eighteenth-century farmhouse with a barn for the animals and eighty acres of land. It was one of the highest farms in Wales, almost above the treeline in the Montgomeryshire hills and was as wild and isolated a home as could be found. The nearest village, Pontdolgoch, was two miles away. It was harsh but beautiful; a few larches sheltered the house from the biting north-east wind and a solitary ash stood by the gate. Each year the arctic tern returned to breed in the mountains around the house.

'Being often very impulsively romantic,' Laura wrote later, 'we hadn't realized that it was 1,500 ft up ... this was to prove a problem in the winter when enforced skiing holidays ensued.' She could not have failed to notice that there were no other inhabited buildings within sight, simply rocky mounds, stone walls, sheep and mountain streams in distant prospect. There was, and is, only one access road to Clogau, a narrow winding track with cattle grids and an incongruous telephone kiosk half way up. The house, a low, grey stone building with beamed ceilings and stone floors, was a singular choice. Bernard, being almost as romantic as Laura, spent many a Sunday before they moved decorating it, with the children, as a surprise. He also had to build almost a mile of the access road. By the time he had finished there were four bedrooms, a kitchen and dining room on the ground level with steps down to a large, open-plan living room with oak rafters, converted from the original barn. There was just one room upstairs, the master bedroom.

The years at Clogau were among the happiest for the Ashley family. They were all pleased to leave Machynlleth as they did not consider themselves an urban family and felt much more comfortable surrounded by space and solitude. The house was both individual and large enough for them to put their own stamp on it. They furnished it with some large modern pieces that blended with the stark surroundings and the children remember occasions when they could not sleep, coming downstairs to find their parents dancing alone in the living room. The Ashleys gave many parties in this house – almost the only period in their lives when they had time to socialize other than for business reasons. The increasing prosperity of the business, too, enabled them to afford family holidays abroad which, in true Ashley style, became adventures. In 1966, the children remember squeezing into Bernard's sports car for a camping holiday in St Tropez; a highly glamorous and international resort which immediately exerted a determined pull on Bernard to enjoy success and its fruits on a European scale. The family went skiing in St Moritz for the following two Christmasses. Laura was never a keen skier but was happy to imbibe the atmosphere, do up the children's laced boots and spend the day with her needlework.

Soon after the move to Clogau the Ashley's youngest child, Emma

Mary, was born at Machynlleth Hospital, the only one of the four born in Wales. Her birth, half-way through the decade, coincided with the moment when her parents, not exactly middle-aged but poised in mid-career, knew a major push was required to get their products out of the household departments and into the customers' wardrobes. This meant for Emma a quite different childhood from that of her siblings. At this critical juncture in the company's development Laura could not possibly stay at home with her new baby, although that was what she strongly advocated for other mothers. How she juggled her life between the mountain retreat, the factory and the new, but still unsatisfactory schools for her older children, required not only a remarkable feat of physical organization but a manipulation of her theories that could not be mere sophistry. At 3.15 pm Laura would always drop whatever she was doing to go and collect the older children from school. Often she brought them back to the factory and continued working while they amused themselves, or chatted to the staff.

Laura convinced herself that the business was not merely 'a family business' nor just an extension of family life. It *was* her family. She was there, primarily, to support her husband but, more than that, she saw the business as the means by which she maintained the family. The paradox is that ultimately the business prevented the family from existing in a normal sense. But in the early Sixties Laura could not foresee that such a dichotomy would arise. The knowledge that her commitment to the business and the family could coexist without conflict, so that she could be with her husband and her children and develop a business all at the same time, made the next few years of unremitting toil not only tolerable but fulfilling in a way that surprised even Laura herself.

By the mid-Sixties Ashley Mountney products were selling consistently well in major stores throughout the world as well as in small kitchen and craft shops throughout Britain. This was partly due to the efforts of a young girl who had been taken on as a textile designer but who was used increasingly as a salesperson. Liz Matson visited every county in Britain and made several trips abroad during her time with the Ashleys. Bernard instructed her on the routine when driving through towns. 'You had to look from right to left constantly searching for a shop that might be suitable to stock their products.' It was while obeying these instructions that she nearly knocked over an elderly man crossing the road. Bernard sometimes came with her on these selling trips, but was of dubious assistance. He would invariably march into a shop without an appointment, munching an apple. If he considered he had been kept waiting too long to see the buyer, usually the time it took to eat the apple, he would quietly put the core in the pocket of a competitor's apron. Liz was well placed to see that the huge demand for the Ashleys' products could never be satisfied by the existing outlets. 'I was out there selling and I knew, you simply could not sell any more. The big shops were as coy as ever in their orders and sending so much back, complaining about the quality. We had approached all the little shops and they were stuffed full. I begged them to open a shop of their own; it was the only way.'

The Ashleys were aware of the constriction preventing expansion, especially in London, and were determined to rectify it. Although many students were buying the shifts and smocks and wearing them as dresses, buyers for the large stores insisted on keeping them in the overall or apron section where they were often dumped in a large circular rail with hundreds of other similar, or less attractive, household overalls. The Ashleys were appalled to discover that, even if all their smocks had been sold, most buyers would not reorder until the other makes had gone too. Even the excellent publicity which the company continued to enjoy at this time could not, it appeared, pierce the conservatism or timidity of the buyers. But it was also, as Laura recognized, partly a question of quality; the uneven finish of the garments made them unsuitable, in a buyer's eye, as smart dresses. Laura spent hours checking seams, putting her hand inside gloves, turning products inside out and inspecting them for the smallest defects. But, instead of criticizing her workers, she preferred to find ways of encouraging them to do better in future, often correcting the mistakes herself if possible. This made for slow progress, but Laura knew she was training an unsophisticated workforce in an area with virtually no industrial background; the situation demanded all her patience and understanding.

One of the most touching examples of this concerns a pensioner employee, Anna Griffiths, taken on at Tybrith. Miss Griffiths, as she was always very correctly known, was descended from a farming family which had lived in the area for generations. She had been a 'postie' all her life, delivering in all weathers to wild and wayward homes. Now, however, she had had to give up due to ill-health and applied to 'Laura

Ashley' for work. In spite of the fact that her only formal training had been undertaken thirty years previously when she had learned how to use a domestic sewing machine for a post as family governess, she was given a job and remained a devoted machinist for more than ten years. 'The finest person one could ever meet,' is Miss Griffiths' verdict on Laura Ashley.

A certain mystic quality about Laura, which she must always have owned, began to have an effect from now on. Her employees wanted to perform well to please her. She did not say much but always had time to listen. She could delegate if necessary, but worked hard herself at the same time. She never avoided eye contact whatever it was she had to impart. One of Laura's great strengths was her ability always to work on a human level and it was this talent, to catch the human scale in everything, to which, most significantly, she was later able to give artistic expression in her designs. As Bernard was constantly planning the next adventure, she would never deter but always encourage him, while at the same time ensuring that the necessary details were not overlooked in the excitement.

Nonetheless, Laura began pressing in earnest for a shop exclusively selling their own products as a way forward. Yet Bernard was more wary than ever of this route, having just emerged from an unsuccessful experiment with a shop in London, on Knightsbridge Green, called 'Boys'. This had been a joint venture with several other entrepreneurs and the shop sold housecoats made up in 'Laura Ashley' fabrics as well as some garments made at Tybrith and others manufactured by the other shareholders. But there was no clear image and it failed disastrously. Bernard considered himself lucky to escape with most of his original investment of £3,000 intact, thanks largely to the intervention of a mutual friend. 'Bernard was a very likeable chap with a wife and kids in Wales who had sunk his only working capital into this shop. I told the others he had to get his money out,' recalled Philip Pollock, a businessman with a wide range of interests who remained a close friend and adviser ever since. After this débâcle, Bernard, typically, saw the company's salvation in machinery; bigger, faster and better. Accordingly he set about finding himself some that he could adapt as well as new premises to house it. He had worked extremely hard building up the wholesale accounts, of which there were now well in excess of the hundred and he was not prepared to see them all jeopardized by the opening of a shop. He believed then, and does still, that his company's skills lay first and foremost as dyers and printers.

6

From Carno to Kensington

In any success story the threads of luck entangle with time to form part of the 'Greater Myth'. Was it mere luck or superior judgement that enabled Laura and Bernard to recruit some local staff of exceptional talent, dedication and above all the will to succeed? As a result of living within the rigours of a farming calendar these people understood the imperatives of the seasons; they knew instinctively that the day did not stop just because it was dark, that work might be slack one day but fraught for the next three. They carried weight in the community. If they were on the side of the English couple with weird habits, then the whole village would be. Meirion Rowlands, one of the Ashleys' most key appointments of this time, was well known as the local prizewinning sheep shearer; he met Bernard over a pint in the pub. Meirion desperately needed more remunerative work and was on the point of leaving his home town. What imaginative job search agency would have foreseen that a champion sheepshearer could become a master garment cutter (and, later, much more besides) but Bernard and Laura did. When Ashley Mountney work was slack, he could be released to help on the farm for a few days sheep shearing again. When the Ashleys needed help with construction work he could borrow farm tractors for them. For, as Emlyn Hooson described Meirion, 'he was a whole hogger – either wholly for you or wholly against you.' Luckily he was wholly for the Ashleys.

Among the Welsh core of the 'Laura Ashley' business was not only

75

Meirion but, shortly to join them, his sister Carol (now Jones), as well as his brother Alan, Phil Morris, Dai Jones, the Hughes family and others. These people cared deeply about the success of the venture because they cared about their own livelihoods, the future of their children and the very breath of their dying community. 'Until you've lived in Wales you don't know what cheerfulness is,' Laura often commented. Both she and Bernard were continually taken aback by the way their staff threw themselves into the Ashley enterprise – although they expected nothing less and, in different ways it was they who inspired their employees to rise above whatever talents they thought they could offer. 'Laura Ashley' was the village pride and joy. Because so many people so badly wanted it to succeed when it did they almost believed it was because they had willed it to. Thus was 'The Myth' born. But the success owed more to hard work and drive than simple luck or faith.

Each day held a different challenge or, as one long-standing employee put it: 'We all lived to go to work.' Many of them will reappear throughout the story, for this Welsh heart of the business always retained a special place in Laura's affections. When mistakes arose, the original Welsh workforce was never blamed; when success registered, Laura appreciated how much she owed to them. From now on 'Laura Ashley' was Welsh or it was nothing.

Bernard had now taken the decision to stay in the area. He approached the county councillor and poet, Francis Thomas, and told him he would not be renewing the lease on Tybrith as they had now outgrown it. 'He gave me twelve months to find him a bigger place,' recalled Thomas. 'I was doing everything I could to keep him because of the jobs in the area.' Thomas's first proposal was a field in Carno, near the Post Office, for sale at £12,000, twelve miles from Tybrith but closer to their new home, Clogau. However, when Bernard applied for planning permission to build a factory on the site he was turned down by the local highways department.

Then Thomas remembered an existing, highly original property, minutes away from the field. Carno Station, a Victorian granite relic of an earlier railway age, had been closed to passengers on 4 June 1965, a little more than 100 years after it opened, and was now for sale.

'Much too small,' said Bernard when he first saw it. But he soon changed his mind when he realized the scope for expansion and the magnificent setting of the building. With a backdrop of endless hills and valleys, a gentle stream flowing across granite boulders in the wings and at the front, facing the road, the Victorian village school,* the dramatic possibilities for a major reconstruction quickly took shape in his mind. In his hands the existing contrast between the building's industrial past and the immutability of the landscape would be sharpened into a creative expression of striking proportions. It was, in short, a perfect location for the myth to be enacted.

The railway building (600 sq. ft.), shunting shed (1,500 sq. ft.) and slightly more than one acre of land were for sale very cheaply at £1,200. Although the track behind the station was still used for freight, trains no longer stopped at Carno. Negotiations with the Railways Board at Swindon were complicated by the existence of a private property on the site. In addition Bernard was bothered by a rumour that a turkey farm was due to open opposite. Turkeys, he feared, would encourage rats and rats would eat his cloth. But the turkey farm developed elsewhere and Councillor Thomas worked arduously to iron out most of the bureaucratic formalities which Bernard hated or ignored.

Bernard immediately renewed a contact he had made with the Industrial and Commercial Finance Corporation Ltd (ICFC) to secure a loan, the company's first major borrowing. After more than ten years of approaching various banks, the company had finally proved its staying power. ICFC lent a total of £14,000; £7,400 for the land and buildings, £4,600 for the plant and £2,000 working capital (increased in October 1967 by a further £4,000). On 23 February 1967, the station was bought and Bernard, having already planned a 3,000 foot extension, immediately embarked on it. It was, much to Francis Thomas' consternation, a question of building first, seeking permission later. 'Laura never got involved in these sorts of negotiations,' he said ruefully, 'but if you ever asked her to help sort out a problem involving Bernard it was always "my husband right or wrong".' Thomas was not the first to learn that criticism of Bernard, to Laura, was foolhardy. Yet Bernard himself shied away from any contact with officialdom. 'He left it all to me to sort out with the planning department and I had to plead that we'd lose him altogether if we made a problem.' Some councillors,

---

* Built in 1851 to accommodate thirty children, the school charges for educating children were 1d a week or 1½d if there were two from the same family.

who saw Bernard only as a source of irritation, might have welcomed that. Not Thomas, who liked them too much. In the event Bernard was allowed his extensions and the only stipulation was that the wall facing the road must be in stone to match the adjacent stone-built bridge, rather than in brick, which would have been cheaper.

Carno was a predominantly Welsh-speaking village with a declining population when the Ashleys moved there. Agriculture was the main-stay of the community, although most other rural crafts had disap-peared. In 1949, according to a survey by the local branch of the WI, there had been five carpenters and wheelwrights, one blacksmith, two masons, two cobblers, one tailor, one dressmaker and three butchers. By 1967 only one butcher, of all these craftsmen, remained. Up to 1939, the local flour mill was in operation and the last iron-rimmed wooden cartwheel was made the following year. According to age-old local legends, the meaning of the word Carno comes from a hill in the centre of the Parish called '*clorin*' because it is shaped like the back of a horse; the Welsh farmers' word for the tail of a foal is '*torir clorin*'. The old part of the village, where the church stands, is down by the heel, or hoof of *clorin*. As the Welsh for hoof is *carn*, folklorists insist that *Ein Carn O* or Carno, by the hoof of the horse, must be the meaning of the village name. There are other, less complicated, explanations;for example Carno is surrounded by cairns and the word may be a derivative of this. At all events, the mediaeval part of the village developed at the junction of the rivers Cerniog and Carno, before the latter reached the Severn, and is grouped around the church and the site of a Roman camp. Markets, held free of toll by privilege of the Lord of the Manor, and the 'Goose Fairs', where poultry and pigs were sold, died out only at the turn of the century. The village and surrounding farms have changed little over the centuries; the Aleppo Merchants Inn, standing on the route of the old Roman road, was first licensed in 1632. Although post-war plans for the village included a community centre, new school, village hall, playing fields and houses, these never fully materialized. With the advent of 'Laura Ashley', this sleepy village was to see more changes in a decade than it had in centuries.

Shortly after moving to Wales, Bernard, who was continually having trouble with the finely tuned engine of his Lotus Elite, had discovered a motor club. Antony Sheppard, a fellow enthusiast, persuaded Bernard to let them recondition the engine. The man who did the job, thereby impressing Bernard greatly, was Dai Jones, working at the time as a service engineer for domestic appliances. 'Bernard gave me four new tyres for my own car as payment but kept saying, "I'm going to open a big factory one day and have you as works' manager".' As soon as the railway station at Carno was theirs, Bernard wrote to Dai offering him the promised job. 'We met one Saturday morning and he asked me what I was currently getting paid. I told him, about seventeen pounds a week, and he offered me a pound a week less with no payment, but free petrol.'

What was the attraction? 'I could see something was there; Bernard had the persistence to obtain the site, he was doing something positive – already he'd got a steel frame constructed for a building where the freight was formerly loaded – he was practical and a great motivator at the same time.' Dai joined and was immediately given more challenging work than he had ever known. Second-hand machinery was scattered around the yard with new parts and modifications arriving daily. The cutters and machinists were to remain at the club house for another twelve and eighteen months respectively but the plan was for the printers to move immediately into the new premises.

Dai's initial role was to install the 3,000 lb boiler, with dyeing and washing machines, in the former railway shunting shed. He was horrified. 'I'd worked with steam but nothing like this. Often Bernard would say "Okay, you're in charge, I'm off," and leave me to it. It wasn't that he wouldn't help, often he did, but he believed that by delegating he brought out the best in people, that they would rise to the challenge, and he had other things to be done.'

Once Dai succeeded in getting Bernard's semi-automatic printer in full working order it could produce 5,000 metres of cloth per week. One of the most important advances, made possible by the move to bigger premises, was the use of reactive, instead of pigment, dyes. Reactive dyestuffs, developed in the Fifties, chemically react with the cotton fibre, under the influence of alkali and heat. Generally they give a good wash-fastness and provide a much wider and brighter spectrum of colours. However, they require a complex treatment for finishing and so a 'wet processing' area had to be set up. This 'wet end' became ever more necessary as the company began to prepare the raw materials itself. The cloth which 'Laura Ashley' bought in 1967 came from India and Pakistan in loomstate and was not of high quality. It required sewing together, then cropping, scouring with just enough caustic soda so that the fabric would not tear, and bleaching with peroxide, which then had to be well washed out. These were all new processes which required space, machinery, an increasing range of chemicals and personnel. But the more procedures which eliminated middlemen ensured that the price of the finished product could be reduced. This increasing vertical expansion of the business also enabled the Ashleys to keep a much tighter control on their product's image. For the next three years there was a constant struggle to buy better second-hand machinery for each stage of the manufacture; sewing, printing, curing, dyeing and mixing. Somehow, Dai, goaded on by a blend of Bernard's impatience and supervision, got them working.

From the start there was no such thing as clocking in; Bernard would usually arrive at 7.30 am, sometimes earlier, and everyone else would be there by 8 am. Although Laura had a demanding toddler at her heels, she broadened her horizons from researching prints and quality control to overseeing the total production process. 'She'd give you a hand with anything that needed doing, from packing, invoicing, cutting and laying to choosing and mixing colours; she wasn't keen on the administration side but she did that too,' Meirion recalled. Still, she never lost sight of the smaller details that made the operation run smoothly. She kept a record of everyone's birthday at the factory and, until the company grew too big, always brought in a cake on the appropriate day.

It was now that she started a canteen, run by a mother of eight, Gwenny Hughes. This was a small enclave at first where homemade soup, fruit and a few other wholesome products were not only provided free, but all staff were expected to partake of them at midday. No fried foods were allowed. Those who lived any distance from the factory were collected in the morning and taken home at night. There were never to be any night shifts at a 'Laura Ashley' factory. If Laura noticed any of her staff wearing clothes in a poor state of repair she would look into that person's wages and family circumstances and see if there was a way of paying them more without upsetting the hierarchy. All her staff believed she genuinely cared for their welfare for no other reason than her deeply-felt need to be surrounded by a contented workforce.

Every able-bodied man employed by the new company was eager to

Laura aged six, in fancy dress as a pierrot. Although living in Wallington she already had a sense of her roots in Wales.

Below: A family group at home. From left to right: Mrs Mountney (Bess), Trevor (on her lap), Francis, Laura, Mr Mountney (Stan) and Mary.

Above: Laura joined the WRNS in 1944 from Merthyr Tydfil and spent most of the next two years in Paris and Brussels. This photograph was one of Bernard's favourites and always sat on his desk.

Right: Laura on her wedding day – a bitterly cold afternoon in February 1949.

Laura at the Old Burlington Street offices of the Ashley Mountney company. The bolts of cloth in the background were Bernard Ashley fabrics ready for delivery to clients, who included Terence Conran.

Bernard's first dye lab in the basement premises at 83 Cambridge Street, Pimlico.

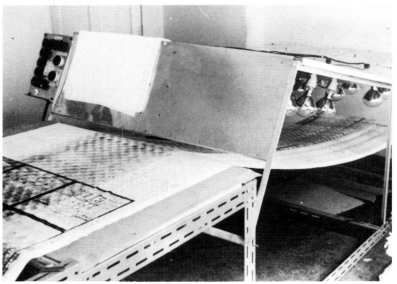

Bernard's first printing machine, built from Dexion, at Cambridge Street, where there was barely room to squeeze around the table. The geometric designs being printed were Bernard's.

Christmas with the children at East Cottage. Friends were worried about how poor the Ashleys were at this time but the children are wearing matching sweaters.

A more prosperous Christmas in Wales at Gwalia House, above the shop in Machynlleth. From left to right: Bernard, Nick, Laura, Emma, David and Jane.

The first semi-automatic printer at Carno in the old shed (1967). The design shown is by Bernard, in three shades of brown.

Above: The first automatic (hydraulic squeegee) machine housed in the 'new shed' at Carno 1970. The old railway shunting shed can be seen in the background.

Laura's striking black and white outfit is set off perfectly against Bernard's Lotus Elite. The striped shift, made out of Welsh flannel, was one of Laura's designs. Although she hated posing for press photographs she never minded when Bernard wanted to use her as a model.

Laura walking on the top of the rugged Welsh hills above Clogau. Although often accompanied by Bernard, as on this occasion to discuss business plans, her solitary walks were one of her most replenishing activities and a valuable scource of creative inspiration.

Above: The first Laura Ashley articulated lorry, with its bold Sixties lettering, would rumble down the narrow lanes from Carno to London only to be attacked by marauding customers waiting for their favourite styles to arrive.

Laura in the sort of formal pose, advertising company products, that she hated. But this gypsy-style outfit suited her well and the tiered skirt was one of the company's most successful styles ever.

A rare shot of Laura at the helm of their boat, *Quaeso*, while Jane tries to read and the sea is calm. Always self-conscious of her wispy hair, Laura invariably wore a scarf over it tied at the back in peasant style.

Above: Bernard and Laura, with their friend Thomas Dunne, waiting to board an Ashley aircraft, Bernard often piloted this himself.

Laura with her first grandchild, Sara Jane, in the conservatory at Rhydoldog, 1984.

Clogau, Montgomeryshire, a Welsh longhouse; as wild and isolated a home as could be found.

Right: Rhydoldog House, Radnorshire, a Victorian rambling mansion with magnificent views.

Left: Château de Remaisnil, Doullens, France, the Ashley's first experiment in grand living.

La Pré Verger, a romantic French manoir in the south of France, hidden among lavender and olive groves.

lend a hand with the new buildings. Spurred on by Bernard's example, Edgar Hughes, Gwenny's son, was often to be seen with pick or shovel in hand, mixing cement, laying concrete floors, building walls or fitting windows. Dai and Meirion were two other company stalwarts who regularly pitched in with building work in their spare time, or else organized a shift system with the other printers, almost all of whom were happy to volunteer for manual labour. So devoted was Meirion that when he came in at dawn once, to get the boilers going, he tripped on a pipe in the shunting shed and broke his forearm. 'The bone was sticking out of my arm but I knew I had to carry on. I was bleeding but I just tried to hide it because it was a terribly busy time.' Today he laughs about the accident. He carried on for two days but finally, in excruciating pain, had to go to hospital when a splint was put on his damaged limb. He never breathed a word to Laura because he knew her concern would force him to stop work immediately. Interestingly, when Laura was told about this incident years later by a researcher preparing an internal history of the company, she could not accept it. The very suggestion pained her so much because the company appeared uncaring and tough; she therefore denied that such a thing could possibly have occurred. It damaged the myth.

Meirion was much in awe of Laura and Bernard. 'You could see there was something special about them. They told you everything about the company, what their plans were, how much they earned and so you felt part of the team. Sometimes Bernard would work all through the night and there was not a day in winter even in snowy, freezing weather when they wouldn't turn up and bring sandwiches and bottles to keep us all going.' He was impressed, too, by the way Laura dealt with disasters, of which there were plenty at that time. 'Once I cut the neckline wrong on three hundred dresses and I thought at first I'd just keep quiet and fill the gap with lace. But, of course, she would have noticed so I told her and we turned the scoop to our advantage. In future that style always carried the "wrong" neckline. All she said to me, very calmly, was, "Remember, you can always learn by your mistakes".'

Meirion was not alone in seeing Laura and Bernard as 'a spare set of parents to us all.' The nucleus of workers who helped transform Carno Railway Station into one of the world's most efficient textile printing plants considered themselves from the beginning as part of an extended family. As the business grew, sons and daughters might be working alongside parents, brothers and sisters. It was a local concern, employing whole families, and everyone knew that in order to flourish they must give it their all. It was their family.

The new factory made it possible for the company to produce increasingly elaborate garments. A third building included a single-storey office which incorporated a design studio and dark room for the first time and enabled Laura to organize her print and pattern research. Liz Matson had been very impressed at how much Laura had taught herself from books; using cardboard patterns she could manage basic grading. But for several years it remained extremely basic, with only small, medium and large sizes remotely possible so long as the styles were kept simple. At the time they moved to Carno, Meirion and Tony were still cutting, with scissors, a mere four lays at a time. Now, however, spurred on by the popularity of the Victorian nightdress, she decided it was time to produce a modified version as a day dress. No market research informed Laura that women were thirsting for long dresses which they could not find. But she believed that the more a woman covered up, the more she was attractive to the opposite sex, while Bernard grasped the idea as a way of using up more fabric. In addition, the finished cloth had a natural, peasanty look, often full of flaws and slubs, that gave it a charm and character which coincided perfectly with the image Laura sought. She was absolutely convinced that what she liked other people wanted too; a canny instinct which she used always as her guiding principle and from which no one could shake her. Dai Jones remembers her single-mindedness being focused for one brief period on the need for stainless steel buttons on blouses. 'She was so hell-bent on them that when I told her I couldn't get them anywhere she said "Well, we'd better make them." I made a few as samples and then she could see that they weren't right so we didn't use them in the end. But if she wanted something she'd have it.'

At other times she could be flexible. Increasingly the dresses were full of lace inserts and pin-tucks, which were intricate to sew. Sometimes she would try to reduce the detailed work in her original design simply to facilitate the process for the machinists. This also had the effect of keeping prices down, thereby benefiting the customer. Each machinist was given virtually an entire garment to produce as a more satisfying method of working than 'production line' techniques. Laura would often send memos to Meirion asking him to let her know if anything in the design was causing problems in making up; if so, she would alter it. Within the year it was evident that the Carno factory was revolutionizing the company's ability to produce cheap, original clothes without any of the problems faced by so many other British industries in the late Sixties. The basic long dress took only fourteen minutes to make, yet none among this motivated workforce considered they were overworked, nor in any way exploited.

In spite of the growing success, there was still never any spare cash as profits were endlessly ploughed back in the unremitting quest for newer, more powerful machinery. While money was usually found for the larger items, there was a continual shortage for other equipment. Dai Jones remembered when he had to go to his cousin in Llandidloes for a bucket to mix the dyes, 'because there was no money to buy one, and money was owed everywhere.' Also the only vehicle was a small van suitable for local deliveries, and so goods were despatched each day throughout the world from Carno's small sub-post office. All items had to be packed so that they weighed less than twenty-two pounds and sometimes there were so many parcels filling the room that it was impossible for other customers to pass through the door; the postmaster would then telephone the Newtown depot to request a special van to come and collect them. Eventually the post office built an extension simply to cope with Ashley Mountney work.

The company was engaged in a delicate balancing act; it could not afford first-rate machinery or transport until it had expanded, but it could not expand (as a wholesaler at least) until it improved quality through more sophisticated machinery. Bernard and Laura nearly became victims of their own success at this point; with the great increase in turnover (sales were by this time around £100,000 a year), the company was falling into the near inevitable trap of a young, fast-growing business. It was forever seeking longer credit from its suppliers, it was never able to be be paid quickly enough by its customers and did not boast adequate assets to borrow permanent capital. They had had accountants to help them in the past but, as a group, Laura never trusted them. One, she felt, was taking advantage of Bernard and her by knowing about the business – he had requested some shares in the company, which she considered an outrageous request; another had called her by her Christian name which was equally unacceptable. She preferred Bernard to work out whatever financial disciplines were necessary 'on the back of an envelope' and Carol Jones, who was 'one of the family' to balance the books. Laura maintained, pointedly, that she could manage quite well with a traditional abacus, which she asked Dai to make her. It was a good example of Laura's humour; no one was expected to laugh.

Finally the Ashleys decided to combat the problem of non-paying wholesale customers by themselves buying a London shop. For a long time Laura had nurtured this dream, but Bernard well knew that selling products in your own shop at the same time as supplying other retailers was a risky undertaking; the latter regarded it as unfair competition. However, he was increasingly irritated by having goods returned, even if complaints were occasionally justified. Without adequate infrastructure it was difficult to ensure that, for example, two small purple dresses went to Harrods and four large green smocks to Liberty's. Rectifying such errors was costly. As Ashley Mountney could not become entirely independent of the wholesalers overnight it was decided to start a subsidiary company expressly for the retailing operation and in 1968, little more than one year after the move to Carno, Ashley Shops Ltd was formed.

The first 'Laura Ashley' shop in London no longer exists. It was swallowed up by London Transport, who owned the site, and became part of South Kensington underground station. Previously, 23, Pelham Street had been a boutique with a mezzanine floor, two changing rooms and an office. The Ashleys decorated it plainly in white and left it as bare as possible, apart from two rails which could hold up to 500 garments. The name 'Laura Ashley' was attached to the glass in modern, bold, white letters. There was never any doubt that the shops would take their name from the labels in the clothes, which, it was hoped, loyal customers would recognize. 'Made in Wales' was also printed on the labels, which further reinforced the authentic country air. On the first day takings were twenty-seven pounds, seventeen shillings and sixpence and for six months many potential customers walked past assuming it was a wholesale showroom.

Then Bernard made two critical decisions; for the first time he organized some advertising and he hired a new shop manageress. Moira Braybrooke was one of Bernard's most imaginative appointments since she had neither retail nor fashion trade experience; she had worked as a secretary in Monte Carlo, had style, good looks and an exotic family background. Looking for a change, she answered a newspaper advertisement. Bernard spotted a dynamic personality and sent Moira plunging into her new job. Perhaps because she had not previously been living in London, Moira observed precisely what it was that dozens of well-bred young ladies were enthusing over; the long pin-tucked nightdresses, which no one else was making, to wear as day or evening dresses. She knew that although the shop stocked a few overalls and smocks and even some children's clothes and sheepskin jackets, it was the long dresses with their wonderfully romantic feel and yards of material in the skirts, that the *cognoscenti* came to buy. No other manufacturer would be so profligate in their use of fabric but the Ashleys behaved as if they had fabric to spare. Often they did.

Buoyed by Moira's immediate report, Bernard spent £200 on some photographs and had posters printed of a model wearing a corduroy maxi dress with a high neck, belt, tucks along the bodice and a full skirt with a wide frill; excellent value at six guineas. He placed the posters around London's underground, giving the little shop as a stockist. The effect was electrifying. Suddenly queues formed around the block with girls keen to grab armfuls of the dresses. The two beleaguered shop assistants were on their feet serving, wrapping and operating the till non-stop for days; they became exhausted. If the changing rooms were full, girls would undress in the middle of the shop leaving piles of clothes all over the floor, such was their desperation to find the print and the style of their choice. Sometimes Moira had to lock customers out in the middle of the day in order to control the numbers inside. When both the *Observer* and the *Daily Express* wrote flattering editorials on the new shop, sales soared to over £3,000 a week. From now on 'Laura Ashley' was always considered good material for hungry fashion editors eager to spot a wayward trend and Moira cultivated close relationships with all the fashion editors of the day. 'The press was always very kind to us, giving us so many free editorials that we never had to pay a penny for advertising. Often we would design something specially; if someone rang and asked if we had a Mexican outfit for a feature on Mexican clothes we'd say "yes" and within a day have a sample made up which fitted in with a Mexican look.' The ability to produce garments at speed and on demand in this way was obviously a vital factor in the early success. No marketing and no forecasting ensured huge flexibility. 'It meant we never had to say "no" to anything a fashion editor asked of us,' Moira joked. Her relationship with Meirion was crucial, too, for ensuring the steady flow of garments from Carno to London. Both would shout at the other down the telephone so much that Laura, fascinated by the interaction of her staff, used to worry on occasion that they were not 'getting on'. To an extent, the stormy exterior mirrored the relationship of their employers, Bernard and Laura; but underneath everyone was shooting for the same goal.

Moira knew exactly what designs she needed in the shop and would tell Meirion to have two dozen of a particular style ready for delivery to the shop within two days at most. But she never dared instruct on colours. 'We just let him use whatever dyes he liked and send us whatever he ended up with.' Dye mixing was still being done by hand, often using the same bucket, without cleaning the dregs in between, for startlingly different shades, so that colour matching was virtually impossible. Thus there could be no economies of scale in case a sleeve cut from one lay of medium blue had to go with a dress cut from another lay of so-called medium blue. Not surprisingly, the 'Laura Ashley' palette was always highly distinctive; from the moment the shop opened it was clear that their prints, either monochrome or two tone, were being produced in colours nowhere else available. These had now moved away from the bright primaries of the early Sixties and included many rustic shades such as mushroom brown, sage green and sludgy blue; colours, which were more reminiscent of the old-fashioned vegetable dyes and perfectly complemented the style of the dresses.

The sudden and dramatic success of the London shop might have caused uproar and panic among the thirty-strong team in Carno. Instead, it generated excitement and renewed vigour. Deliveries to London were mostly undertaken by Meirion or Dai Jones, and occasionally, Bernard. At first they managed with an old Hillman Minx estate, but they soon traded up to a Ford Transit van. They would load it for Pelham Street after a day's work in the factory, drive there and back in a night, and report for work as usual the next morning. There were certain weeks when a driver went every night, others when they could get by with three deliveries a week. 'But we didn't mind a bit, a job here was so much more than just a means to an end, it was never a case of them and us. We're not exactly country yokels, but all the same, selling garments in London, yes, to be honest, it was very exciting,' Dai Jones admitted twenty years later.

Seeing what 'Laura Ashley' has become today, such remarks do not seem out of place. But in the context of the mid-Sixties, when Britain's chaotic labour relations were deemed to be among the world's worst, such good-natured willingness to work long hours, doing all kinds of jobs, for sums of money that were not vast, are extraordinary. There was hardly a corner of British industry in the Sixties which did not suffer strike action of one sort; much of it lengthy, acrimonious and ultimately futile. Yet there never was, and still is not, a trade union at 'Laura Ashley'. Bernard and Laura maintained that their door was always open and while the company remained small, it always was. Nobody ever felt the heavy hand of management versus employees. The couple worked at the same tasks as their staff, they dressed in the same way, educated their children at the same schools and ate in the same canteen. Not surprisingly, they were rewarded by deep loyalty and an overriding will to succeed. It is largely this ability of the entire enterprise to pull together which gave rise to, and strengthened the myth: somehow, 'Laura Ashley' represented all that was best in traditional Britain.

In those early years Laura believed that the prints were more important than the styles. They had chanced upon a look which was popular and yet could be varied in dozens of different ways; the neck could be scooped, V-shaped or square, the sleeves could be full, tight or removed altogether (so that it became a pinafore), and the waistline could be moved up or down. Only the length was a non-variable and so every style retained the same 'look'. The pinafore version naturally needed a blouse and items in unbleached white cotton were the cheapest of all to produce. This realization led to several white calico garments; fulsome petticoats, frilled blouses and fancy nightdresses being the most obvious, all of them generous with material. Moira is convinced that 'at this stage there was no conscious effort to recreate the past in the styles – one thing just led to another – but there was in terms of the prints; with old reference books proving far and away the best place to find ideas.' By 1969 Laura was spending much of her time poring over old books – the endpapers of novels were a rich source of small prints as were old plates, teapots, and patchwork quilts, in fact anything that caught her eye in a variety of odd shops. And she had begun to form a unique library of prints she liked. One of the most popular motifs at the time the shop opened was of swans and lions, which came from an old, heraldic design; another was a Persian print showing a fantastical dog in a jungle of giant thistles. There were also several prints of buds and flowers in the range, but these were by no means predominant, nor, yet, was their ultimate significance to the company glaringly apparent.

Laura was never one to swim with every fashionable cross-current that came her way. If a woman found a style she liked, why should she not keep it for ever, as long as it was practical and comfortable? For herself, she had by now evolved a working wardrobe of a plain skirt, in navy or beige with matching cardigan (usually well worn and full of holes in the elbows) and a toning plain shirt. This, in essence, remained her favourite outfit until she died. But she did keep abreast of fashion eddies, for example by subscribing to the fashion trends and information service, Infovogue, and by reading as many magazines as she could discover. In this way she developed her instinctive talent as a fashion editor; she could instantly take a detail from this and an idea from that, while keeping well within her overall style. The year the shop opened she hired a new dress designer, Jacqui Smale, fresh from the Royal College of Art, and told her how sensible she thought it was to wear uniform because this removed the agonies of planning what to wear each day as well as the decisions about accessories to go with the clothes. Perhaps she was attracted to Jacqui's work because she had just won a prize for designing a new uniform.

Laura gave Jacqui a clear brief about the sort of dresses and blouses she wanted and sent her to the Victoria and Albert Museum to research styles. 'I had to adjust my ideas because my previous designs were sharp little miniskirts ... rather severe.' Although Laura would phone Jacqui every day she would usually ask for another dress 'along the same lines'. With her sewing machine on the half-landing of the Pelham Street shop, she worked mostly at making up samples to send to Wales. Although Jacqui went to Carno periodically and helped teach Meirion and others how to grade, a skill she had learnt at college, Laura wanted Jacqui to be based in Carno as one of her growing design team. This included Phil Morris, who had been apprenticed to a graphics printer for four years when he joined the company and who was immediately sent by Bernard on a further course in fabric processing. Then he was drafted into Laura's studio where his technical expertise was critical in strengthening the developing team.

Phil soon became one of Laura's closest associates but even he recognized that 'she wasn't an easy person to work with, I think anyone will tell you that. But I learned how to, over the years. You could never impress yourself or your own ideas and feelings on to her. You had to make her feel she was coming up with the original idea. She had this absolute conviction that what she liked, other people would too. Amazingly, her touch was almost always right.' Phil's discovery of Laura's need to believe she had decided whether or not a new idea would be successful was an essential prerequisite for anyone who wanted a good working relationship with her. Those who understood this might leave a swatch of fabric lying around so that Laura could pick it up and believe she had discovered it herself, even if they had been trying to persuade her to use it for months. She would never be coerced into something that was not wholly hers because she was deeply concerned lest the image of the company would be irreparably diluted. Since the product bore her name, it became of paramount importance to her to maintain an image of which she approved.

With the London shop flourishing the Ashleys could afford to worry less about oppilative buyers. However, one unexpected new problem emerged. For months they had had difficulty in reconciling the accounts until they realized the extent of shoplifting. The Ashleys, determined to stamp it out, adopted an active watching policy. Surapee (Su) Karnasuta, a young Thai who helped Moira run the shop, had several Thai friends who were happy to train their eyes on potential shoplifters and were not afraid of speaking authoritatively to anyone they suspected of helping themselves. Another unforeseen dilemma which now surfaced was how to satisfy the demands of the new customers for winter-weight, or seasonal clothes. Until now it had been enough to produce smocks, nightdresses and long dresses in cotton for stores which would carry supplementary ranges by other manufacturers in different departments. But a shop selling only summer-weight clothes in November looked mildly ridiculous. Miss Griffiths remembers costly experiments with machining wool at Tybrith which ended in disaster as the fabric had stretched and shrunk in all the wrong places. A heavy investment in new machinery was needed before Ashley Mountney could offer wool garments. Bernard ingeniously proposed a range of dresses in 'double cotton', or a double layer of fabric. Although somewhat bulky and unflattering, it was not unsuccessful as it blended with the current trend for layered clothes and endorsed the rustic air of a bygone age that other 'Laura Ashley' clothes were now describing. As they would not consider offering anything that was not made of 100 per cent natural fibres, they managed to complete the range by producing dresses in brushed cotton and cotton corduroy.

Part of the attraction of shopping at 'Laura Ashley' was finding uniquely eccentric clothes. The peasant look was a potent image, but there were others. The magic was being able to step into a 'Laura Ashley' dress and imagine you had found something out of a dressing-up box. You had put on much more than a dress, there was such a vivid aura of theatre and drama surrounding it. And all of this for just a few pounds.

But personally, the decade did not end well for Laura. The phenomenal success of Pelham Street pulled both her and Bernard increasingly into the capital. Bernard was happy to drive up and down several times in a week, but Laura felt the need for a base. At first, they took a flat in Chelsea, opposite the Royal Hospital, but in 1969 they bought a beautiful nineteenth-century house in Paulton's Square, originally built for army personnel. It was but a short hop from their first rooms in St George's Square but represented an enormous leap in lifestyle. Laura's frequent absences in London meant that her baby, Emma, was often left behind with Gwenny Hughes. Although Laura had great faith in Gwenny, she never doubted that it was a mother's place to be with her child. For one who was convinced of the merits of control, both control of self and regulation of one's environment, she was discovering something beyond her range of command; her children. Inevitably, as the older three grew up and away from her, Laura suffered.

David, feeling that he was learning nothing at Newtown Comprehensive and that his parents' lives were increasingly centred on London, took a unilateral decision; he left Clogau, moved into the family flat in Chelsea and enrolled at Holland Park Comprehensive, the most renowned, free-thinking state school of the day. When he wrote home to Jane telling her how wonderful was his new independent life style, she followed. Laura's two oldest children thus fled the nest while still in their teens, and she was powerless to respond. Meanwhile Laura and Bernard underwent a change of heart over educational priorities and wanted to send Nick to the nearby, old-established public school, Shrewsbury. To bring him up to the required standard he had to go to a boarding preparatory school, which he loathed so much he escaped over the wall and hitchhiked home. Laura could not force him back and, in a desultory fashion, he was allowed to follow in his siblings' tracks. It was as if, because she bore them so much love, the actions of her children had the power to anaesthetize some of her most cherished convictions.

At the same time as running two homes, Laura was still combining many roles in the factory. In the autumn of 1969, aged forty-four, she found herself pregnant yet again and, utterly exhausted, went into hospital for an examination which resulted in a miscarriage. The experience left her physically and emotionally drained and a few months later she returned to hospital for a hysterectomy. In the event, the operation went smoothly, but factory staff say they saw a new uncertain side to Bernard during those tense, waiting days. She slowly regained her strength in the latter part of the year, just in time to cope with a winter season and no designer. Jacqui Smale had left before Christmas as she had recently married and could not, as Laura wished, move to Wales. Laura was not in a great hurry to find a new designer if only because it was dawning on her that the company needed more of a skilled copier than an original artist. Some of Jacqui's clothes bore the label 'Designed by Jacqui Smale for Laura Ashley' and Veronica Papworth, fashion editor of the *Sunday Express,* had written flatteringly about Jacqui's work. In future, all designers at 'Laura Ashley' were to remain anonymous and the company image was kept under close control and scrutiny by Laura. The Ashleys were already highly conscious that they were selling a brand, which happened to bear Laura's name. They knew that designers would come and go but the real strength of the company was the creation of one brand with which the public could readily identify.

To get them through the Christmas crisis, staff in London were instructed to send down a variety of commercial patterns and magazines which Laura adapted herself. Somehow a collection for the next few months was cobbled together and gobbled up by the hungry customers.

7

Internationalization

'If you went to a summer party in 1970,' said Joanne Brogden, Professor of Fashion at the Royal College of Art, 'you could guarantee that most women would be wearing a long "Laura Ashley" skirt or dress. Perhaps Mrs Ashley understood best what English women want, which is to feel not too conspicuous but, rather, pretty and comfortable. And if they have a lot of money they probably don't want to show it. If she is unique, it's in the way she introduced fashion for wearing and for the houses we live in.'

The Seventies was truly Laura Ashley's decade. Not because she was a clairvoyant forecasting trends which suddenly came true, but because this was the moment when her consistently held belief that clothes were part of an overall way of living was now applauded by the market. She had always devoted considerable time to patient observation of her surroundings, her staff and humanity in general and, now, her assessment of women's needs and desires precisely matched the throwback mood of the Seventies. That she achieved it just when the company was set for major expansion, was an accident of timing that Bernard was determined to exploit to the full.

The publicity given to the company in the Seventies was out of all proportion to its size; but magazine and newspaper editors recognized that Ashley shops and their products offered something quite new. The bold geometrics of Courrèges, the pink plastic and psychedelic horrors of Parisian and other designers, had had their day. Seventies' youth was full of uncertainties and tenderness which was reflected in the trend for romance and nostalgia, fabrics that swayed and moved; women wanted to dress up. The film *Butch Cassidy and the Sundance Kid* further reinforced the nostalgia boom. 'I can't imagine any girl not wanting to look like Katharine Ross,' wrote one fashion editor early in 1971. The way to do so, she recommended, was to wear long 'Laura Ashley' dresses with wide sashes and lace-up fringed boots. 'At an unbelievable five guineas,' the mass circulation *She* magazine told its readers, 'you can't afford to miss this full value summer dance dress to add enchantment to your evenings. "Laura Ashley" prints are not only inexpensive, they are exclusive and in fine natural cotton (takes beautifully to starching) strewn with pale and perfect posies.'

Such was the power of the press that it quickly became apparent that 23 Pelham Street could no longer cope with the demand. The Ashleys annexed Number 25, to be used only for selling fabric (at thirty-five pence per yard) as the factory was still producing far more than could be made up into garments, while Number 23 was used just for children's clothes. New premises, around the corner at the top end of Fulham Road, were acquired to serve as the outlet for adult clothes. At 1,760 sq. ft., this new shop was the largest and smartest yet. It was in a row of green marble facades, but although the elegant exterior had to be maintained, inside the Ashleys continued their policy of minimal decoration with maximum stock. Again the shop looked more like a warehouse 'with only the clothes to make ... a forest of colour', wrote Veronica Papworth in the *Sunday Express*. The stone-floored basement was converted into a huge, communal changing room, one of the first of its kind, and Bernard thoughtfully provided a large leather armchair for bored husbands or partners. A long queue of customers greeted the shop's opening on 4 May 1970. That year, total sales for the company were in the region of £300,000, of which £250,000 came from the shops.

At the same time Gwalia House was closed down and replaced by a quaint shop in the historic market town of Shrewsbury. Originally intended as an outlet for the excessive number of seconds that were still being produced (both flawed material and finished items), it was selected mostly because of its convenient location for Bernard on his route from London to Clogau. It cost a mere eight pounds a week to rent. But neither he nor Laura had time to oversee it properly and the first few months were disastrous. One day Bernard arrived to find crisp wrappers littering the floor and the assistants sitting around smoking. Furious, he immediately closed the shop, fired the staff and the entire provincial retail spread of 'Laura Ashley' might have ended there. But Laura herself quietly went in the next day, spent hours cleaning up the mess and advertised for a new manageress. Bernard agreed to give the shop a second chance and hired Jean Revers. Not quite knowing what to expect other than that she wanted a new job, Jean turned up for work promptly on a cold, wet, Monday morning but found no one to let her in. Finally Carol Jones, arriving in a great hurry, apologized but could not stay as she was doing the payroll. 'See you next Saturday,' she called out as she handed Jean the night-safe wallet and left.

That, however, was exactly what attracted Jean to the company. 'No one ever checked up on you, they just trusted you so you felt you had to prove yourself.' She immediately set to and tried to establish some order. 'The shop was in an awful muddle,' Jean recalls. 'There was no system at all in the company, they would just offload whatever they felt like whenever they wanted. You dreaded anyone coming in for fabric because you knew you wouldn't be able to get more than three yards without a fault.' Jean so enjoyed the challenge of her new job that she asked her husband, Peter, then a watch salesman, to help her move the heavy rolls of fabric, put up shelves and pictures and generally bring some order to the store.

'We were busy smartening things up one night when BA knocked on the door. He was driving past, saw a light on in the shop and demanded to know what was going on.' Bernard could not fail to have been impressed by such spontaneous enthusiasm; equally, Peter felt Bernard was 'obviously a man of excitement heading a most intriguing company. I could see that he needed someone to deal with the administration leaving him free to run his company.'

Within a few months Peter, too, was offered a job, initially to help Bernard market home furnishing fabrics on a wholesale basis. Bernard was keen to re-enter the contract market with the country furnishing cotton and a decorator cotton, which was half-way between cotton and sateen. He had, still, many contacts in this field and it was yet another approach to coping with the surplus capacity produced by the Carno factory. But, increasingly, their own shops were also a highly successful means of serving this end; many young couples were buying the light-weight fabrics, because they were so cheap, and using them for furnishing.

In 1971 the Pelham Street premises were threatened with demolition as London Transport wanted to re-develop the underground station. To replace them a lease was taken on 71 Lower Sloane Street. At the same time, an exceptionally pretty 'Laura Ashley' shop opened outside the capital, in Bath, one of the most popular tourist centres in the country, particularly for Americans. Buying a 'Laura Ashley' dress was like buying a small piece of old England to take home. Jean Revers, who had dramatically improved sales figures at Shrewsbury, was invited to run the Bath shop, a beautiful old narrow, timbered building on three floors with a small flat on top which the Ashleys were converting, tempted by the possibility of staying there themselves.

The shop was well-located, close to the ancient Abbey and Roman Baths. But there was a further appeal; the City boasts two excellent museums with a wealth of textile resources; the American Museum and the Museum of Costume. Laura found enormous fulfilment in discovering old print references and Brian Jones, a soft-spoken, young artist who had recently joined her design team in Carno, proved adept at transferring them on to fabric. Virtually self-taught, Brian Jones was to become a mainstay of Laura's design team, always having an instinctive feel for what would appeal, or not, to Laura. She always felt unnerved when she researched at the august Victoria and Albert Museum and became only too conscious of her lack of formal training. Junk shops and smaller museums became a more satisfactory hunting ground for her. In the event, however, the Revers moved into the half-converted premises at 12 New Bond Street, Bath. It was they who oversaw the Ashleys' first venture into environmental selling, whereby the country charm and old-world air of the house perfectly complemented the products on sale within. The shop's three glass doors and old-fashioned set of windows were all adorned with window boxes and hanging baskets and for several years it won a Bath Festival award for the best floral shop facade in the City. The Bath shop became an important centre for all Ashley operations as the second floor was used as an office as well as a workroom for two machinists. Here samples were made which would be sent to the London shop for testing. If they proved successful, they would be despatched to Carno for mass production. On the ground and first floors, products were displayed in a more domesticated, less austere atmosphere than in London with a deliberate attempt to make customers feel that they were shopping in a private house from an earlier century. The basement, again with its original flagstones, became a large communal changing room similar to the one in Fulham Road.

As the retail side of the operation was now increasing in importance, one of Peter Revers' principal tasks was to find new store locations and Jean's was to hire staff for them. In 1972 another fabric store opened at 40 Sloane Street, and, more importantly, the first shop in Europe was taken in Geneva; Bernard's idea. There were no marketing plans nor sales projections. It was just an adventurous, yet instinctive choice of base from which to plan an international assault. As he had always maintained good relations with a number of Swiss wholesalers, the products were well known and well received there. He recognized that the strength of the Swiss franc would be an important factor in developing other European stores, and he knew that Geneva, although not in the forefront of the fashion world, attracted a number of the internationally rich and famous. So he set off one day with Moira, as she spoke French, and they stayed in Geneva until they had organized the shop. It was an instant success and the staff took great pleasure in reporting back when the actresses Audrey Hepburn and Sophia Loren both travelled from Italy to patronize the establishment.

Both Bernard and Laura developed an accurate profile of their London customers. Although Laura always prided herself that her clothes suited any woman from fourteen to forty (plus), there was a distinct 'Laura Ashley' girl emerging. Sixteen-year-old Sara Freeman liked to spend Saturday afternoon shopping and had just discovered the new shop in Fulham Road. After a long session trying on clothes, she was walking out with her purchases when a man tapped her on the shoulder and asked her to go back into the shop. 'It was Bernard, who had been watching me from his office and asked me if I had ever thought of a career in modelling.' Sara was slim and pretty with long, straight hair, good bone structure and no make-up. Epitomizing the natural English girl Laura had in mind for her clothes, Sara became the first 'Laura Ashley' model, a prelude to a highly successful modelling career. She was soon invited back to the house at Paulton's Square, where she found Laura 'motherly, warm, interested in what you were doing and a marvellous person to chat to. There was no fuss, you just became part of the family immediately and did everything together.' Sara often stayed with the Ashleys in Wales and, at first, Bernard took all the photographs. Bernard had always been intrigued by the possibilities of photography – Cartier-Bresson being an early idol as much as Hemingway – now he had an opportunity to indulge his aspirations. Laura was always around, but in the background. Sara recalls, 'She was there as a mother. I never saw Laura working at the business. I feel it was an enormous privilege to have known them because they made work such fun. I never enjoyed any later professional modelling jobs as much.'

One day another unusual customer was spotted; a man buying a selection of dresses. Tom Trevaskis, an Australian manufacturer looking for ideas in Europe, made no secret of his intention to copy certain features of the dresses he thought would be popular in Australia. He returned a few days later to meet the proprietors and Bernard, recognizing there was a limit to their own international expansion at this stage, and ever keen to find outlets for the masses of cloth being printed, immediately proposed to Trevaskis that they worked together, not in competition. The two men struck a deal and subsequently Trevaskis took a 50 per cent partnership in a new company to import 'Laura Ashley' fabrics and make them up locally according to agreed patterns and styles. Shortly after, a similar deal was negotiated with a Canadian businessman, Joe Yanow, and 'Laura Ashley' shops were soon dotted around the major towns of Canada and Australia.

Laura herself took no part in these business arrangements. Perhaps she was not interested. Probably she was, but she knew this side of the company belonged to her husband and any involvement on her part would seem to him an interference. She never encroached on anything that she (and he) deemed his territory, although he was not so circumspect in offering his opinion on design and colour. One of the more experienced printers remembers Laura asking him at this time to 'have a go' at producing a pattern she liked. When she saw a test of it she was extremely pleased and told him to run off a few hundred yards. 'Well, just as we finished the boss came past in a hell of a state. We three all went rigid. We knew he didn't like it. He just took out a knife and slashed the silk screen and that was that.' Laura, who watched this scene with the faintest flicker of a smile, said nothing. 'We felt sorry for her but he just didn't want that pattern,' recalled the printers. The employees were occasionally terrified of Bernard 'as if he had one over him,' as they described it, but they all knew that however much he might stamp and shout while the anger lasted, he could go for a walk and come back as if nothing had happened. Laura, however, was much less straightforward. If she were annoyed she would say nothing but her anger might last for weeks, sometimes months, becoming more intractable for its lack of outlet.

Jane believes that her mother was often stressed to the point of despair at this time, '... that she suffered all the torments and tribulations of every working mother without anything in her background, education or make-up having prepared her for such an emotional wrenching.' Although by now she had had twenty years in which to accustom herself to Bernard's outbursts in private, and, in a curious way this display of his male aggression was also a powerful magnetic force for her, she was nonetheless acutely embarrassed by any public display of his temper. 'I never intended to belittle or humiliate her in public. My impatience and intolerance were always directed against things outside the company and Laura knew that. But she was always there, with me, to protect me and sometimes she'd get caught in the blast,' Bernard explains. Laura tolerated his tirades because she loved him, and she forgave him everything as one forgives a child. But the same level of tolerance did not always extend to her staff, who may have fallen short of her high standards or overstepped the bounds of power. It is important to see her occasional contretemps with staff within the context of her relationship with Bernard; almost everyone who worked with her was aware that she had two, sometimes quite distinct, sides. She was, unquestionably, a mother figure, full of care, concern and interest, and this is how her friends saw her. But as an employer, she could be demandingly difficult, with an unyielding, steely core, possessed only by those with utter conviction in the rightness of what they are doing. Overall, she inspired great loyalty, respect and love, but her home life was often fraught and it is impossible to appreciate the extent of her achievement in commercial terms if unaware of the friction in her domestic life.

The sudden and massive expansion of the company's market in the early Seventies had several repercussions. At the beginning of the decade the Welsh staff had already swollen to 90, but within eighteen months had reached 130. After Jackie Smale's departure, most of the new clothes were created by Tim Gardner, a freelance designer who subsequently won an award as Romantic Designer of the Year. The company's next full-time designer was an unusually talented Thai women, Sonny Vipatasilpin, a friend of Su, the first manageress of the Pelham Street shop. Sonny had been Thailand's foremost classical dancing teacher, with a school of her own and a television programme. She had some peripheral experience of design through the theatre but her appointment as 'Laura Ashley''s principal designer was typical of Bernard and Laura's preference for those without formal vocational training who, they believed, would approach the job with unblinkered vision. 'In any case,' Su explains, 'all women in Thailand knew how to sew.'

Sonny, it turned out, knew more than that: many of her ideas arose from her exotic background and, dovetailing neatly with Laura's romantic vision, these designs remained top sellers for years. From now on the media began to talk about a 'Laura Ashley look', which sometimes meant a milkmaid style and at others a Victorian nursery maid, but the appeal was predominantly pastoral. Laura had learned, from the antique dress in the window of Gwalia House, the pulling power of a loss leader and she was not above producing one sample dress, never intended for general distribution, for the press, always hungry for a fashion article around which they could build a story. This helped enormously to develop in the public mind the idea that 'Laura Ashley' was a place where idealized longings for rural relics could be indulged, where clothes with bustles, tiers, smock aprons, frills and puffed sleeves could be found. Not only was there plain cotton but now lace, lawn, twill, corduroy, crepe, velvet, silk and some wool were all being used in the fabrication of these follies of fashion. In the early part of the decade 'Laura Ashley' was selling a bustle-backed wedding dress in cotton seersucker for a mere ten pounds fifty. A famous designer was charging £600 for a comparable design.

Laura often went for long walks on her own into the hills behind Carno railway station. Sometimes she would come back with a posy of flowers, other times she would just spend an hour deep in meditation. When Bernard was there, they walked together, and discussed every aspect of the business but, more often, she walked alone in the Welsh hills refining and reiterating silently her philosophy of life.

Fashions are forever fickle; but to Laura they contained many constants. She believed women should have a sensible working wardrobe and, abhoring idleness, wanted to sell clothes for the working woman. The ideal working dress would, therefore, be one in which you could reach up high to bring down the best china, bend down low to pick up the dropped toy, feel comfortable in for walking around the park and pushing a pram or playing ball, not worry about if baby food was deposited on it, move around in easily with a baby on your hip and cover up totally for rolling out pastry or helping with painting. In other words, Laura's idea of the working woman was one who worked at home, and her needs should be catered for so that she could look attractive in the environment in which she naturally flourished. Laura wanted her shops to stock a complete wardrobe for this working woman, (the 'capsule wardrobe' of her Wren youth) rather like lists sent out by boarding schools before term. She wanted one pinafore, one skirt, one dress, perhaps two blouses, one nightdress, an apron, a swimming costume, a coat and a jacket. 'Many of our customers could not understand why we might have only one style of nightdress or long-sleeved blouse, but it was because Laura was trying to evolve the most perfect example of that particular item and believed it was more important to have one good example of each than several skirts and dresses,' Moira explains.

During her walks, she doubtless ripened her belief in the moral purpose of clothing. Although compromises, inevitably, were made, Laura was, almost instinctively, anti-fashion and anti-design; 'more is less' being a long-standing Ashley maxim. Being poor, she knew from experience, did not necessarily mean being without taste. Interestingly, her attempt to impose, however gently, a universal level of good taste made her clothes unacceptable to many art students, who perceived a 'Laura Ashley' outfit as death to individualism. Conversely, most other students, as well as former 'women's libbers', with whom Laura might have thought she had nothing in common, warmly welcomed her clothes. In their eyes, a 'Laura Ashley' dress, with its known emphasis on 100 per cent natural fibres, together with its cheap price and universality combined a soundness both ecological and ideological. The women's movement was maturing too, as it slowly swung back to the acceptability of some women choosing not to work outside the home. This was tolerated as long as they did so out of a sense of liberation at being at home, i.e. through choice not force. The non-radical and less aggressive values of the women's movement, second phase, fitted well with the 'Laura Ashley' style. Furthermore a 'Laura Ashley' dress was not made according to a man's stereotype of how a woman should look, although Laura believed that the covered-up, 'floaty' look was what men liked. Many of the dresses looked as pretty and attractive on fatter or pregnant women as on their taller and slimmer sisters.

Laura was not the first English designer with a puritanical streak. From Ruskin, to Morris and even Terence Conran, there is a discernible tradition which mixed design with ethics and social theory. Laura certainly brought a missionary zeal to her work; it was yet another stepping stone which enabled her to cross the gulf from working at home to working outside without associated guilt. The roots for such zeal can be traced to the many dress reform movements of the nineteenth century of which the shared goal was to alleviate the pressure of fashion on dress, both for men and women. Many of the reformers of the 1870s and 1880s believed that women would earn both a new respect, if they could eschew the frivolities of fashion, and a new freedom which would liberate them to perform a useful role in society.

Mrs Amelia Bloomer, an American, whose eponymous, bifurcated undergarment was considered revolutionary in the early part of the last century, was passionately concerned with showing women that they could combine beauty with utility. Although later reformers in England were concerned with the weight of fabric for maintaining body temperature, most were appalled by the emphasis on spider waists achieved through tight lacing and corsets. The result was restricted movement, fainting fits and even curvature of the spine. Not long after Mrs Bloomer's crusade, the women favoured by pre-Raphaelite painters also took up the cudgels on behalf of dress reformers and wore loose-fitting dresses with low-set sleeves and dropped shoulder lines for maximum movement and comfort. Probably the loudest voice raised in favour of dress reform in the last century was that of the German, Dr Gustav Jaeger, who for sanitary and hygienic reasons, wanted men and women to wear natural, undyed wool next to their skin. Women were permitted corsets only if they used no force to preserve the shape.

Dr Jaeger may have been considered an eccentric, but the Rational Dress Society, which won so many adherents at the International Health Exhibition in 1884, continued the battle on broader lines. Laura would have approved of their aims, which almost a century later, stood as a beacon for her own philosophy; they were 'to protest against the introduction of any fashion in dress that either deforms the body, impedes movement or injures health ... and to promote the adoption according to individual taste and convenience of a style of dress based upon considerations of health, comfort and beauty and to deprecate the constant changes of fashion that cannot be recommended on any of these grounds.'

But the greatest blow to the dictates of fashion on women's dress came with the World War I. Although Laura Ashley had, unconsciously, much in common with the nineteenth-century dress reformers it is ironic that their efforts towards change were entangled inextricably with the organized struggles for the rights of women; women, to be taken seriously, had to dress in a more robust, sensible manner, they stated – an argument amply demonstrated by their usefulness in wartime. Towards the end of the twentieth century, Laura believed that the pendulum had swung too far and that women were far more likely to achieve their ends if they showed more feminine charm, prettiness and selflessness, as she herself practised. But her belief that all women, regardless of wealth, should be offered clothes that were artistic and beautiful, not brash, sexually offensive or uncomfortable, would have made her a worthy member of most of the nineteenth-century dress reform movements.

In spite of her preference for high necks and concealment, Laura once allowed a bikini to be added to the 'shopping list' of essential items. It was only when *The Sun* newspaper displayed it on a girl in a highly provocative pose that she realized how easily the purity of the image could be sullied. Another magazine featured her popular lace insert blouse on a well-endowed model who wore no bra underneath, with quite a different effect from that intended. She decided therefore that *The Sun* was never again to be offered 'Laura Ashley' publicity material and reinforced as tight a hold as possible on the image. Only a family member could be trusted to do this. It was in this spirit that Bernard gave Jane, at eighteen, a professional's Hasselblad camera and appointed her company photographer, the first of their children to work for the company. 'It was typical of his deep-end philosophy,' says Jane, fondly. 'He threw you in and you either sank or swam.' Jane, who had a natural feel for mood and background which complemented the clothes, swam more than competently and her black and white images of windswept models against bleak moors or stark beaches created for many who saw them on the white shop walls their indelible image of 'Laura Ashley'. Today, most high street shops use photographs of their clothes to win over customers but in the early Seventies, the concept was startlingly new and original and Jane's work was highly acclaimed by other professionals.

Behind, or perhaps in front of, all the ideals and theories there was a sound technical base which, under Bernard's tutelage, was also entering a phase of significant growth. Almost as soon as they moved into the Carno premises they had outgrown them. Between 1968 and 1972 seven major extensions were added to the original railway station buildings. The most dramatic breakthrough came in 1970 as Courtaulds, the textile giant, was upgrading its machinery and selling off cheaply equipment which had been built to last for years. Over a two-year period, 'Laura Ashley' bought from Courtaulds two Stork flat bed printers, one Buser printer, 'the Rolls Royce of them all', two pad mangles, a step and repeat machine and a 15,000 lb. boiler. 'We bought it, dismantled it, brought it back and re-erected it,' Dai Jones vividly recounts. 'Bernard had always wanted a Swiss Buser and as we only had to pay £1,500 for it he was very impatient to see it work, like a small boy with a new toy. Laura was very excited too because until then we could only produce two colours but now, suddenly, we could print eight; it was revolutionary. But of course, we still didn't have all the machines we wanted.'

The new machinery prompted a reshuffling of existing facilities at Carno. A 13,000 sq. ft. building was erected for the machinists and cutters as well as for garment distribution. The big second-hand machines and new boiler were stored in the vacated building and a two-storey building was put up with a canteen at the front and offices at the rear. However, even all this was not enough. In April the first offshoot factory opened in Machynlleth. This time the company converted a disused cinema to house twelve machinists. One further purchase was a source of great pride to Bernard; a thirty-two ton Scania articulated lorry which cost £6,000. It was painted purple with the company name in white and made the journey to London twice weekly. Laura, knowing how much this vehicle meant to Bernard, had a miniature of it made for her husband, which he kept in his office. The driver would begin his 220-mile journey from Carno at 4 am and would arrive punctually at 10 am, often blocking the whole of Sloane Street. A crowd of eager customers would be awaiting his arrival outside the shops and attack him for the particular colour, size or style of dress they had been waiting for. One day when the driver arrived at ten minutes past ten an angry customer berated him: 'You're late, you should have been here ten minutes ago!'

With such dramatic (for them) technological advances, it was inevitable that furnishing fabrics would soon be on sale in the shops alongside the dress weights. Bernard had been told this was a confusing mixture – reminiscent of the old drapers' shops – and would never work as the products would attract different customers. He proved them wrong. However tentative these beginnings, it was instantly clear that furnishing fabrics would be a growing market; customers had almost demanded them by making do with narrower width, lighter-weight dress fabrics. Bernard, acutely aware of the volatility of the fashion market, was convinced the company must diversify into the more stable home furnishing sector as soon as possible. Now, not satisfied with the immediate success of the furnishing fabrics, Bernard revived his twenty-year-old plan to produce wallpaper, using designs taken directly from fabrics, and sent Meirion and Dai Jones to Holland to buy a paper printing machine. 'This is like printing money,' Bernard told them. For Dai Jones, it seemed more like printing headaches. 'We knew nothing about what sort of paper to buy, we just tried to learn from books. At first the 100 gsm paper we bought from Norway and Finland was much too weak and we got hundreds of complaints from all the shops. Then the machine started printing lines all over the paper and we had to send someone into the shops to remove all the faulty rolls.' But in spite of the problems, there was never any question of giving up. Dai knew only too well that the company mentality was to persevere until they got it right. Quality finally improved with the purchase in 1974 of a wallpaper-coating machine.

By 1973 there were eleven shops to supply in Oxford, Edinburgh, London, Bath, Shrewsbury, Geneva, Amsterdam and Paris. Of these, Paris was the most significant as both Laura and Bernard had always loved France, yet were terrified of it. They feared that if their products were not welcomed in the French capital, everything they had built up might be lost. Yet they could wait no longer to tackle Paris. They took a small boutique on the Left Bank, where hitherto there had been only antique shops, correctly recognizing that the little street, Rue des Saints Pères, was full of 'Laura Ashley spirit'. To run it they chose a nineteen-year-old English girl who spoke French, had been at school with Jane and a Saturday assistant in Pelham Street for the past three years. Pat Yot had never been entrusted with such responsibility before but she had become a friend of the family; to Bernard and Laura loyalty and energy mattered far more than experience. 'It was incredible, it was like a bomb going off,' was how Pat described the opening; just as in England at the beginning, there were days when customers had to be locked out and long queues formed. Suddenly, '*Le Style Anglais*' was what every young *Parisienne* girl wanted.

As a result of the burgeoning international network, many of the European staff came frequently to Wales to see the centre of operations. The farmhouse at Clogau became too small and too isolated. Not only did they need somewhere to put up visiting employees (and, increasingly, the necessary but not always welcome journalists) they now needed a showcase for their home furnishing ideas.

'Like everything else Bernard does, he suddenly decided he needed a large Welsh farmhouse TODAY and so they bought Rhydoldog,' a friend recalls. Aesthetically not a beautiful house, Rhydoldog is a large, predominantly Victorian, rambling mansion with some Edwardian additions, grafted on to a seventeenth-century farmhouse base. Its beauty lies not in its architecture, but in the magnificence of its views as it sits in splendid isolation on top of a steep hill looking down the unencumbered views across fields, moors and woodland to the river valleys of the Wye and Elan. Laura once said she hated the thirty-roomed house, which she considered ugly, and then felt guilty about hating it. Her more considered view was that it was 'the sort of house you become fond rather than proud of. Its mellow character is compounded of its age, its comfortable lack of pretension and the various roles it has to play as farm, design studio and home.' But at first it seemed to them magnificent. It offered Laura and Bernard endless possibilities for decoration inside and, after more than twenty years of marriage, it was the first large house they could plan together, yet another incentive towards developing the home furnishing side of the business. The opportunities for walks and picnics outside in the grouse-filled hills were equally limitless. The name of the house means, literally, water running over stones, and a moment's quietude brings to life the sound of many waterfalls tumbling all around the 800-acre property. There was plenty of silence for Laura and Bernard at Rhydoldog, marred only occasionally by David and Nick motorbiking their way through the sheep. It became more than a family home but a working farm and, they hoped, an inspirational headquarters for their international design empire.

'Our inspiration is totally with rural life as it can be lived,' Laura wrote some years later. 'We expect that women will want to cook and sew and launder even if they are also reading Homer or studying Italian painters.' In a rare discussion of her design philosophy, Laura wrote; 'You could equate the company with a first-class nanny in a *fin de siècle* nursery. Innocence, discipline, high standards and above all a kind of scrubbed, simple beauty. Or you could visualize the farmhouse kitchen towards midday. The morning's cream is quietly clotting on the stove, the gleaming copper pans are being put to use and the farmworkers are filing in to a meal which is pure poetry; vegetables plucked from the soil within the hour, fresh baked bread, farm butter, eggs, game and fruit. The farmer's wife will be wearing cotton, freshly starched.'

One of the first changes Laura made to Rhydoldog was to set up a telex room and offices at the end of the corridor on the ground floor. But, apart from that nod to twentieth-century technology, she tried an experiment of a different sort; to see whether it would be possible to live here, as in some undefined time-gone-by-period, the life she was ruminating over. To this end, she hired two young graduates as her personal assistants, who were to live at Rhydoldog.

'But it was an impossible position,' one of them pointed out, 'and very stifling because she felt you had to be part of the greater family and do everything with them. For example, we would often go on expeditions to Hay-on-Wye looking for French, nineteenth-century pattern books but if you found any yourself you could not possibly claim originality. That would definitely not be popular with Mrs Ashley.' One of the first tasks of the day was for the girls to prepare freshly squeezed orange juice. Laura asked the farm manager, Dai Davies, to find her a good Jersey milker and taught herself how to milk the cow. Soon, however, she did not have enough time to do this although someone had to relieve the poor beast, and the fresh creamy milk often sat in a gleaming churn in the corner of the kitchen untouched until it went rancid and had to be thrown away. Bernard liked the milk, and that for Laura was sufficient justification for doing anything. But nobody else really liked the rich, unpasteurized taste. 'Laura took life very seriously – not in the sense of discussing world politics but just her own life. She expected everyone to live up to her own high moral standards and there was an overwhelming feeling that if you did not, you had somehow failed.' By the end of the year both girls concluded that the nineteenth-century atmosphere of Rhydoldog was not for them, and left. Soon after Dai sold the cow.

Dai's family had been working on the farmlands around Rhydoldog for generations. But Laura Ashley was of a breed he had not met before. 'She was so determined and so curious about things. She liked to think she could do it all. She had to conquer everything to satisfy herself.'

He did not object to fulfilling her 'romantic notions about this and that' if it meant searching for a butter churn and separator but he drew the line at finding her a hacking pony. 'Apart from the damage it would do to the ground I knew it would have to be ridden every day and then if it bolted or got stuck in the mud it would be my responsibility.' She listened to his advice and bought instead a Welsh pony with the vague idea of attaching it to a trap and doing the shopping in it. That, too, proved impractical but Dai was impressed by the way Laura managed, without any fuss, to get most things done the way she wanted. 'She would often come and have an afternoon cup of tea with me and then pick my brain as to what BA had asked me to do that morning. If she didn't like it she'd just tell me to say to him, "I didn't have time." She would never have a confrontation but she would get things done her way.'

Of the children, only Emma really grew up at Rhydoldog, although the others came back at weekends. On moving here Laura had crises of conscience about how best to educate her youngest child. Emma had a spell at a small, local Welsh school then she had been sent to one of London's most exclusive girls' preparatory schools, off Sloane Square. When they bought Rhydoldog Laura tried a new experiment. Using a specially devised PNEU (Parents National Educational Union) course she tried teaching Emma herself at home all morning. In the afternoons mother and daughter went for long, nature-based rambles when Emma had to identify and discover things. Both Emma and Laura loved these times; Laura in any case spent hours on her own just sitting in the garden or fields, thinking. But it was far too unstructured and anti-social a method to be a total success in educational terms. Finally, they consulted an educational psychologist who advised the parents that, in view of their constant travelling Emma's needs would best be served by a boarding school to provide her with some stability. As they were certain about only one thing, their fourth child was not going to Holland Park Comprehensive, they followed the psychologist's advice and Emma, from eight years onwards, had a happy, if conventional education at boarding school, first at Knighton House in Dorset and then, at thirteen, moving to the more traditional Cranborne Chase.

After fifteen years in Wales, the enthusiasm which Bernard generated among his staff showed no signs of diminishing. Dai Walter Jones (no relation) was given a job at 'Laura Ashley' after being hospitalized for five years with a serious illness and with little prospect of finding employment elsewhere as he was approaching retirement age. Nonetheless, he joined the company in 1970 as a sewing machine mechanic but was soon moved to work on one of the large printers. From the first he would often stay behind 'after hours', telling his mates he 'just wanted to finish this run' because he knew the machines were capable of producing more material than they were currently achieving. Eventually, he built production up to about 3,000 metres a day. 'I always walked the seven miles home, but that day the Old Man and Peter Revers came past in the car and offered me a lift. "What've you been doing, young Dai?" they asked. "Oh, only cleaning up the printer," I replied. "You think we don't know what's going on? You've got the machines going to 3,000 a day, we know. Go to the first pub, Peter," Bernard ordered. When we got to the pub my hands were so swollen and red from picking up the jug and throwing it all day I could barely pick up a pint to drink.' In spite of the pain in his hands, as he drank with his boss Dai felt only the excitement of having achieved his goal. 'He always recognized what we've done; there was never any them and us,' Dai recounted proudly.

The speed with which the Ashleys were opening new shops and the steady expansion of the Carno factory should not mask the continuing difficulties. Jean Revers was horrified at the sight of huge bonfires in the fields at Carno; there was so much unusable fabric it was just burned. This wastage offended Laura too, who thought the fabric was quite good enough to be used somehow and decided to try selling remnants. These became so popular that on delivery day customers would fight wildly for bags of them. 'In the end we practically gave them away,' she said. From this, the idea was derived of 'patchwork pieces', which then led to a demand for specific colours in the bags,' 'and suddenly we realized we had created a bit of a monster.'

The 'patchwork pieces' saga was not one that would quietly die. It represented for Laura thrift, history, craft, usefulness, prevention of idleness and a host of other qualities which her childhood and subsequent work at the WI had encouraged her to prize. Preparing the 'patchwork pieces' from remnants was an ideal occupation for her continuing band of outworkers; Laura considered it an essential part of her duty to keep feeding these women, many of whom lived such isolated lives in the hills that they might go for days without talking to anyone. This activity was something she was the most proud of, one of the first things she would tell new friends about her work. Helping women to stay at home yet giving them an occupation, some money and a branch held out towards the wider community were all worthy goals in Laura's eyes. But the issue also epitomized the emerging dilemma for Laura, caught between the dictates of commerce and social responsibility. The 'patchwork pieces' could never be economically viable because they took time to cut, arrange and bag, yet were never sold for more than a few pence. They used up space in the vans, required time to unload and ultimately made the shops look messy. Bernard soon took against the idea and Laura fought doggedly to keep them, believing that her loyal customers were entitled to receive the benefits from any advantage like this. After all, it was inspiration from the patchwork quilts in 1952 which had proved the original impetus for the whole company.

8

Rationalization and Remaisnil

I n April 1974 an advertisement appeared in *The Sunday Times* announcing that 'Laura Ashley' was seeking a financial controller. The need for such an appointment was not obvious to Laura. Bankers, book-keepers and accountants were all beneath contempt, she felt, and as they had managed perfectly well until now without an in-house accountant, she could not fathom the need to change. Bernard, however, realized that unless someone with a sound financial background took the company's problems in hand, its continued existence was threatened, although he too showed little enthusiasm for the idea. Like most new companies, they were overtrading alarmingly and expanding so fast that there was never adequate working capital. But Bernard always believed the lack of cash to be merely temporary. 'We just need some help to get over this short-term cash crisis, that's all,' he informed the new financial controller, Welsh-born accountant, John James.

John James joined 'Laura Ashley' in August 1974 and took a rather different view of the problem. During 1973–5, in the wake of the oil crisis and the Middle East War, the company had had a borrowing facility from the Midland Bank of £100,000 yet they were, in fact, overdrawn by some £300,000. Only Carol Jones' dogged loyalty had staved off creditors for so long. But now the situation had become critical and the Bank's regional director for Wales called an urgent meeting of the shareholders. Laura did not attend; quite possibly because Bernard forbad it. But she was not interested in any case. 'She felt the only thing that made the company work was good design and hard work, nothing else. People like me represented an alien world for her,' explains James. It was a heated meeting, and one banker remarked to Bernard: 'I hope your new financial controller will keep tight reins on you.' 'If he does that he'll have to go,' Bernard joked.

James faced such intractable problems that after a few months he nearly quit. But he found himself in a double bind; the bankers said they would withdraw their support if he left and this would have killed the business instantly. But also, he was drawn towards Bernard, whose vision and single-mindedness he greatly admired, and a business which he felt had great potential for further growth. Increasingly, he found himself estranged from Laura, who, in the subsequent eleven years, 'never once asked me how things were going. Whenever things went wrong she would blame us and say that we were causing Bernard difficulties.' Bernard had to act as 'go-between' as Laura would only accept bad news or limitations to her independence from him, certainly not from an accountant who was later to describe her designs as 'itsy-bitsy prints' necessary to camouflage the bad quality of the fabric.*

The first summer of John James' control saw the company with neither cloth to make up winter clothes nor money with which to buy it. Between them they managed to organize £50,000 from ICFC on a three-month note and rapidly tried to straighten out the balance sheet. Meanwhile Bernard was in London opening the biggest 'Laura Ashley' shop yet (4,200 sq. ft.), in Harriet Street, London, SW1. It soon became a phenomenal success, and was closely followed by the opening of a major factory in Wijk, Holland, 'bought with borrowed money that was not available to the company', James commented. It was the company's first foreign manufacturing plant, used to make up printed cloth sent over from Wales. James was in a quandary. If he tried to slow the pace Bernard would complain at being given 'no financial options'. One of his first, and most basic suggestions was that prices must be raised. But this struck at the very heart of what Laura was hoping to achieve and she quashed the suggestion with ferocity. 'I can see what you're doing,' she told him icily. 'You're trying to make

---

* *Financial Weekly*, 23 July 1987.

excessive profit.' It took him three years before prices were increased adequately to meet the needs of the business.

John James had more than one showdown with Bernard, too, since a crucial part of his role was controlling the cash flow. This would sometimes draw Laura in and she would spring tigerishly to Bernard's defence, especially if some long dreamed of project of his was under threat through lack of cash. She was in favour of sacking the accountant; no one had ever stood in her husband's way before. When Bernard wanted to buy his first boat Laura was faced with an interesting conundrum as she was still frightened of water, could not swim and felt appallingly seasick on any small craft. Overriding these fears, however, was her maternal instinct to indulge Bernard with whatever it was he wanted and she urged him to buy a boat. But in 1975 Bernard himself recognized the time was not right to buy a yacht. And after that, James felt his task easing, slightly. The following year, he became Group Managing Director for Laura Ashley Ltd.

James recognized that, while Laura's shaping of the product range was crucial, it was up to him to design a corporate structure to support it; otherwise the company could scarcely expand and might even cease operating altogether. Until 1975 there had never been formal, regular board meetings, merely *ad hoc* occasions when, for example, they needed to fire someone. From now on there were regular board meetings and Laura was appointed Deputy Chairman in between Bernard, Chairman, and John James, Managing Director. She used to attend the general discussion part and make her views known as to where the next shop would be. For example, she was deeply opposed to opening in Manchester, as she did not think her type of customer lived there, but preferred to be associated with the older university towns or cathedral cities such as Bath or Edinburgh. At one board meeting she proposed introducing padded coat hangers 'but that was never going to turn our fortunes', according to John James. In his view, maximizing sales was not her highest priority. She knew other people in the company were responsible for that. Her most valuable role, especially as the company grew, was maintaining image.

Board meetings were often embarrassing for all concerned. Sometimes Bernard would make his wife leave the room, telling her, 'This is boys' business' and she would meekly obey. No one else was allowed to overrule her in the boardroom. But although she accepted a dressing-down from him in public, and indeed made a point of telling people 'Oh! BA takes all the real decisions; I'm just the assistant to the Chairman,' in reality, they discussed everything together afterwards and she often managed to achieve what she wanted in the privacy of the bedroom. Confronted by a more formal, corporate approach to the business, Laura retreated to the outer circle only to launch an attack on the inner circle. She knew that, as long as she applied it with care, she had great power over Bernard. She once admitted that she would have loved a career in politics and believed she was now being forced to draw upon all her native political skills to ensure that her design ideas and her control over image were not submerged in the drive to reduce the debts. Laura also took positive steps to boost her designing team and hired a graduate from the Royal College of Art whose brief was imperceptibly to modify the Victorian image.

Lynda Kee-Scott's clothes had to maintain the traditional English country-girl look, but were required to broaden the appeal. Lynda found working with Laura a great stimulant; 'She never stopped thinking of the company and would often spot something in a book that attracted her; she would know instantly how it could be adapted. She was so enthusiastic about what she saw and liked that she could transmit her ideas even if the appeal was not immediately obvious to us. She knew what was right and wrong in fabrics just the same as she did in life, there were no grey areas.' Lynda never felt that Laura, however persuasive she might be, encroached on her autonomy as a designer. But if, somehow, a dress escaped Laura's approval at design stage and slipped into production, then she would spare nothing in her attack. Once Laura went into the Paris shop and discovered a simple dress with drop waist and wide pleats, which she hated. She complained that it was not feminine – a woman should show off her waist – and therefore did not convey the right image. She insisted that she had never seen it at the design stage. Furious, she walked out of the shop with bundles of the offending garment over her arm and telexed Carno to withdraw the pattern from production immediately.

Lynda always accepted the importance of having someone with a strong concept controlling the design outflow and never found Laura's unspoken guidelines stultifying. But she admits there was room for rationalization in other areas; 'at first clothes were never costed properly; in fact we may have been underpricing', she explained, 'but for

Laura the most important thing was that everyone was working happily together'. Laura acknowledged the need for hiring designers with their own ideas but rejected the need to be told by either accountants ('grey suits' as she termed them) or shop managers what she could or could not sell. She held firm because she knew that the road to compromise was without signposts, that the possibilities for getting lost were manifold and that it was paved with flawed imitations of the truth. Her uncles had taught her well.

The more successful the shops became, the more the branch managers reported back on those lines which sold well, thereby wielding a power which Laura did not at first wish to accept. Within limits, Laura was prepared to accept their comments, if, for example, they told her that brown sold better than blue. But when they started to tell her that customers preferred some synthetic mix materials (they creased less, washed better and were cheaper) she considered such input was dangerously overstepping their authority. Laura was adamant. Customers must be able to know that a garment with the label 'Laura Ashley' was made of 100 per cent natural fibres. No mixes. No compromises.

Increasingly, the Ashleys were hiring a new breed of staff; qualified and experienced. Hitherto they had deliberately promoted internally, which served to reinforce the already strong personal loyalty. To an extent Laura found the superior knowledge of some of her employees unnerving but she was also prepared to learn from them, her own tastes changing subtly in the process. The experience of the French shops was particularly important in this context.

On the same day as John James joined the company, Anthony Marangos took control in Paris. 'I knew nothing about shops or garments but I was an Englishman in France who spoke French and they trusted me,' recounts Marangos. 'They had a wonderful pioneering style and pride both in what they had achieved and in what they could teach you. If they liked you they believed they could teach you to do anything and by God! you'd do it as well as anyone. They were a formidable couple with both guts and style.' But it was clear to Marangos, just as it was to James, that the store openings and continuing publicity were creating a level of business which the financial resources of the company simply could not support.

Two months later the Ashleys hired their most professionally qualified applicant to date in the retail sector. Liza Wanklyn, an American living in Paris, had graduated from design school and had worked for Jean Muir and Givenchy before applying to join 'Laura Ashley'. Because she had been exposed to the luxury end of the market, much of what she found at 'Laura Ashley' appalled her. 'They hadn't tested the French market at all before opening and so everything was just delivered from Wales, hung up and not thought about. No one arranged it by length or by colour, there was no attempt to market the products,' Liza Wanklyn remembers vividly. Of course, the untidiness was part of the English charm. Nonetheless, France was a very demanding market, as both Laura and Bernard were well aware, and once the freshness and newness of the product had worn off, it was critically important that the merchandise was of the highest quality. When in January 1975, Liza was appointed Director for European Merchandising, she set about organizing some improvements. The French shops were the first to use the dark green exterior, which became an instantly recognizable hallmark of 'country' quality, and were also the first to have architect-designed wooden interiors. 'Laura had a very practical eye for what would sell and a very shrewd idea of pricing. She had a wonderful sense of period and could adapt an idea brilliantly but her lack of formal design training handicapped her in other ways. Sometimes clothes would arrive with the sleeves backwards or the pocket on the wrong side; someone with formal training would never have allowed garments with such a poor finish,' Liza maintains. A harsh criticism, perhaps, since Laura was no longer running the factories on a daily basis. But, as she was the first to recognize, the products bore her name.

Home furnishings, by their very nature, were subject to fewer of these problems and when they appeared in the French capital, with a big new shop on the Right Bank, in the fashionable *seizième*, it was yet another conquest. Such shops, offering coordinated fabrics and paper, had never before existed in France; hitherto it had been possible to hire an interior decorator who would go into a home and suggest exclusive fabrics at exorbitant prices. But for the average home-owner to find good taste cheaply, displayed informally, and feel certain that he or she was not making a mistake because it was already arranged and coordinated, was quite new to Parisians.

In spite of these initial advantages, furnishing fabrics, as clothes, were badly in need of overall direction and it was also in Paris that a young woman who had no formal design training but had worked for the exclusive Colefax and Fowler, was hired. Carolyn Warrender, twenty-four when she joined 'Laura Ashley', had a very clear idea of what was needed. 'They had a range that was selling, but with no one actually involved in planning it; it was just a question of whatever anyone thought was pretty going in with no production schedules, no set ranges for satisfactory colour matching.' Carolyn found her most difficult task was persuading Laura of the necessity for such schedules. If a particular print was not selling, it would be removed from the range; but then, if Laura especially liked it, she would put it back in. Carolyn recognized that Laura had excellent taste. 'I never saw one thing she wanted that did not sell,' but nonetheless insisted that this undisciplined approach was unacceptable for a customer trying to furnish a house, who might have kept a sample for six weeks only to find she could not reorder the same fabric. 'Laura found the new formalities extremely annoying. Sometimes she would say "This is my company and if I want it, why can't I have it?"' But Carolyn, backed up by Phil Morris, hammered away at the point that furnishing fabrics were not like clothes, where customers did not expect to come back for more of the same. Laura had not focused on these difficulties. Although, ultimately, she accepted the need for pattern books, production schedules, yearly reviews by committee and other organizational disciplines, she disliked intensely the way these formalities intruded into her own sphere of influence and destroyed the spontaneity of her collection, which had always been one of her greatest strengths.

Carolyn became Laura Ashley's personal assistant, a role which necessitated an extremely close relationship. This enabled her to see Laura both as a warm and caring friend, but also as a difficult busi-nesswoman. 'In fact, she really wasn't a businesswoman; marketing was such a nasty word to her. She was, fundamentally, a good person but the side we all saw at work was the side that could not cope with the constant expansion of the business. All the difficulties were symptoms of her struggle to cope with the development of what the business had become,' Carolyn believed.

Enjoying their European success, Laura and Bernard were spending an increasing amount of time in France, which they had always loved. They bought a flat in the capital, Nick attended art school for a while there, and Laura made a very close friend of a woman whose unusual shop had been opposite the Ashley's first boutique on the Left Bank.

Anita Saada had children of similar ages to Laura's and was to become a staunch source of support to her over the years. One of Laura's favourite meals from this time on was couscous, which Anita taught her how to prepare. The French open-air markets held great appeal for Laura, as did the Left Bank *bouquinistes* where she often found appealing old prints among the musty volumes. Although she never mastered the accent, she was learning to speak quite competent French, teaching herself out of books as ever. At the same time she was engaged ever more knowledgeably in researching fabrics and starting to build an impressive library of art books and textile samples and references. She developed some useful contacts in the antique textile field including one dealer whose name she would never divulge, even to her own assistants in the company.

Quite by accident, she had produced a brilliantly simple brainwave for home furnishings; using in the same room the monochrome positive/negative wallpaper and fabric. She and Phil Morris together had hit upon this virtue out of necessity since the machines could still print only one colour and new machinery for multi-coloured printing was much too expensive. There was no momentary flash of inspiration; it was typical of Laura's talent to turn a disadvantage into an advantage. The wispy lines of one of her most popular prints of the mid-Seventies, wild clematis, were ideally suited to this reversing treatment. When the background was off-white, the pattern was unobtrusive enough to be used as wallpaper in several features advertising other products and 'Laura Ashley' gained much incidental publicity in this way. When the background was, for example, sage, plum or navy however and the flowers off-white, the pattern was transformed. The slight and subtle variation offered by reversing the colours of background and foreground on 'Laura Ashley's' tiny prints became the leitmotif of a generation. The simple designs burst upon a tired market which offered little else but large floral designs often in rather garish colours. The cleverness was in using the wealth of old prints lying around ignored and simplifying them to make them fresher and give them a contemporary feel. For years, 'Laura Ashley' had the field to themselves.

Although Laura loved her Parisian existence she was aware that the staff at Carno also needed to see her. Perhaps she never realized quite how deep-seated was this need, but shop, as well as factory staff, could not fail to be impressed at the way both she and Bernard always knew their names, asked with interest about their home life and would always try and help if there was a problem by sending taxis, flowers, hot meals or whatever the crisis demanded. When José, the Portuguese housekeeper whom they had promoted to become a shop manager, had nowhere to live, they bought her a house, oversaw the extensive repairs and stocked it with furniture.

Just occasionally staff felt that her concern for their welfare bordered on the intrusive. She was, for example, appalled to discover from reading a shop diary that one of her unmarried store assistants was visiting a family planning clinic. But she would often tell friends how keenly she felt a responsibility not just for her employees' jobs, but for their health, their mortgages, their children's educations and the entire survival of the rural community in Carno. She did not exaggerate. And yet, Laura found the working environment there increasingly difficult. While accepting in principle the need to delegate, her inner fury, not always expressed, if something were not carried out to her wishes, was great. One unfortunate decided to fill the reception area in Carno with tropical plants, a major gaffe as anyone who knew Laura realized; she found their artificiality an affront. On another occasion, Phil Morris knew that, had Laura been consulted, she would never have agreed to a particular print being produced with a border. Nevertheless, one of their licencees had requested this and, since it was a lucrative contract, Bernard had told him to go ahead and produce it. 'Just make sure Laura doesn't see it,' he warned Phil. However, when Laura discovered a reference to the border in a telex, she immediately confronted Phil. He explained that it had been approved by Bernard, which of course, by implying criticism of her husband, compounded his crime. 'She did not speak to me, at all, for six months after that,' Phil said. Bernard never knew of the rift between Phil Morris and Laura. Her fortitude was such that she did not need to unload on to him her emotional worries. But, keeping the matter to herself was also a way of protecting her husband: she wanted to believe the incident was all Phil's fault, not Bernard's.

John James, in addition to the financial complications, faced a welter of other unexpected difficulties. One of the more intractable problems was how to dispose of the effluent in an ecologically acceptable way. As production at the new factory had accelerated beyond anyone's predictions, no one had stopped to consider effluent. 'Most textile plants are built near a big sewerage plant, not in the middle of the countryside like ours,' explained Dai Jones, whose responsibility it soon became to find a means of solving the problem. 'No one had ever realized the amount of water we would need,' he added. One of the first attempts to treat the effluent involved building a small lagoon, the idea for which Dai discovered in a book. When that did not work they tried pumping or spraying it on to neighbouring fields, hoping it would filter through the ground by natural causes. 'But we were producing so much effluent it flooded and we had to rent a small piece of land specifically for effluent disposal,' explained Dai. That too proved inadequate and the company then commissioned a disposal plant. But on 13 January 1975 'Laura Ashley' was convicted and fined at Newtown Magistrates Court for discharging waste matter on to land. The Severn Trent Water Authority brought the prosecution as the water had run off into a local water course, polluting rivers which boasted some of the finest fishing in the area.

Came the summer of 1976 and the factory was hit by a new problem as the whole of Britain suffered from one of the worst droughts on record. Just as the company was about to enter a crisis period through shortage of water, Meirion Rowlands, then Production Director, thought to use copper divining rods to search for new sources of water in the hills he knew so well. Under a dry bank in a nearby field he discovered a spring. The farmer whose land it was gave 'Laura Ashley' rights to transport the water and 20,000 gallons were ferried daily to the plant. Without this additional source, production in Wales might have stopped entirely.

The drought had aggravated the effluent problem as the company was forced to rent tankers to carry away the effluent which was an even more costly, though temporary, solution. Laura, although embarrassed by the prosecution and the £90-fine, was never involved in seeking a solution to the effluent disposal problem. It fell into the business category and was therefore Bernard's province, not to be encroached upon. She cannot have failed to be aware of the situation as the land reeked of the smells and both water and land were often strikingly coloured. For Dai, John James and others involved, the problem was one of the most frustrating of the expanding years. Even when an expensive filtration plant was finally installed it proved inadequate. In 1978 the company was charged with five further separate offences relating to effluent and on this occasion Newtown Magistrates imposed fines totalling £450. Eventually a more effective pump was installed which removed both offensive chemicals and colour. But the effluent saga had lasted for nearly eight years and although the court appearances were relatively few and Laura herself never became directly involved, the publicity was unwelcome for a company which claimed the Welsh countryside as the key to its philosophy.

Given all the attention the company was attracting it was inevitable that someone, somewhere, would find something to criticize. An article in the *Daily Mail* lambasted the attitude of shop staff in the new Harriet Street branch. Laura was only slightly worried by the adverse publicity but she was bitterly hurt, as if this were an attack on her personally. She responded with a round-robin letter to all her employees, thanking them for their contributions and enthusiasm and reassuring them how highly she thought of them all. 'The *Daily Mail* article was just provocative journalism and our lawyers are in fact dealing with it,' she consoled them. But after a further month's reflection she changed her mind and wrote to Moira that it was up to her to do something about 'the incompetence of your staff at Harriet Street [which] is now causing BA and myself sleepless nights'.

During the mid-Seventies Laura travelled around Europe a great deal, imbibing what she saw and able to take ideas and incorporate them into her collections. She and Bernard could come and go as they pleased, partly thanks to Ruby and Molly, two local women who kept Rhydoldog clean and checked each day for telexes which might announce the Ashley's return, in which case the beds would be aired and food prepared. While she was away Laura would send Lynda or Moira detailed written descriptions, as she had never learnt to draw, and expect them to adapt her suggestions. 'Here in the South of France,' she told Moira, 'a lot of baggy blouses are being worn with jeans ... which reminds me! I think we shall need some ... cotton and wool mixture for winter with everything going so floppy and baggy.' In her notes to designers, with accompanying photographs, she would tell them, 'We definitely need a version of this,' or 'This will be the trend for autumn,' or 'These are the sort I am after.' Wherever she was the telexes would clatter with instructions for Moira based on either what she had seen or read. She was already turning against the frills of earlier years, partly because they consumed so much factory time. 'I do want to have very simple things,' she telexed Moira. 'They look good and take so little making-up time [which] therefore gives us a price advantage on the market.' But this change was chiefly because her international exposure was making her more sophisticated. Her own clothes now, although comprising the same plain skirt and toning cardigan with a cream shirt, were bought, more often than not, from Yves St Laurent's Rive Gauche, or Sonia Rykiel.

Everyone who worked with Laura at this time agrees that, as a fashion editor, she had a sure instinct about forecasting trends, a canny feel for coordinating colour and fabric that was invariably right, and knowledge of which of the latest details could be adapted to the 'Laura Ashley' look. It was hardly surprising therefore, that she resented, but grudgingly accepted, being told by those on the shop floor, or in administration, what customers wanted. From the start the Ashleys took all the decisions (and risks) from design to manufacture and marketing. Having enjoyed a remarkable degree of freedom for several years it was now hard to relinquish areas of control. Hers was, and always had been, an autocratic empire where the customer would be presented with what to wear. Although she embraced the need for each collection to be a little different in order to move forward, she would often be upset that what she considered a beautiful print could not be included in the collection for ever. However she did not work in isolation of the sales figures and shop reports, which she read avidly and, as she wrote to Moira: 'I feel that we hit it in many respects but we don't seem to repeat the exciting things fast though.' The blame, she felt, should be laid at the door of 'the planners who are playing too safe to the provincial market . . .' She pointed out that adding sales from stores outside London 'could be a killer', since the provinces were so much slower to react to new trends.

Laura had always been able to identify gaps in the market and fill them. Yet this could never be done by interpreting yesterday's sales figures, which gave information only about products already in the shops. The increasing reliance on managers' reports as a means of deciding what the shops should carry infuriated Laura and complicated her ambivalent feelings towards her shop staff. Although she put them firmly into the category of 'workers', rather than 'idlers', and therefore to be praised, they were not quite on a par with the Welsh factory workers, or designers; nonetheless they stood on a higher plane than accountants, clerks or corporate planners. When she discovered, in the summer of 1977, that 5,500 metres of plain cloth was 'hanging about in Helmond and they don't know what to do with it', she was appalled and gave orders for it to be made up into suitable garments immediately. 'I really don't think anyone in this firm understands finance,' she telexed Moira.

Laura's instruction that shop staff must wear 'Laura Ashley' clothes made sound business sense and was, after all, no hardship. But there were also emotional reasons behind the rule as it was also a way of reasserting her authority. Thus, the girl in Geneva who continually mixed 'Laura Ashley' clothes with her own, and the girl in Paris who agreed to wear a 'Laura Ashley' shirt, but left off her bra, must have known that their futures with the company were blighted. That she did not do so herself was beside the point. 'As I work with the prints all day I would get so bored if I wore them as well,' she once told an American interviewer, who expressed surprise to find her in such plain clothes. At the front of Laura's mind constantly was the realization that these shops bore her name and everything in them must therefore reflect what she stood for. With an empire of such a size, it was a difficult but not impossible task she had set herself.

The outside world could not guess at the disturbing cross-currents. It saw a company which, by 1975, had a turnover of five million pounds, employed 1,000 men and women worldwide, had forty shops, three factories and which was profitable enough to own its own jet. Bernard had needed little persuading to buy the first company aeroplane, a twin-engined Piper Navajo for £95,000, which carried six passengers and two pilots. 'Laura Ashley' was painted boldly on the side. Many in the company, not only Laura and Bernard, were required to undertake extensive travelling. Yet flights were expensive and with company headquarters deep in Wales, connections were difficult.

It was this success story which prompted the Prime Minister's Office to inform Laura that her name was on the forthcoming list of Queen's Birthday Honours; she was to be offered the OBE if this was 'agreeable'. David remembers the day the letter arrived, and the ominously quiet discussion which ensued between his parents at Rhydoldog. He remembers, too, seeing a crumpled letter in his mother's writing in the wastebin later that day. Laura declined the offer of a public honour, knowing it was the only way to salvage her husband's personal honour, which was the more important to her. He was, she felt, as deserving of recognition as she; he was the Chairman of the Company. But above all, the letter had been sent to Ms Laura Ashley, a form of address she detested. She wrote back, declining the offer, signing herself, 'Mrs Bernard Ashley'. She contented herself by having the official offer letter framed.

In Britain in the mid-Seventies, there was a keen debate as to the merits of remaining in the Common Market, and Laura was invited to take part in a government-sponsored television film proclaiming the benefits of the European community. The film was intended to show that all the best names in Britain favoured European unity. Among those who had agreed to take part were Harold Macmillan, Marcus Sieff, Trevor Howard, Henry Cooper, Terence Conran and Marjorie Proops. One of the production team then proposed Laura Ashley. 'It was an obvious choice, partly because of all the business they were doing in Europe and also because the public was fed up with the same old faces; here was someone fresh at last,' recalls Peter Batty, director of the film. Laura, however, declined on the grounds that she was not nearly important enough to share the limelight with such august people. She was, Batty believes, genuinely shy and nervous. Then Bernard suggested taking part himself, an idea which was vetoed however, as his was not the name associated with the company.

Several months later, Batty was asked to make a film about any successful British company to redress criticism that television programme makers were obsessed by those in difficulties, of which there were many in the Seventies. He remembered the Ashleys, who appeared unstoppable in their ascendancy, and this time Laura, together with Bernard, agreed to have a documentary made solely about them. Batty found Laura still rather reserved. 'She was an earth-mother type who couldn't quite believe in all her success. What she was doing seemed to her all utterly natural. She was rather embarrassed by the aeroplane and constantly worried about whether or not people had enough to eat.' Whenever the film crew opened a cupboard in a shop to store some electrical equipment, they found it stocked high with food. Hot meals, slopping all over car boots, were delivered around to the shops. Yet Batty noticed that in spite of her reserve she had a way of inspiring people to do things for her. 'She even got the "sparks" peeling potatoes. Most film crews want as little to do with their subjects as possible, yet the Ashleys immediately became involved in our lives and we in theirs.

They took trouble to make sure our rooms in the hotel were the best and the result was that this was a very happy film to make. Everyone liked her very much,' said Batty.

Today, Batty admits that perhaps they liked the Ashleys too much. The documentary showed them in and out of their aeroplane, discussing store openings around the world, managers flying in, telexes flying out and telephone calls from San Francisco. It showed a family picnic in the Welsh hills with Laura commenting that all her children were still at home; 'they won't go away like other people's children do', a part of the myth she believed herself; the background music played cash tills ringing to the rhythm of dresses being folded and packed. Not surprisingly, reviewers treated the film harshly, complaining of a lack of critical input. Batty recognises that he could have taken a sharper look at the derivative nature of the designs or examined some of the problems likely to face the company in the future. It would have made good drama to pit Bernard's projection of mass production against Laura's fears that this would threaten to destroy the ethnic and cottage industry appeal upon which the business was based. But no producer would ever have succeeded in making Laura disagree with her husband publicly, let alone on a television film.

The filming lasted three and a half weeks and took place in Bath, London, Brussels, Paris and Carno. 'The Rise and Rise of Laura Ashley' was screened on 14 December 1976 and marked an important turning point for the company. Not only a household name, now it was a household face with household heart as well. But if Laura was, once more, stung by the criticism, Bernard was furious. 'Sure it was an hour-long commercial,' he wrote to Batty, commiserating. 'What else do they think we are running here, a pansy shop? It is a pity some of those guys do not get up and learn to do commerce in the way that the rest of the world has to and put to advantage their expensive educations which are paid for out of general taxes.' The film's message – the continuing success of this homespun cottage industry with a modern technological core – seemed borne out a few months later when the company won a Queen's Award for Export; over a three-year period they had increased exports six-fold. The presentation ceremony was held in Carno, at the factory, with the Lord Lieutenant of the County deputizing for the Queen. Later in the year, the Queen, as was custom-ary, gave a reception at Buckingham Palace to which three representatives of the firm were invited as an additional way of marking its achievement. Neither Laura nor Bernard were able to attend this ceremony as by that time they had exported themselves. The Ashleys sent their apologies, along with Moira Braybrooke and the oldest and the youngest company employees.

* * *

There is a story, apocryphal no doubt, told by his friends that Bernard, having decided it was time for another move, walked into the offices of a prestigious estate agents one Saturday to see what was available. Disgruntled at not being attended to immediately, especially as he wanted to buy a large country mansion, he stormed out and decided to buy an estate in France instead. Such restlessness had been a hallmark of Bernard's since infancy and Laura at least shared her husband's ability to make decisions quickly. They came home, packed their bags, left Wales for good and set up in Brussels until they found a new house. They consulted a map of France and worked out the ideal point between London, Paris and Helmond in the Netherlands. Having located the spot, which had to be served by a nearby airstrip, they rang Anthony Marangos in Paris and told him to call back in half an hour with the largest houses closest to the spot. 'Well he rang back with three; one was too far west; the other had bungalows; the third was the right one. We didn't even look at the others. We rang Anthony before lunch and told him to buy it. Bernard and I always agree,' Laura later told the journalist, Maureen Cleave.

In the late Seventies the Ashleys were travelling around so much and had so many different houses that it was hard for them to know where home was. Bernard loved moving, and they had now spent nearly five years at Rhydoldog which was as long as he liked to spend anywhere. Also, this nomadic existence was bringing them into potential conflict with several different tax jurisdictions. There was an argument which insisted they should have one commercial base for tax purposes. It was also weighing on Bernard's mind that they were opening more and more shops in Europe and yet the European commercial scene was not as stable as that in the UK. The company had opened a record fifteen shops in 1978 bringing its total to over seventy outlets worldwide. Yet morale in the European shops was never as high as in their UK counterparts and they often had to beg for a booster visit from their patrons. In addition, the heavy tax rates of the late-Seventies would have made it virtually impossible, had one or other of the pair died, for the company in its entirety to be passed on to the children, Laura's most cherished ideal. Given the conventional wisdom that any change in tax affairs should be put into effect before 5 April, allied to Bernard's natural impulsiveness and Laura's love of buying and doing up old houses, the haste with which the Ashleys moved out of Britain in the spring of 1978 is easily understood.*

But it was a haste they paid for dearly in emotional terms. Laura found herself repeatedly hurt by accusations in the press that they had become 'tax exiles' and tried to point out how the decision to live abroad had, on the contrary, been forced on them by their peripatetic lifestyle on the one hand and fear of punitive estate duty rates on the other. It was, she tried tirelessly to explain, not a selfish move but the only way to preserve the business. Henceforth Laura insisted that home was wherever Bernard was, and she accepted stoically and with cheerfulness the many unpleasant aspects of the move. But there was no doubt she hated leaving her family behind and being away from Wales. 'I left Rhydoldog for ever', Laura was to write later, 'on an early April day when the wild daffodils were smothering the banks of the old water garden and thousands more nodded to me all the way down the lovely driveway to say farewell.' It was the only public, albeit circumspect, acknowledgement of her sense of loss. 'She never said anything, never complained, you just knew how much she hated being away,' said Trevor Maddocks, who worked closely with her in Carno.

And so they moved, with no master plan in mind, first to their small flat in Brussels. It was from here that they rang Anthony Marangos, and inspected the house, or rather château, which he had found for them in Picardy, North East France, between the towns of Arras and Amiens. Remaisnil itself is but a hamlet of five or six cottages, a few alleyways and a simple parish church to serve its sixty-five inhabitants. Across the road from the church, at the end of an impressive avenue of mature limes, stand the black wrought-iron gates of the Château de Remaisnil. Only those who know what they are looking for will stumble

---

* The highest rates of income tax were at 98%, capital gains tax at 30% even on unrealized capital and death duties were levied on estates as low as £15,000.

upon it and this seclusion exerted a strong appeal on the Ashleys. It was surrounded by thirty-five acres of flat countryside on the edge of the Somme valley. Memories of the country's former sadness as a battlefield and burial ground make it depressing for many English; Bernard and Laura, by contrast, conscious that both their fathers had fought in this part of France in World War I, found this link with their native country comforting.

The house was in need of total renovation and would not be habitable for nearly a year, but the Ashleys moved into a hotel in Le Touquet from where they hoped to oversee the extensive repairs to the exterior and interior. Of course, the builders never worked fast enough for Bernard. In the beginning, a team of French builders was hired, but when they did not respond to his treatment of them as an army detachment, he fired them and barked orders at Anthony instead. After this they employed Welsh builders and had everything sent over with them including paint, sandpaper and Polyfilla. But the Welsh builders were unhappy about staying in a small French village without fried eggs and sausages for breakfast and although the local hotelier was eventually persuaded that this fare was absolutely essential, the Welsh contingent did not see the job through and a third firm, French again, was then brought in.

The eighteenth-century Château de Remaisnil is magnificent by any standards; it was by far the grandest home the Ashleys had yet lived in and it presented them with numerous challenges of a personal and artistic nature, not least of which was learning to speak French. Laura was often to be seen with a heavyweight nineteenth-century French novel in her hands, but this pursuit held little appeal for Bernard.

Although a château has existed on the site at Remaisnil since 1572, the present brick and limestone edifice dates from around 1760 and was built for Theodore de la Porte and his wife Henriette de Cerf Wintershove of the House of Flanders. The de la Porte family owned several properties in Picardy and were related by marriage to the noblest and richest families in the area. By the time the Ashleys bought the twenty-two-room château, it had seen a variety of owners and fortunes, yet although remarkably close to the battlefront in both World Wars, had escaped any major damage.

It comprises three main parts, the central living section with two wings slightly set back, as well as several outbuildings, and the old kitchen quarters, the '*commun*', linked by an early twentieth-century underground tunnel. The white tiles in the tunnel are the same as those used in the Paris Metro, both supplied by a M. Elby, who owned the château from 1909. The '*commun*' was used formerly as servants' quarters and kitchens. The mansard roof and dormer windows were added in the nineteenth century but the predominant style of the château interior was Louis XV rococo, with traditional Picardian emphasis and additions. Before embarking on any decoration Laura was determined to research the château's history as thoroughly as possible to establish what was original and what should be preserved. One of the most attractive features for her was the garden, comprising ten hectares of parkland, which they converted to pasture and brought over their own flock of texel sheep. Around the château itself were neatly laid out formal gardens with mature trees, age-old fountains and sweet smelling bushes as well as a neglected, sunken, walled garden. This had become a wilderness of weeds and bushes but hidden deep inside was a derelict conservatory demanding to be restored.

Life at the Novotel in Le Touquet was comfortable enough at first. Bernard and Laura escaped on to their sailing boat for much of the summer, a yacht they had been enjoying for some years now, and they pottered around Mykonos in Greece. But at the end of the summer, they had to return to Le Touquet. As the days, weeks and months dragged on and the fine weather turned to biting snow, preventing builders or delivery vans from approaching Remaisnil, the frustrations for Laura and Bernard became at times overwhelming. One of the lowest moments for Laura was an interview she agreed to give to Susan Raven of the *The Sunday Times*, for 'A Life in the Day of' series. She did not deny having said anything which she was quoted as saying. She was simply embarrassed at being revealed to the public. In the article she was at pains to point out why they had to stay out of England until the following April, 'not because of tax', she insisted, 'but in case either of us drops dead, which would mean the company having to be broken up'. The article described her current routine of constant travelling, discussions with designers flying over to see her, and her concern to exercise more and lose weight. She disliked the photograph of herself in shorts, which she thought made her look fat; in fact she looked remarkably fit for a fifty-two-year-old. But what upset her particularly was the last sentence: 'I should go and work for a week in one of my shops but – though I could even sleep on the factory floor – I can't understand people working in shops.' She was still naïve enough not to realize that ideas tossed of the cuff could sound quite different in the cold print of day.

Those who worked for 'Laura Ashley' at this time found it a mixed experience. Overall, the degree of responsibility and independence, the rapid and inexorable growth of the company and the originality of the product, made it a continuously exciting and rewarding place to work. Yet it was also exhausting and frustrating. Even within London the operations were spread over a wide area with, for example, designers at Greenford, south-east London, fittings in Battersea and pattern-cutting in Kilburn. In addition, there was the studio in Carno and Laura herself in France. This meant many of the staff could be travelling for days on end, racing against deadlines, and, just when they were at their most exhausted, might receive a summons to fly to France the next day, which usually meant leaving at 5.30 am. 'All the people who worked with Laura in those years experienced the rough edge of her humour at some time or other, usually when you were so run down and exhausted, after four or five days travelling with no proper sleep, that you could not fight back.' Laura's anger would usually come in an icy blast on the telex for all to see, invariably concerned with a project she had decided she no longer approved of. 'It was like a burning spear going through you, you felt sick for three days. She could denigrate one's whole being into nothingness,' is how a senior member of her design team described it. 'I would forgive her because I would feel she was really unhappy to behave like that.'

Bernard explains Laura differently. 'Her authority was so complete, she never had to lose her temper, like I did. If she said "Don't do something", you didn't do it and you didn't argue. She always gave orders with a smile, but the more she smiled the more quickly you acted.' To Bernard alone Laura admitted she was unable to compromise, a talent she rated highly in him but was unable to foster in herself. In difficult days, her obduracy increased.

Carolyn Warrender noticed a change in Laura and Bernard too. 'Those were not the same people I had known; they were homeless, with no nest around them and no children. They were so unhappy that life lost its perspective for them.'

Desperate to have Christmas in their new home, they were at least able to move into the '*commun*' of the château in November. They were without hot water and numerous other comforts but they had a base they could call their own. The Novotel, sorry to lose its famous customers with their constant stream of visitors, threw a huge farewell party for them.

9

America

One autumn day towards the end of 1973, Bernard was driving through Oxford and, as was his wont, stopped off to see how things were at the local shop. He was in an expansive mood, and enjoyed chatting to the sales assistants. Twenty-three-year-old Jill Yate took the opportunity of telling her boss that, although she had had a wonderful year travelling around Europe, she was beginning to feel homesick and would soon be going back to the United States. 'Well, let me know when you're off,' Bernard told her, 'because we're going to open in the States very shortly. You could run the shop for us.'

It was typical of the way the company operated in the early Seventies. Of course, there was no business plan for opening in the US; it was merely a dream, long nurtured by Bernard. Of course, Laura took no part in such a major business decision; the empire builder was Bernard. Laura harboured a vague suspicion that America was full of neon nastiness and immoral movies, but she encouraged Bernard's plan. And then, of course, Jill Yate knew very little about retailing or the fashion industry; until a year before, her main interests had been rock and roll and the Beatles, and she fell upon the job at 'Laura Ashley' as representing part of the faded Sixties pop culture she loved. But what mattered, as Bernard well knew, was that she was young and energetic and would feel charged with enormous responsibility and will to succeed in return for being offered this opportunity to take 'Laura Ashley' to the States. Finally, of course, there was no market research pointing to where in the entire continent would be the most suitable place to start. Since Jill was returning to San Francisco that seemed the obvious location for the new shop. Also, there was a bias against opening immediately in New York as Bernard and Laura wanted to avoid the limelight in case they failed.

Not that anyone in the company seriously questioned whether the new outlet would be successful; they had seen American tourists (although not necessarily Californians) on holiday in England 'going crazy' over the designs and assumed people would flock to them in the States. Peter and Jean Revers were so excited by the project they decided they would try living in America for a while as the new venture would clearly need a business manager. Jill returned in the spring of 1974 and was told to look around for a suitable site. A few months later the Revers and their baby daughter set off for San Francisco. 'We didn't know anything about America, but it felt right. We were so full of our own importance we thought Americans with bulging pockets would come and find us wherever we were,' Peter Revers explains.

Jill, charged to find the oldest building in town, located one of the few pre-earthquake buildings in downtown Jackson Square, part of the financial district. It was a large basement, with no street-level exposure, and although sales for the first two days were excitingly high, the next few months were a disaster. She sat in the empty shop for days willing people in off the streets. With Laura still opposed to advertising, ('too commercial') their options were few. After nearly a year, when they were further buffeted by a major recession which affected the entire country, Bernard wanted to close down and cut their losses; but with a ten-year lease on the shop there seemed little point even in doing that. Having never visited America, the Ashleys had scant grasp of the cultural differences or geographical distances involved; in the UK no two stores were more than 350 miles apart. Bernard would sometimes call from London and say, 'Peter, why don't you go down to New York for the day and see all the magazine editors?'

Peter and Jill slowly began to realize the markedly different requirements of their American customers. And yet the shop was being sent exactly the same merchandise as was being sold in England. American women, they learned, did not much care for murky colours but wanted bright yellows and apple greens, vibrant colours which were hardly used at all in Europe. Even the all-white cotton garments, the mainstay of the inventory, posed an unexpected problem in the US because these items had to be ironed, starched too if possible; many Americans do not even possess an iron, let alone use one. Also, they found, American women have different shapes from their English sisters, being less curvaceous around the hips, and therefore they prefer a more tailored line. Further disparities appeared on the home furnishings front; the standard English width of 21-inch wallpaper rolls was unknown to American decorators, who worked with a 28-inch standard, mostly vinyl, paper. Vinyl, a man-made composite, was anathema to Laura. These variations would have been impossible to rectify without buying expensive new printing machines, unthinkable, as home furnishings were still at an experimental stage in England.

How much to vary the product according to the market was a problem which hit at the very heart of the business. Bernard and Laura's attitudes were still coloured by the historical evolution of the business, manufacturing led, and believed their shops existed only to absorb the manufacturing capacity. They had invested heavily in their branded products and in the machinery to make them. The rationale behind Laura's views was that her heart was in Wales, or, more specifically, in the factory in Wales, and this obliged her to do everything within her power to maintain that factory at full capacity. Six thousand miles away, Jill and Peter felt they too had made an investment of their time and the company's money and pleaded with Bernard for a little longer to educate the American customer. 'We knew it could work but we needed a better location and a lot of word of mouth.' Bernard advanced $30,000 'to do or die with' and, early in 1976, Peter bravely used half of this to open a second shop on Union Street, a prime commercial location in the centre of San Francisco. He went down to the docks to buy a lorryload of timber going cheaply, had the building sandblasted and refitted, and insisted on some adjustment of the merchandise to suit the customer profile. This time, it was the long-awaited triumph.

In 1975, Laura visited the United States for the first time to see the San Francisco venture for herself. It was the first time she had travelled beyond Europe and she was captivated by the beautiful city and continually remarked upon the quality of the light and the gentle colours which bathed the buildings. As a result of this visit, and those to the South of France, she introduced several brighter and lighter designs in her next collection. The following year she went to New York, to a large party given by Bloomingdales to show off four rooms decorated in 'Laura Ashley' fabrics. Bernard did not accompany her so she invited David, then studying engineering in Newton, near Carno. David's apprenticeship with another firm had irked his father who believed the family company could teach his children all they would ever need to know. The ensuing breach upset Laura, who missed having her eldest son at home and was constantly trying to find ways to retain as much contact with him as possible. David refused his mother's invitation at first: 'To a dedicated anti-capitalist, as I then was, New York was everything I didn't approve of. But when she said we were going by Concorde, that, to an engineering student, was it.' Thus, at a stroke, Laura cleverly brought her son back into the company and family.

In New York, Laura was fêted as a brilliant female entrepreneur. However much she might have wanted to remain aloof from publicity the female press corps had already identified her as the 'Woman Head' of a multi-million dollar international corporation and, through the same lens, saw her therefore as challenging a man's world. They compared her, in advance, to similar women in the States who had manifestly succeeded but when they interviewed her, and found how she differed from the stereotype, they were even more intrigued. What lessons could be learned from this sweet-talking, gentle-faced Englishwoman with so much success behind her? The party at Bloomingdales was an orgy of mutual congratulation. By this time Laura was thrilled to meet famous people and be treated as a celebrity among them – a contradiction within herself which she never outgrew as she did not seek the limelight and took pleasure in deflating those whom she considered did.

At this particular party, Gloria Vanderbilt was another guest of honour whom Laura was excited to recognize. 'David, let me introduce you to Gloria Vanderbilt,' said Laura, summoning her son to her side. But when she realized her son did not appreciate who was this doyenne of New York fashion she said out loud: 'Oh David, I can see you don't know who Gloria Vanderbilt is, do you?' David well knew that his mother found this sort of joke, at Ms Vanderbilt's expense, irresistible. But, on other occasions Laura could laugh at herself just as easily because she was constantly amused by the transience of fame and never took her public for granted.

Bernard, appreciative that Laura in New York would be treated as a queen of design, an extraordinary superwoman who had singlehandedly achieved it all, accordingly decided not to go on this trip. He insists today, however, that the prominence of his wife's name never worried him. 'I always found it very funny when I was referred to as Mr Laura Ashley, especially as I hated my own name, Bernard.' At all events, he was shrewd enough to realize how perfect was the name – timeless, classless and English – and never contemplated changing it.

Eventually, Peter rid them of the first, hapless shop in San Francisco and, in 1981, felt ready to open in New York. New Yorkers were familiar with the 'Laura Ashley' name because the products had long been sold in Bloomingdales and Macy's. For some years now they had licensing agreements with some major US companies to produce 'Laura Ashley' designs on sheets and other home furnishings. This arrangement was partly to help overcome a technical problem since Laura Ashley machinery was not capable of producing sheeting to the required width, and coordinated bed linen was a must for American designers. But it was also an appetiser by way of preparing the American public for the full range of 'Laura Ashley' products to come. But their own store on Madison Avenue at 64th Street, at the epicentre of the city's wealth and elegance, was still a giant leap. Upon its success might depend the entire future of the company. Because import duty (35 per cent on ornamented goods) and freight charges, had from the start pushed prices up in the US, Peter now decided to make a virtue of necessity and deliberately aimed for an exclusive designer image with corresponding price tag. Naturally, this did not please Laura who thought the designer status was a disadvantage 'because people aren't so likely to think of us as a neighbourhood store; that's what we want to be. It's rather like knowing your mother is always the same,' she told reporters.

They opened, from scratch, within seven weeks to see 800 people fight their way through the store on opening day, building up to 1,000 by the first Saturday. Once the New York store established itself, quickly followed by others, Laura's treatment as a superstar by the US press increased. When occasionally they asked her what was the marketing strategy or the business plan and she said, openly, that there never had been one, her patent naturalness and honesty made the whole thing appear even more of a fairy story. This was self-perpetuating. Journalists treated her with such awe and respect that she soon thrived on interviews, developed her eccentricities and refined the mythical aspect of the success. She especially loved any opportunity to contradict those interviewers who assumed that, as the company which bore her name was so successful, she must be an ardent feminist. 'I only work part-time,' she told one. 'I'm just a housewife,' she laughed to another.

The American press lapped up her homespun philosophy and whimsical reaction to success as an integral part of the 'Laura Ashley' empire. No market advisers could ever have dreamed up a better ploy because Laura was only enunciating theories she had always believed in. 'Our products can help give people a calmer, more well-ordered existence,' she told one American interviewer. Offered such a vast platform on which to air her philosophy of life, she found she warmed to her theme and lost any remaining traces of shyness. She was described in US newspapers as a tycoon who was quaint, genteel and steeped in the worlds of Beatrix Potter and Jane Austen. And she responded by telling them she was no tycoon, just a wife and mother with an unusually clear view of the world. 'Frankly, I make clothes for women to look sweet. I like sweet women,' she said in one syndicated interview. 'I see women's role in life in the light of sweetness. Men should be the hunters. Women are keepers of the hunters: it's a straightforward, set philosophy of mine.'

Later, she subtly modified her views so as to accommodate, not alienate, American feminists. 'A woman sees the home as her base and she dresses to complement that environment almost as part of the decoration. Of course that doesn't mean that she doesn't leave her home to work, it just means that the home is where she visualizes herself, wherever she is ... Man goes out into the world and brings back what a family needs to survive but he doesn't find a reflection of himself in the home as a woman does.' The new emphasis, nonetheless, did not alter the pivotal position. Women, in Laura Ashley's world, have no existence except in terms of their relationship to men; this was not sacrificial, it was fulfilling. Thus her choice of the quaint word, 'sweet', is no coincidence; sweetness is the quality Victorian men were taught to prize in a woman above all others. Laura found other themes in Victorian novels to bolster what she already believed; for example the home was viewed as a haven isolated from the trials and tribulations of the 'real' world and women presiding over the home were to make it as attractive as possible to persuade men to stay there rather than, for example, drinking in a pub all evening. Laura, who had a horror of pubs, dedicated her life to improving home comforts.

Contrary to his expectations, David found the atmosphere in New York stimulating and exciting. He wanted to stay, and told his father what he thought was needed to capitalize on the enormous potential of the US market. Bernard, harder on his own son than he might have been on any other twenty-three-year-old in the company was not keen, telling him he had no business experience. But he relented. David, involved initially in finding new store locations, decided to stay on the East Coast with the next shops opening in Boston, Mass., Westport, Conn. and Washington DC. From now on the American venture was not seriously in doubt, but as margins were tighter, there was not, even here, an immediate cash surplus. John James remembers doing the accounts with Peter Revers on his kitchen table in 1977 to save the company the expense of hiring an outside firm of accountants.

From the first, image was recognized as the vital factor which would decide the future of 'Laura Ashley' in America. Two years after storming New York, Laura and Bernard hired a young girl of impeccably aristocratic background and 'English rose' looks as Director of Publicity for the US company. The image Sarah Callander projected for 'Laura Ashley' over the next few years could not have been a more perfect match. Sarah understood instinctively the romantic feel of the product, coupled with Laura's personal philosophy of being true to oneself as a woman and letting everything revolve around the home. And yet she subtly steered her boss towards a more sophisticated version of this.

Fuelling the aristocratic Ashley appeal in the US was the considerable publicity given to the shy, young fiancée of Prince Charles. The then Lady Diana Spencer, who had shopped at 'Laura Ashley' from the age of fourteen, was regularly photographed in frilly, feminine blouses in white cotton or lace, preferably with a high ruffled neck. Even after her wedding, the Princess of Wales continued to shop at 'Laura Ashley', albeit with a bodyguard, and whatever items she brought received wide coverage. 'Laura Ashley' sales everywhere were boosted by this royal connection but the effect in America was electric. Could it be that young girls who wore 'Laura Ashley' dresses might become princesses themselves?

But the greatest fillip to 'Laura Ashley's' success in the US came from connections with the British Embassy in general and with Lady Henderson, the Ambassador's wife, in particular. Mary Henderson, Greek by birth, had first come across Laura Ashley in Paris when she and her husband had been posted there in 1975. As a great admirer of 'Laura Ashley' dresses, she often wore the long, British-made cotton dresses to Embassy functions – once she found she was clothed in the same fabric as a sofa – an embarrassment which she carried off with great panache. Thus, when she was hosting a major fashion show in Paris, featuring the best British designers, she invited Laura to attend, even though she was not showing Ashley clothes. The two women became immediate friends. When, in 1979, Sir Nicholas Henderson was posted to Washington and within two weeks of moving was told that the new Prime Minister, Margaret Thatcher, was to visit, Mary Henderson wasted no time in asking Laura if she could supply certain fabrics at cost price with immediate delivery; Laura naturally obliged. The Lutyens house in Washington had forty rooms, nine of which are bedrooms. She wanted, she told Laura, to create the atmosphere of an English country house and chose a blue and white vines fabric. In return, the Hendersons agreed to open the new 'Laura Ashley' shop and Bernard and Laura went to stay at the Embassy for the occasion, sleeping in what had become known as the 'Laura Ashley' room at the Embassy.

At the end of 1982, Lady Henderson conceived the clever idea of giving the Embassy in Washington a facelift by inviting several top British designers including David Hicks, David Mlinaric, Jean Munro and John Stefanidis, each to decorate one room. They were to give their advice free as the Government would pay for the work. Since all materials were to be British it would be a major boost for British products and the finished house would serve as an exhibition showcase, providing excellent publicity for all those involved. Laura Ashley was one of those invited and was genuinely thrilled to be considered on the same level as these 'famous names'. 'She was always quite stunned by her own success,' recalls Mary Henderson, 'because to her it was so obvious that people preferred to live in an atmosphere of comfort and tranquillity. She offered a freshness and uniquely British quality that makes her comparable to William Morris, I believe.' David, by this time Senior Vice President of 'Laura Ashley Inc.', understood the importance of Mary Henderson's friendship. 'They were always totally supportive of the company and the publicity from the Embassy could not have given us a better boost or image.'

By the end of the Seventies 'Laura Ashley' had sufficiently entered the American consciousness that when a small toy factory in Kentucky was threatened with closure, the Governor, John Y. Brown Jr., immediately contacted Laura Ashley and suggested they took it over. Laura liked the idea, partly because it was a way of avoiding import duty, but also because the eastern Kentucky women who worked at the factory were similar to the Welsh women she had first hired in the Sixties; rural, with strong ties to family and community and skilful seamstresses by upbringing. From then on all the white items of clothing sold in the US were made in Kentucky. With 'Laura Ashley' shops opening at about the rate of ten a year and Peter Revers' avowed aim to have one in every state, the new factory was crucial. In September 1979, the first 'Laura Ashley' store in a shopping mall opened in Chicago's Water Tower Place. Others in shopping malls followed as David managed to persuade his mother that such locations were essential in America because of the long distances from homes to towns. In 1980, three 'Laura Ashley' shops opened in Atlanta, Georgia, Baltimore, Maryland and Costa Mesa, California, and Laura derived great pleasure from travelling to the West Coast to attend the opening of this shop. She was flattered to be told that she must be an artist from the way she dressed, until David added 'they tell everyone that'. She performed with great natural charm in a television interview and marvelled at all the stretch-limousines she rode in.

By the end of 1980 there were thirteen 'Laura Ashley' stores in the US, not one of which took less than $400 per square foot annually in sales. Average sales per customer were running in excess of $100 and the company goal for forty-five to fifty stores within the next five years seemed easily achievable. David instituted an address book for mailings and comments in the front of the Madison Avenue shop and when the addresses were analysed, the Ashleys learned that their store had one of the highest customer profiles in the City, after Tiffany's.

One aspect of the American success which pleased Laura above all was her eldest son's achievement in creating his own niche within the company. Several journalists questioned him about whether or not he had found it hard being Laura Ashley's son and his answer told them more than they had realized. No, it was not hard being her son and he had no problem answering to his parents, because, in fact, he reported to Peter Revers. It had, however, been tough being Bernard's son, until he removed himself from his direct sphere of influence. Able to prove himself on his own ground, his relationship with Bernard improved and deepened and Bernard was the first to respect David's proficiency. Laura had been perceptive enough to create the means of achieving this.

It was clear from his success that he understood his adopted country extremely well, a fact underlined by his marriage in June 1979 to a wealthy New York Jewess, Susan Adler. There was, however, no grand wedding for Laura to attend as the couple married quickly and quietly. David was the first of her children to wed and Laura got on well with her first in-law, welcoming her into the family as well as the company. Susan often came over to Remaisnil for meetings. On 30 October 1980, Laura celebrated the birth of her first grandchild, an American baby called Sara Jane. Bernard announced that he wished to be known as an uncle, not a grandfather.

10

France and Family

Laura's absence from Carno endowed office politics with a new dimension. Exactly one month before her departure she hired, according to the advertisement, a 'fashion co-ordinator'. She explained to Deborah James, chosen from 300 applicants, how she wanted 'the design system to be as perfect as it could be so that the accountants could not spoil it' – 'accountants' having now become for Laura a generic term for anyone not on the design team. She once reported to Robert Landgrebe, marketing manager, in a voice of genuine shock that she had just been on an aeroplane with three accountants 'and do you know, they tried to talk to me about design'. Landgrebe, only the second graduate employed by the company, had taken over Peter Revers' job when the latter went to New York and had responsibilities for scheduling and managing shops, but knew better than to express an opinion on artistic matters.

Deborah James had run her own business, a shirtmaker's called Deborah and Clare in Beauchamp Place, and having recently experienced her own troubles with accountants, was extremely sympathetic to Laura's attitudes. She also found herself naturally in tune with Laura's taste and, although her job specification was to oversee the entire design structure for clothes, Laura advised her that she 'had been brought in as a flanker to Moira'. Later, Deborah thought she understood more precisely Laura's vision of company structure while she was abroad; 'she had Moira to sell more, Meirion to produce more and me to do it better'. Deborah was never certain whether it was a case of 'divide and rule' or 'design and rule'.

Deborah told her new boss what she believed the company needed: 'Principally the clothes were an insult to the country girls they were trying to portray ... they weren't suitable for country wear but they were selling very cheaply to secretaries in towns. 'Laura Ashley' had a loyal following among country people who, I felt, were being let down.' In Deborah's view the quality of the clothes had to synchronize with the quality of the image. She made two other trenchant criticisms; one was that the colours had to be controlled by introducing a system which would not permit a forty to fifty colour range. The second concerned the shops; 'They were still like a jumble sale inside with everything crammed on the rails.'

Laura was quite happy to let Deborah set in motion her improvements and chivvied her on. Yet general strategy, however serious a concern, had to give way before the immediate problem of the winter '78 collection. For Deborah this meant travelling to Remaisnil once every two weeks, often accompanied by Phil Morris from Carno. In the first year Laura wanted to see everything herself so the colours, prints and designs were all taken regularly to France for inspection. Mere geographical separation did not lessen her perfectionism; she once asked Phil to reprint a design thirty-eight times until she was satisfied with the colours. But after a while Deborah and her assistant worked out a system through which everything passed and which was regulated by a strict design timetable; this was sanctioned, but not directed, by Laura.

Deborah maintained that if the company wished to keep hold of its original and still loyal customers, now in the thirty-plus age bracket, and looking for more elegant attire, it had a lot of ground to make up. In fact, all British fashion retailers were being forced to recognize the ageing of the baby boom generation and at 'Laura Ashley' there was already a move towards broadening the appeal of the clothes to an older, more sophisticated market which spent less freely on personal adornment but demanded more in quality and style. Laura's own experience was also decisive here. 'Now in her fifties, she found most of the clothes were completely unsuited to her personally and you do lose interest if you cannot wear what you are producing,' Deborah commented. She believed this was a prime factor encouraging Laura's shift away from garments towards home furnishings. More significant was the greater scope for historical research offered by the latter; clothes, Laura recognized, could never draw upon their historical antecedents to the same degree.

Whatever the varying demands on her time, Laura was determined not to delegate print research. Hitherto she had been so tied up in the day-to-day mechanics of the company that she was often forced to consider time for research as a luxury. In addition it was only very recently that the company had the expensive machinery necessary to translate some of the more sophisticated effects she wished to produce, and even this was being constantly updated. As her knowledge of European art history increased and now that she had found the Musée des Beaux Arts in Paris where she felt comfortable and was treated with respect, her talent for recognizing saleable patterns, ripe for rediscovery, flourished. 'I knew she went to a certain museum but I didn't know where else she went, nor any of her sources, nor what she paid for things. You couldn't possibly ask her anything like that. You knew it was hers and she guarded it jealously,' Deborah said.

Her exposure to and enjoyment of French museums and antique shops was a key element which enriched her life in France. She was collecting many valuable print references and sources, far too many to be used at once, and had special archive cupboards built for her which occupied a tall, cavernous room off the first floor landing at the château where she often worked. Although Laura's formal education finished prematurely, she showed a remarkable capacity for intellectual growth in the middle years of her life: many of her ideas were changing so fast that her colleagues often found it difficult to keep pace. Laura thrived on the expanding horizons now before her. Yet she could not have done so without the help of a young French countess, Sybille de la Borde. Sybille was the single most important element which eased daily pressure for both her and Bernard in France. For several months before the Ashleys moved in, the locals of Remaisnil speculated about what to expect of the new English châtelaine. 'Laura Ashley' was sufficiently known in France to excite great curiosity and Sybille was tempted to offer her services as a general assistant. She knew the château well, as her uncle and aunt had formerly owned it. Within a few weeks of the Ashleys moving in, she drove up, knocked on the door and welcomed them to the area. If there was anything she could do to help she would, she said, be only too happy. 'I had never worked at all in my married life and I'm not a natural businesswoman. But I loved their products and was dying to work for them.' Bernard refused her offer at first; he did not think her English was fluent enough. Then, on 31 December, he rang back in desperation at the slow progress on the house, and told Sybille they would like her to start the next day.

It was largely Sybille who effected the Ashley's smooth transition to an often closed French provincial society. She introduced them to their neighbours, her own family and friends as well as to the best local craftspeople and services; her husband performed a valuable role in selecting wine for the Ashleys. 'Laura was more like a friend than an employer, she was so kind to me and did so many thoughtful things. Bernard's character, quite the reverse of hers, was so magnetic he made life exciting every day.' The Ashleys fully appreciated how much they owed to Sybille and treated her with great respect and kindness; *faux pas*, which from other members of staff would have met with icy reproofs, went scarcely noticed. 'They were so patient with me at the beginning until I understood English better; they would ask one of the secretaries in Wales to type a letter if I couldn't. If my children were ill Laura would send me home immediately and I was even allowed to smoke in their presence.' This last was a major concession as smoking in the company was, theoretically, totally forbidden. Sybille was an exception, but Laura liked to believe that she had persuaded her at least to cut down.

Halfway through 1979 the Ashleys finally moved into the main part of the château; it was not completed for another two years and was to prove a far more major project than anyone had realized. But even when there were teams of twenty or thirty workmen 'tripping over each other', as Laura told a friend, with beds scattered all over the place and no curtains, 'it still has a very romantic atmosphere'. She found it less romantic when one of the workmen blundered into the bathroom while she was still in the bath. 'Luckily it's a very old bath and only my shoulders could be seen,' she managed to joke.

Laura's natural adaptability enabled her to settle quickly. Her life at Remaisnil in the first years had no routine; she continued to travel regularly around Europe overseeing shops as well as production in Helmond. She was constantly at the telex machine, her old wartime

found working a pleasurable state. It formed part of her dream; she had the perfect home, the perfect family, the perfect husband, the perfect life and the perfect job. In Laura's world dreams *did* come true. But of course the dream glossed over the differences between the public, perfected self and the private, often anguished individual. Remaisnil became the staged version of her perfected life, the culmination of the myth which was such a potent force for customer and company alike and without which the art could not flourish.

Laura was an efficient stage manager, ensuring that the myth remained undisturbed. If Bernard was busy with flying lessons then she could be left in peace to get on with her work; once he was back, if he wanted her to go somewhere with him, he would just say 'Come on Laura, we're going,' and even if she were in the middle of a meeting, she would put away what she was doing and go. Her ability to remain utterly calm in such circumstances was extraordinary. Just because she had to leave a meeting suddenly did not mean she would relinquish her authority. Phil Morris well remembers such an occasion. 'As she got up to go past she said: "Give me a ring and we'll do the Home Furnishing Collection tomorrow." Everyone else thought the decisions had been made but in fact we totally re-did that season's collection in a waiting room at Brussels airport, just the two of us.'

1979 signalled a turning point in the Ashley's existence. To the outside world they had arrived on the international scene as self-made, jet-setting millionaires. However much they may have disliked such labels they were unavoidable as the dramatic jump in their lifestyle was to have an equally powerful, and highly visible, effect on the company. The move to the château influenced the types of fabrics and products which from now on bore the 'Laura Ashley' name and so the company grew, organically, by producing a more exalted range. Laura believed, as fervently as ever, in the universality of her own experience. But this was becoming harder to justify. During discussions on the type of fabric suitable for 'Laura Ashley' sheets she stuck to her insistence on 100 per cent cotton. When a colleague pointed out how difficult and time consuming these would be to iron, Laura countered: 'Oh, but surely everyone sends their sheets to a laundry these days?'

However, some fabrics to which Laura now aspired were, she knew, too lavish for her own company to produce. For example, she decided to decorate the main drawing room of the château in a plain, but luxurious salmon pink silk, in stark contrast to the small flowers and sprigged cotton in the other rooms, yet absolutely in keeping with the style of the house. An English interior designer flew out especially to plan and make the curtains for this one room, and the heavy silk drapes with thickly ruched pelmets, magnificent tassels and braid trims cost several thousand pounds, exceeding by far the means of most of her customers. Laura had always aspired to the very best within a certain budget; her budget had now expanded. She hoped it would not be too long before 'Laura Ashley' was itself producing material of this calibre. 1979 was a time of personal change, too, because the move abroad was followed by a major restructuring of the business which Laura eventually accepted, having first found a means of making it workable to her.

The single event which marked the dividing line was the company's twenty-fifth anniversary celebration in April 1979. After a year abroad, Laura and Bernard drove up to Rhydoldog in snow to find that Ruby and Molly, as a welcoming gesture, had put out the French flag on the lawn. They sat down to a celebration champagne lunch with Dai Davies, the farm manager, and set about opening the heaps of telegrams and congratulatory letters 'so that we really felt on top of the world'. They visited all the factories and shops they could squeeze into their brief, allotted time and the highlight of their visit was a Silver Anniversary Ball when 700 people gathered at the leisure centre near Deeside, Queensferry. They were entertained by the Royal Artillery Band, the Brendan Shine Show and comedian Harry Secombe, who captured the poignancy of the occasion by singing 'We'll Keep a Welcome'. The festivities were capped by an emotional presentation of a set of Bohemian cut glass from the staff to Bernard and Laura. They, in turn, gave each employee five pounds. By the end of the evening Laura had shaken everybody's hand and found something to say to each one.

After twenty-five years of manufacturing, but a mere eleven retailing, company expansion worldwide had reached seventy shops. In order to foster the feeling of family among such large numbers of staff the first edition of 'Laura Ashley News' was launched. It was inevitable that as the company expanded, so did the role of accountants and planners and Laura, however rueful, never once proposed that expansion should be blocked. After months of discussion, it was decided in 1980 to appoint Deloitte Haskins and Sells, management consultants, to produce a five-year corporate plan for the Laura Ashley Group. As a result of one recommendation, the company was no longer to be totally run from Wales, but broken up into smaller profit centres; four separate operating divisions were proposed, each with its own board comprising the principal managers within that division. The stated aims of the restructuring were partly to reduce the recent increased level of borrowing, but also to make individuals more accountable and profit conscious for the areas of operation under their control. The latter was not a goal which Laura espoused, nor was she comfortable working in such a formal setting.

The most dramatic symbol of the changing nature of the company was Laura's estrangement from the main board of the company which bore her name. In 1980 she stopped attending board meetings, which she considered a pantomime; those things which she really cared about she managed to achieve quietly away from the meeting, in discussions with Phil Morris or Deborah James. Although she often maintained that it was her own choice not to attend, she told an American interviewer 'I would love to go to board meetings where he [Bernard] is chairman but I'm not invited. I guess it wouldn't be right for me to differ with him. But at home it's the petticoat rule.' On another occasion she explained: 'I'm not allowed to go to board meetings.' She told a reporter from the *Chicago Tribune* 'I'm titular head only. What would be the point of my disagreeing with my husband at a board meeting? We do talk about the agenda at breakfast before he goes and he will hear my point of view.'

Once the Deloitte's plan was implemented, Bernard remained Chairman, John James Group Managing Director, and a new role was specially created for Laura. No longer Deputy Chairman, she was now, officially, Design Director, to be concerned with the artistic philosophy of the group as well as to oversee the development of the new product collections. Her seat on the board was never formally revoked; it was just that it was clear she was not to use it. Laura responded to this repositioning of her responsibilities neither by loudly insisting that she have more formal authority nor by sweetly surrendering the vestiges of power which she had. In effect she was working harder than ever and enjoying a supreme burst of creative energy since she could now release her talents into producing fabrics and accessories for every aspect of the home, while leaving Deborah in charge of garments. Her cherished ambition was that her customers should accept that 'Laura Ashley' was not just for bedrooms, nurseries and other upstairs rooms but was indeed suitable for every room in the house, however grand. Living in the château gave an enormous fillip to these aspirations.

Laura was in excellent health and neutralized the effect of the plan in a number of ways. In the first place she sharpened her political antennae and manipulative skills. She requested all telexes to be collected and sent out to her each week. On a particularly difficult issue she had a habit of canvassing everyone privately, except the person directly involved, so that when the matter was finally aired she would already be in command of all views. Typically circuitous is the way she used Bernard. When she heard that a particular decision had not yet been implemented she telexed Moira, complaining: 'BA would be very annoyed if he heard it had not been done.' In her arguments with John James over powers allocated to her design group she wrote, also in a telex: 'This company has always been design dominated,' and then bolstered her argument by adding 'see memos from BA leaving no doubt whatsoever.' She went on: 'The image has obviously been watered down these last seasons and the situation must be reversed.' James responded by supporting the role of the merchandisers, of whom he said, 'I do not think they are changing the LA image – I can only think they are enhancing it by ensuring the best level of stock service to the shops.'

Another method of retaining control was by keeping a firm grip on hours of work. There were no written rules but nobody ever worked beyond five o'clock in her presence; at this point formal business ended regardless. Bernard, just as much as Laura, disapproved of working endlessly round the clock. However, those who came to Remaisnil for meetings could not but be struck by a paradox; they were expected to remain in the château for meals and afterwards, until they retired to bed. Going out to find exciting nightlife was distinctly frowned upon. Yet discussion during the evening was about the company and little else and samples of fabric were passed round the table at most meal times. 'The company was an ever present reality that always hovered over us,' one close associate commented.

Laura's insistence on punctuality for meal times became something of a fetish, not because she was herself preparing meals which risked being spoiled; she rarely had time for cooking any more. It was something far deeper and was not merely affectation. Meal times anchored the day and as such had a major place in family life. Destruction of such routine was a step towards destruction of the family itself, and by a short step the company, which was extended family. Everyone knew how important punctuality was to Laura; she believed if you arrived late it could only be because you had not started out early enough. Eventually she put her feelings on record. 'If either of us calls a meeting here it must be assumed, unless otherwise stated, that the persons invited will arrive mid-morning for a day's meeting; lunch is at 12.30 pm French time and dinner 6.30 pm French time. Yesterday, to our consternation and when in fact we had cancelled other plans for the meeting, eight people arrived here at 2.00 pm for a meeting we had anticipated would commence at 11.30 am at the latest. We also had to provide them with lunch at 2.30 pm. Please do not let this happen again,' she wrote to John James.

Meals, meal times and the paraphernalia associated with them had always loomed large in the Laura Ashley ideology. Whether or not she was cooking, she regularly donned an apron as a symbolically matriarchal gesture that she was in charge of domestic arrangements. The fixation with aprons spilled over into her business life too as she insisted that her shops should always stock aprons. Even when whole batches of these ended up on sale rails Laura was not given to ter-giversation.

Parallel with this ideology and another means of countering the increasingly corporate nature of the business was the way she fostered the involvement of her own children and their friends. David was, by this time, playing a major role in developing the fast-growing US retailing operation; Nick was taking a larger hand in design strategy and had built a team of extremely young, artistic friends around him. These included Sasha de Stroumillo, just nudging eighteen when she joined the company and Tottie Whately who, together, designed brilliantly original room sets for shop displays and catalogues. Both were given a free hand to indulge their imagination and produced some of the wittiest and talked about windows in London, several of which featured life-sized stuffed animals or eye-catching visual puns. Window displays were becoming controversial within the company; Laura liked to see windows full of antiques and atmosphere, but increasingly found herself at loggerheads with more prosaic minds who wanted products and price-tags. Laura's preference for young, wholly committed staff invariably paid off; she knew they were less likely to criticize, were unshackled either by experience or domestic ties and would exude energy. Michael Howells, a painter friend of Nick's who stencilled the occasional floor and otherwise assisted in certain aspects of window display, found both Ashleys refreshingly open to suggestions, keen to encourage young staff and always trying to give them their first break.

Emma too, although still at school, was now provoked to make a contribution. Concerned at the way neither she nor her friends wore 'Laura Ashley' clothes (too many frills, too much lace, all up to the neck and down to the ankles, they said) Laura asked them to come up with suggestions for the sort of outfits they would like to wear. The result was 'Emma's Collection' of baggy clown dungarees in vibrant primary and luminous colours, dots and stripes. Arguably, had an outside designer proposed such items, Laura would have found them unpalatably modern. Nonetheless, they did so well that from then on Emma was asked to contribute on a regular basis.

Laura's relationship with her eldest daughter was less straight-forward. Jane had been hurt by her parents' occasional references to her in newspaper interviews as being a 'difficult child' or other remarks prompted only by Laura's nagging worries about what the future might hold for Jane. At the same time, she never swayed from her view that Jane's photography had great artistic integrity and supported her within the company whatever the criticism. She was proud of her daughter's originality and if Jane's work was becoming less commercial Laura was unconcerned. Commercialism was not a quality she rated highly, but protection of one's children from outsiders was. But inevitably, others in the company were pressing for a greater commercial awareness. One of the worst clashes was over a batch of photographs Jane had taken in North Africa. She had used inexperienced girls with no make-up, she had shown their deliberately unshaven armpits, she had dressed them in creased and crumpled frocks – the mood shot taken to its logical conclusion, perhaps, as well as an echo of her mother's antipathy towards using professional models, but a far cry from the traditional 'Laura Ashley' image of strawberries-and-cream-tea on the lawn. Whatever Laura privately thought of these pictures, revolutionary in their way, she insisted they be used. She was deaf to the arguments of those who told her that they would detract from the product, that they promoted only ugliness. Those present at the meeting were in no doubt of her overriding philosophy: 'I own the company, my daughter took the photographs, therefore you use them. If you do not like the photographs we have produced you are free to leave the company.'

Laura herself was in any case developing more pronounced tendencies against commercialism. From about 1979 onwards she started to buy Welsh tweed from the Cambrian Woollen Mill in mid-Wales. This started as a small venture in the mid-Seventies, as a result of Laura's determination to produce cloth woven from wool from her own flock at Rhydoldog. After much negotiation, the Welsh Wool Marketing Board agreed to a special arrangement whereby the Cambrian Mill could make up the Ashley's own wool into cloth as long as this was not sold, but used only for demonstration models and pattern samples. Laura often visited the Cambrian Mill, owned by the British Legion since 1927 but run for the benefit of all local disabled people who then, as now, make up 80 per cent of the workforce. 'She liked the quality of the product, but she was extremely sympathetic to our aims as well,' recalls Eric Hetherington, former sales manager. 'It was partly the Welshness of it all which appealed to her – the wool is grown, spun, woven and made up here in Wales, but it was also her feeling that in the commercial life everything was grab, grab, grab and here was a little corner of the world where she could do a bit of good.' Whenever possible, Laura tried to visit the Mill personally and Hetherington was struck by her ability to pick a 'winning' cloth instantly from the fifty or so patterns he would show her.

Laura Ashley bought substantial amounts of tweed from Cambrian Mill and although they paid the regular price, the company drew upon its charity budget to subsidize this at the rate of a pound per metre. Laura saw it as a project for saving jobs and therefore helping the survival of the rural community. It was a perfect example of one of her most cherished values; retaining something of the past for use in the future. But she was sensitive enough to let those at the Mill believe that they were making a competitive offer. They were startled when, several years later, they learnt about the subsidy. 'Thanks to Mrs Ashley we employed more people, the weavers were paid overtime and we enjoyed an Indian summer for a good few years. She was a wonderful friend.'

In the early Eighties, she organized a venture which above all else satisfied her craving for rescuing the past with no obvious monetary benefit. Shortly after her move abroad she had written to the then

Director of Manchester City Art Gallery, Tim Clifford, asking if she could view some of the Museum's early nineteenth-century cotton samples and take photographs. Clifford replied that he would be delighted, he was a great admirer of hers, and would she join him for lunch when she came. The lunch, however, was not a great success as Clifford had unknowingly double booked; his other guest was David Hockney. Laura was greatly amused by Hockney but the pair did not have a great deal to say to one another. However, Clifford invited Laura home to meet his wife and she spent the night at the Clifford's home admiring their eclectic collection of artefacts. Jane Clifford was enchanted by Laura's capacity for instant, warm friendship as well as her wisdom about life, and it was not long before a mutually rewarding project was born, which was immensely gratifying to Laura personally. 'You must have a higher goal in life than merely making money,' she was fond of telling people. She really believed her company had this greater purpose.

The Gallery of English Costume at Platt Hall, Manchester, part of the City Art Gallery and also run by Clifford, was badly in need of money and publicity and Laura offered to remake their collection of decaying dresses for an illustrated lecture. Her enthusiasm did not, however, encompass all the complexities that would be involved in such a project, from researching the fabric to preparing special screens for printing and educating machinists to make up the dresses in a traditional way. But she knew that Platt Hall had the finest collection of nineteenth-century dresses outside the Victoria and Albert Museum, and reason told her that undertaking such an unusual project would provide a unique opportunity to learn about historical fabrics and keep her company in the forefront of its competition.

Overseeing the project was Anne Wallwork, a television-trained period costume cutter specifically hired by Laura for the project. Initially, Laura told her to start making samples at the Leeswood factory in Cheshire, but, determined that no one should interfere, did not inform anyone else there what Anne was doing. However, it soon became clear that Laura could not secretly organize such a major undertaking while based abroad, and, in desperation, brought in Deborah. She, realizing the potential of the project, begged another year and set up the operation openly in the company's London workroom at Clapham. Here Anne worked with a team of machinists instructed to make four copies of each of sixty dresses selected from the years 1770–1870. Laura insisted that they be made up as near as possible in the original manner, from the cutting and colouring to the hand-sewn hems; historical accuracy was to be paramount. After eighteen months and thousands of pounds expenditure, Deborah and Laura realized that an illustrated lecture was ridiculously inadequate. They approached choreographer Patrick Libby, who created a lavish theatrical presentation using students from the Royal Northern College of Music and Northern Ballet school to perform six scenes inspired by everyday life of the period. These included a harvest supper, preparation for a wedding and a visit to the seaside. The atmosphere was recreated not only through dance and costume but also by authentic contemporary music. The show, on 22 and 23 June 1983, was deemed by all spectators to be a major success. It generated widespread and unusual press coverage. Suzy Menkes, then fashion editor of *The Times,* described Laura in a major feature as 'The queen of printed cotton ... who has nurtured a nostalgia for a vanished rural world.'

Such a show cut across many of Laura Ashley's established principles. In the first place she had always consistently opposed fashion shows for her company; she did not approve of professional models wearing 'Laura Ashley' clothes since they were not representative of her real customers; furthermore, she had moral objections to catwalk cavortings as being sexually provocative; 'Laura Ashley' clothes were not designed with sexual provocation in mind. This was based on a deepseated disapproval of flaunting one's body, inherited from her childhood in the Welsh valleys.

And yet Laura's simple, but devastatingly effective attitude towards sexual attractiveness contained an essential contradiction. She believed that the more a girl covered up the more exciting she was. This was not a moral, but a pragmatic approach. She herself is described by her own husband as 'a very demure, but passionately sexy woman'. Bernard maintains she recognized this 'seeming hypocrisy' within herself and often laughed at it. By turning the show into a theatrical display, Laura felt comfortable; it was so far removed from reality that it could be viewed as a staged drama with no intention of portraying a 'Laura Ashley' customer in real life. It was only her ability to view ball gowns as an aspect of theatrical dressing up, not real, everyday life, that allowed her to accept these highly frivolous and glamorous garments now becoming a staple product of the company.

The second problem was her aversion to handing out money to charity; although she enjoyed being able to help specific ventures in a practical way she hated the idea of charity balls or making large cash handouts. 'I prefer not to show in charity,' she instructed Moira 'as not acceptable to my principles (excuse for people to drink champagne etc and the needy get what's left).'

In spite of the altruistic intentions of the Platt Hall project, there were many long-term benefits. Anne Wallwork was retained on a permanent basis to help with some of Laura's more exotic ideas. Five of the print dresses and a cloak were put into general production and the rest, acting as powerful crowd pullers, went on display at various 'Laura Ashley' shops. An illustrated book, *The Fabric of Society*, was published to coincide with the event and the company's credibility was enormously enhanced by the entire venture.

Laura could indulge these less directly profit-generating activities partly because of their invariable spin-offs but also because she knew others were taking care of the money-making imperative. The company was enjoying a phase during which new products were constantly being introduced so that in January 1981, partly to keep customers aware of the ever-expanding range and also to enlarge the buying circle, the company initiated twice yearly catalogues. Here, for the first time, the prints were given pretty names instead of numbers. The seventy-two-page catalogue took months of planning and discussion before its format was agreed and the final version appeared in five languages. Products were shown individually and in room settings with the complete new collection showcased on the right-hand pages so that all the designs and colours could be seen at a glance. Among new items advertised were Italian floor and wall tiles, bedlinen, lamp bases, shades and luggage. 'I suppose they are nice,' Laura commented to a friend who saw some prototype suitcases lying about the château one day, 'but they are not my idea'. The catalogues were, above all, a crucial means of showing the customer a total lifestyle. Laura believed everything in the home should contribute to a pervading sense of calm and peacefulness; the same calm and peacefulness she had first discovered at her aunt and uncle's home in suburban Wallington.

The first 'Laura Ashley' fragrance, produced in France and packaged in a floral box designed by Nick, was another venture contributing to the total 'Laura Ashley' woman. A few months later 'Laura Ashley' soap arrived too, but in greater quantities than anticipated. Sybille, told to order 5,000 bars, had inadvertently ordered 50,000. Panic-struck once she saw her mistake she immediately confronted Bernard with the truth, apologized and offered her resignation. 'He kept quiet for a long time working out how long soap could keep for, then he just said, "Well, we'll have to sell the things." For several years every drawer in my house was bulging with soaps.'

Bernard decided to produce perfume after being constantly solicited by cosmetic manufacturers wanting to use the 'Laura Ashley' name. Typically, his reaction was to beat the professionals at their own game. There was also an element of romance in the story as he wanted to create a fragrance especially for Laura. Bernard approached a well-known Swiss firm, who sent a 'nose' to study Laura. The result was two fragrances, which Laura liked equally, so they decided to introduce them both calling them, simply, Number 1 and Number 2. Having created the venture, Bernard was less interested in running the day-to-day operation. 'He just said to me, "You're French, you must know about perfume," and handed it over,' explained Sybille.

A grand ball in the château seemed the obvious way to celebrate such exciting new departures, especially as the decoration was, finally, complete. Nick, by this time leading a glamorous social life in England with his girlfriend Arabella (Ari) Campbell MacNair-Wilson, daughter of a Conservative Member of Parliament, proposed that since nobody wanted a purely business party for journalists and other promotional appendages, each of the children should invite their own friends. There were some special members of the company who classified as friends too, including Mariel Angel from Lyons and Anna von Meiss from Geneva. Laura wanted to include her seventy-six-year-old mother, Bess Mountney, and sister, Mary Coates, and several family friends such as the Pollocks and the MacNulties. The organization for the event fell to Sybille, who was expected to invite some of her friends and family to lend an authentic French air to the proceedings.

'It was a mammoth task,' Sybille recalled, 'because it was really the first big party Laura had given in her life. She was nervous and excited all at once just as if she was a young girl going to her first ball.' At first Laura was quite happy to hand over all the arrangements to Sybille, but then, in the last few days, she wanted to be in on everything. There were coaches to arrange from Dover to bring over the English contingent, there was breakfast and lunch the following day, there were marquees to order and decorate with flowers, most of which Ari undertook. And there was the dancing. Sybille booked a disc jockey who had been highly recommended, 'but he was a bit too French for Bernard and Laura', Sybille commented drily. There were also some complicated sleeping arrangements to juggle: all Emma's friends were to stay in the '*commun*' while most of the rest of the young people brought sleeping bags and pillows to put down on the marquee floor. The adults were mostly farmed out, by special arrangement, to Sybille's friends' châteaux. Bernard declared 'No Smoking' throughout; but Laura, pragmatic as ever, rather than countermanding him, simply had fifty ashtrays placed strategically around the château.

Laura wore a long, grey satin dress with a big bow which was especially made for her in a more girlish style than she normally allowed herself. She looked young and pretty and relaxed for the first part of the evening until a ghastly sense of anti-climax set in when she realized that many of the young English guests had arrived well watered and rowdy after their coach trip, soon to become hideously drunk on the Ashley's generous provision of champagne and wine, with a few dainty canapés and other elegant nibbles. There was a lot of noise, much broken glass and Bernard and Laura could only guess with horror at the disreputable behaviour until they found evidence on the lawn the following morning. Bernard in a state of disgust, left the proceedings early and went up to bed. Laura, desperately disappointed, tried to be a polite hostess for as long as required but when she finally retired found Bernard had locked the bedroom door. With all the bedrooms allocated she had nowhere to sleep. The maids found her the next morning hunched up in the laundry cupboard on the landing, dozing lightly. The following few days were a nightmare. Nick was briefly fired, Sybille, upset by the tense atmosphere, crashed the car, and Laura was frequently in tears. But it blew over. Nick's friends wrote that it was the best party they had ever been to, a truly unforgettable occasion.

11

Anguish and Authenticity

Laura soon managed, in her customary fashion, to eliminate the nastier aspects of the evening. She remembered only how beautiful the house had looked, how exciting were the preparations, and what fun it had all been, hadn't it? She was soon telling Sybille: 'We must have another party, we so loved that last one.' In fact they did not host another major ball until Christmas 1983, by which time they had learned from their mistakes. On this occasion, the guests were predominantly French, the music predominantly English and the dinner a sit-down at small tables of eight. Although Bernard again retired early to bed, this time his wife was not forced to sleep in a cupboard.

Anyone close to Laura could not fail to notice her ability to ensure reality remained in the next room. Even her needlework, at which she constantly prodded during bumpy aeroplane journeys, was not really undertaken in order to produce a fine object but as an aid to entering another world of deep thought and reflection. It was not necessarily a world of fantasy. Her daughter Jane was keenly aware of Laura's inner life. 'My mother was always shutting herself off from reality and from nastiness; she was idealistic, which in commercial terms may have been a very good retailing idea but which I, as a rebellious teenager, found difficult to live with.' Jane often tried to shock her mother into facing some of the world's uglier problems, but Laura did not react in the way Jane might have expected. She simply was not interested in problems on a global scale, but saw events in relation to her own family or, specifically, her own daughter. She worried about Jane, but comforted herself that anything her own daughter believed in must a priori be acceptable. In any case, her intense loyalty dictated that she would never discuss intimate family problems with outsiders. Jane is convinced that this refusal to unburden herself to friends led to increased frustrations for her mother. 'But I think it ties in with her romanticized view of the world; if she didn't talk about her problems, then she didn't have any.'

For all their differences in outlook, Jane forged a secure bond with Laura and, perhaps, came the closest of anyone to understanding her. 'My mother used this romantic outlook as a strength on occasions to escape from the world. Yet by doing so she was also making difficulties for herself. I think my father found that frustrating too. He dealt with it either by going off on long trips or by challenging it and then an argument might erupt,' Jane explained. But it was often a rather one-sided argument since open dialogue was something from which Laura always shied away. 'The main conflict they always had was that she wanted to work more and he would not allow her,' according to Jane. True, Bernard did want her to be a housewife and mother but at the same time this was Laura's interpretation of what he wanted and she believed deeply that it was wrong to challenge a husband's authority. For all her championing of old-fashioned standards, she was embroiled in a most contemporary dilemma, which, by circumventing, she never directly confronted, and thus was life made tolerable.

In spite of an inauspicious beginning, Laura and Bernard succeeded within a few years in developing an absorbing private life in their adopted country. In some ways this was easier in France where there was not the same interest in accents or parentage. If Laura dropped in conversation that a piece of furniture had been in the family for generations, who was to argue? Bernard particularly enjoyed the dinner when he served his aristocratic French guests with wine from some dusty old bottles he said he had found in the cellar. 'Ah, Château Margaux '48,' one of them exclaimed with great excitement. However, Bernard had filled the bottles with supermarket plonk, considering this adequate revenge for having been told by the same neighbour that his new perfume was 'rather bourgeois'.

Sometimes the Ashleys mixed their French and English friends with amusing results, such as the occasion when they invited Terence Conran and his wife Caroline, the cookery writer, who were inveighed against by their French dinner companions, claiming it was an audacity for the English to write about food as they knew nothing about it. They often flew out their friends such as the McNulties, Cliffords or Pollocks, to stay for a weekend, and the friends invariably shared the aeroplane with baskets of food and Jenny, the cook. Venetia Pollock, during one such weekend, was particularly struck by a scene at a French market. She and Laura were chatting while Bernard went to buy a khaki-coloured safari jacket. 'He's already got several exactly like it at home,' Laura joked, 'but I won't say anything because he so enjoys buying them.' As Venetia commented: 'Laura was clever; she knew her husband so well, just as she knew public taste in the Sixties. She realized what we all wanted was to wear pretty, long dresses, so she produced them.'

Laura's sensitivities to her husband's needs had prevented her, as a teenager, from scolding him or his gang for drinking or smoking; she merely laughed. She was not going to start lecturing him now and, in any case, insisted that she never saw her role in life as a reformer. However much, privately, she may have hated seeing her husband drink, or hearing him swear, she would never rebuke him in front of others. In public she insisted that gambling was the worst of all vices, much worse than alcoholism, and Bernard, a risk-taker perhaps, was no gambler. In thirty years, if she had not learned to turn a blind eye to Bernard's excesses, she had learned nothing. She excused his erratic behaviour because she assumed it was linked to business pressures and that it was part of the aggressive masculinity which she prized. Friends might be appalled, and employees embarrassed at how little Laura resisted Bernard's will. If she tried to experiment by wearing a little more make-up than usual, Bernard would be furious and despatch her upstairs to wipe it all away. Without a murmur she would do as he bid. When he burst out against some restriction, delay, inaccuracy or bureaucratic procedure that was choking him, Laura sat with her hands neatly folded staring straight in front of her, a controlled tear welling in the corner of her eye, but never even near to a response. To some observers, it seemed that Laura's provoking passivity acted as a stimulant for Bernard's aggression. In complete contrast to Laura, Bernard had never seen the need to control his temper. If he wanted to smash a telephone or hurl invective it cleared the air and nothing further would be said. If, however, Bernard was having an argument with someone else Laura might then join battle in full support of her husband. 'However much I ranted and raved, she always knew I loved her,' Bernard said.

A serious conflagration threatened when the *Daily Telegraph* fashion writer, Avril Groom, was flown over to Remaisnil for an interview with Laura. Bernard insisted on seeing her copy before publication which irked Ms Groom. She declined, telling him that if he wanted advertising, this had to be paid for. She boldly insisted, 'I have never let anyone I interviewed check my own copy before publication.' Bernard asserted that unless she agreed, the interview would not proceed. Fiery criticism of the British press then followed from Bernard, with Laura contributing nothing to the debate. Groom stood her ground and, eventually, as a way out of the impasse, telephoned the Woman's Page editor in London, who advised her that, as she was already in France, she should do the interview and would have to send it to the Ashleys for their approval before publication. The following morning, Sara Freeman, the model the Ashleys had provided, appeared ready for the shots, but Bernard announced that Laura would not be coming down. 'She is unable to give an interview to someone who has been so rude to her,' he told Groom curtly, but agreed to furnish her himself with the few facts she needed. The following day, Moira telephoned the *Daily Telegraph* with profuse apologies for the misunderstanding. Sybille, who witnessed Laura's behaviour with journalists, believed she always felt under attack by the English press. 'She was very proud of her success, not guilty, and did not like being made to feel so,' one friend explained.

Laura found an occasional outlet in humorous accounts of their lives related to close women friends with an infectious laugh. Once she was driving home from a riotous party in the French countryside in order to allow Bernard to sleep on the back seat. However, after a series of wrong turnings, Laura lost her way and, an hour later, ended up where they had started. Bernard soon awoke and asked; 'Aren't we home yet?' 'Oh no, you've only just fallen asleep,' she was able to tell him. He was in no fit state to know. She delighted in retelling this anecdote, which she found hilarious. Laura passed on her belief in the need to minister to the man you love to Nick's girlfriend, Ari. 'She told me she always put the most beautiful girls next to Bernard when setting the table for a party, and that I should do the same, because you want to give the best to the man you love.' If ever Ari and Bernard had a tiff, Laura would take Ari on one side, explain all Bernard's good points and the difficulties he had encountered and then 'make me write a letter saying how I respected him.' One of Laura's favourite psychological ploys, to pre-empt criticism, was telling people how like Bernard they were themselves; Ari, Tim Clifford and her own daughter Jane, all came into this category but were, in reality, quite dissimilar.

For all Laura's inner calm there was a thread of tension running through her body clearly visible, for example, in the way she sat; legs neatly but uncomfortably crossed, back ramrod straight on an upright chair. Just occasionally the tensions spilled over, such as when she berated Moira publicly about the way she was feeding her first child. Moira had given birth just eight weeks previously and had started to wean the baby early in order to attend the Spring Collection meeting at Remaisnil without the child. But, after a while, she had to excuse herself from the discussions to express some milk and Laura was furious. Whatever Laura's motives – Moira believes she expected her to take injections or pills to dry up her milk supply entirely; Bernard believes she was opposed to mothers returning to work so soon – the atmosphere was charged. 'It was a very acrimonious meeting, mostly about why we were changing lengths: the merchandisers were saying the customers want this and the designers were fighting their case and, as it was the first collection prepared without Laura present the whole time, it was not surprising that difficulties should surface,' Moira explained.

Through her iron self-discipline, Laura had managed to control some of her phobias, such as fear of cows, small insects and mice, but she never obliterated the memory of how she had suffered in younger days. Several colleagues remember her habit of turning a design to one side and the other and back again lest anything in it could be viewed as a tiny insect or wild animal's eyes, thus creating horrible fear for an imaginative child. Once she turned a pattern on its side and discovered it could be viewed as a swastika; it was therefore rejected.

Yet Laura failed to conquer fully her fear of water or enclosed places and was never able to use underground trains. She felt embarrassed about this when travelling around London with younger colleagues as they frequently had to resort to a taxi if no bus were available. None-theless she was determined not to let her fear of water prevent her from accompanying Bernard on their now frequent sailing holidays. Bernard's latest vessel was a magnificent fifty-five-foot yacht, *Quaeso*, which they kept moored at St Tropez, alongside the family's small boathouse in the restored village. Extra guests could be put up in the boat itself, which had a permanent skipper and crew, enabling Bernard and Laura to escape at short notice to idyllic, inaccessible Mediterranean islands. Laura still could not swim and often groaned with seasickness. Sometimes she used to lie flat on deck, hoping the overpowering fear and nausea would leave her. Other times she would go down to the galley to prepare a meal, which might have taken her mind off the water but rarely did. But she never complained, nor suggested they should not go. Laura was not tough, but possessed a strong character and would see this sort of action not as a sacrifice, but as an act of fulfilment, she was able to project herself through her husband. That Bernard, since 1981, had had an entry in *Who's Who*, while she had no listing was of no concern. What was his pleasure became hers. For her, the only supreme sacrifice would have been in giving up her husband. Sybille sometimes told Laura gently, 'You spoil him far too much, you know.' 'Yes, I do know,' she replied after a moment's hesitation; 'but I love him.'

Laura, having grasped the necessity of a calm private life for herself, tried to make it an attainable goal for all through her products. Unencumbered by centuries of intellectual debate on the relationship between art and life, Laura saw clearly the effect of beautiful surroundings on the psyche. One of her closest allies and friends in the last years of her life was Jane Clifford, whom she had met during the Platt Hall venture and to whom she now offered a new job as historical adviser. As Laura's personal taste was moving away from the little cottage sprigs, Jane believed it was important that she was not deluged in an avalanche of everything that was vaguely old; that, for example, French eighteenth century was not mixed with Welsh nineteenth century. She was therefore dedicated to bringing authenticity to the nostalgia for which 'Laura Ashley' was renowned. Because of family commitments, Jane Clifford, like Sybille, had never felt able to work before. Only Laura's secure philosophy of family life enabled her to combine the roles because she was given school holidays and other crucial times off. 'There were often terrible panics about getting things done in time,' Jane recalled, 'but Laura would never let things fuss you. She was a tremendously calming influence.' She wrote to Jane at the start of her employment: 'There are two things I beg you to do: get your time each day in the fresh air and strictly limit the hours you spend on your work, which I have always had to do anyway with such a large family and it does make sense in the end. Then there will be some days when nothing seems to resolve and so I always forget those days and do something else completely – I am sure it must be something to do with electricity in the air.'

One of Jane Clifford's first tasks was to prepare the uninhabited rooms at Rhydoldog for a major feature in the 'Living' section of *Vogue*. As a result of her research, the drawing room was turned into an authentic Victorian Gothic chamber with mustard and red wallpaper copied from a Harewood House original in Leeds City Art Gallery collection. A brownish red curtain fabric discovered on the footboard of a bed was originally from Clifton Castle and the pelmet design was taken from a nineteenth-century pattern book. Jane Clifford made other changes in the house. She designed a print room based on an eighteenth-century concept, by cutting out black and white prints and their hanging bows and pasting them on to an apricot Regency background. No one imagined many customers would actually copy this precisely, but it was an inspiration, or guide, to show what could be done. 'Laura always understood the importance of a brilliant idea to entice customers into the shop, even if their courage failed when it came to buying. And she understood that authentic decor need not be confined to the country mansion; the whole idea was to bring good design down to the lowest levels,' Jane Clifford said.

After Rhydoldog, Jane was invited to undertake a second phase of decoration at Remaisnil and, as one of her first gestures, removed a series of framed modern posters which Bernard had positioned up the main stairway; the focus of the hallway henceforth was a magnificent eighteenth-century Brussels tapestry. Jane and Laura went on numerous shopping trips for antiques to Paris and, slowly, all the rooms in the château were redecorated in fabrics more in keeping with the building's style and history.

The 'Ritz Bedroom', for example, 'so named by the Ashleys because the bath in the adjoining bathroom was exactly like those in their favourite hotel, the Paris Ritz', was furnished with some choice pieces of Louis XV vintage. The plain walls were painted in a typically French eighteenth-century green, a colour picked up in the rich, floral design of the fabric, copied from an eighteenth-century Lyons silk, battened to the adjoining wall, and used for the opulent bed coverings. Many of the decorative touches – bows, tassels, swags and rosettes – were derived from old prints, but adapted to contemporary needs. Next door was the 'Louis XVI Bedroom', in which the bed and curtain fabric was also inspired by an eighteenth-century Lyons silk and which took many of its period details from an 1801 mezzotint. The gilt chairs and sofa in this room were upholstered in their original Aubusson tapestry.

Laura was now discovering the art of interior design. She realized that she achieved her most impressive results when faced with an empty room; this forced her, she said, to feel the sort of fabric and decor that was required. Her fame was such that, in the early Eighties, the company received numerous offers from owners of beautiful houses who wanted to have them decorated in 'Laura Ashley' fabrics and then allow the company to use them in its publicity. 'She used houses and rooms as decorating laboratories,' explained Tony Lambert, former Vice President of 'Laura Ashley' Home Furnishing in North America. 'There's no other person who would first fall in love with a house and then do up the house inspired by its period details, putting everything in its proper place according to the house's architecture, history and setting. The selection of print and design according to the house was not the usual way round but it was much more luxurious and that way we produced results that were unique. No one else would go to those lengths or have the same passion about things.'

Recognizing that selecting the fabric according to the house was producing outstanding results, Laura encouraged Jane Clifford to oversee the decoration of both a four-storey Victorian London house and a Cotswold stone farmhouse. Some very stylish fabrics emanated from these experiences, as well as two books recounting the transformations. With the introduction in 1983 of twelve-colour printing as well as a heavier weight of high quality cotton fabric and brocade, everyone now finally accepted that drawing rooms and dining rooms were just as suitable 'Laura Ashley' sites as bedrooms or bathrooms. The new prints still took their inspiration from the past but were more likely to be derived from the printed silks of eighteenth-century Lyons or the pattern books of Victorian designers and architects than the simpler fly leaves of books upon which Laura had formerly relied.

Large flowers and multi-coloured chintzes, the traditional fare of the aristocratic cluttered English country house, now abounded within the collection; they required large windows and large rooms.

This led to a debate within the company as to whether the role of 'Laura Ashley' was to demonstrate the sort of rooms 'Mr and Mrs Average' might own, decorated only to those standards to which they could aspire, or should it display exotically luxurious settings, thus attaining an often impossibly high level in taste and quality. Laura was supported by her US colleagues; their market, with its penchant for 'designer' status, and, to an extent, the continental European market, inclined strongly towards the 'reach-for-the-moon' view. But the UK, the most down-market of the three centres, was always pleading for more banality, fearing to risk losing touch with the moderate market who comprised the core customers.

The partial answer to this dilemma was for most of Laura's exotic ideas to be available in a special, higher priced 'Decorator Collection'. There had been a 'decorator showroom' in Sloane Street since 1980 which, as Carolyn Warrender remembers, Laura initially viewed with some unease. 'We realized that decorators were buying our fabric and wallpaper in bulk and asking for a discount, as was available to them with any other brand.' There was considerable pressure to accede to this and, therefore, for about two years, a Decorator Showroom, for trade only, existed in Lower Sloane Street. 'But Laura was unhappy that if the company could afford to sell to decorators at a reduced rate, then the public should be allowed the products at that price too. She was genuinely concerned to help the customer and found it difficult to see any other point of view.'

Yet by 1982 it was clear to Laura that if she wanted to see the exciting results of her latest researches used in people's homes, she could no longer rely on her traditional customers. The general public still looked to 'Laura Ashley' for tried and tested colour schemes and patterns. 'Towards the end, Laura became quite frustrated at the way her customers would not keep up with her ideas; they lagged behind in a way she found infuriating,' Robert Landgrebe explained. Having believed initially that a good print should be available in the collection for ever, she was now constantly urging her colleagues to be more innovative. The obvious solution was to launch her most original ideas through a separate collection available in interior design shops throughout the country. She knew that decorators, always searching for something new, would quickly make use of them, and hoped the more adventurous of her customers would too. Thus the Decorator Collection, into which she plunged more and more of her energies, was not only a useful device for slicing through hidebound public taste, but gave Laura a focus once more for her creative effervescence.

While belatedly fulfilling her curtailed general education, she did not neglect her ambition to master the French language. She pored over nineteenth-century French texts; Proust and Victor Hugo with leather covers and tiny print were favourites, and she listened to teach-yourself French cassettes. When, in the summer of 1983, she went to England for a few weeks, she took a French companion whose role was to instruct her during every spare moment. Her continual quest for learning prevented her, and the company, from stagnating; but none-theless 1983 seemed to Bernard and Laura an appropriate time to take stock. Neither partner could fail to be aware of the interest in their company which, more than once, threatened to result in a book chroni-cling their success, especially as Laura had just finished working on the first *Laura Ashley Book of Home Decorating*.*

Work on this had started in 1980 and at first Laura seemed excited by the project; but the finished product did not please her. It was largely a practical book, aimed at the DIY market, as until very recently this formed the bulk of purchasers of 'Laura Ashley' fabrics. But during the two years between the time when the book was first mooted and its publication in 1982, the company had transformed itself and the book did not reflect the grander style of living which Laura was now espousing.

In spite of its success – the book quickly sold out its first edition of 60,000 – Laura dreaded the thought of another book which failed to represent the company as she saw it. Far better therefore, like everything else the company had ever done, to produce it themselves. Towards the end of 1982, Bernard was half-tempted to revive his old profession of writer and tackle a company history himself. But he found flying and sailing both more invigorating and he kept procrastinating. They decided, therefore, to employ an English graduate from Cambridge to document the 'Laura Ashley' story. Marianne Brace spent eight months

* Octopus Books, 1982.

168

taking the Ashleys back to Pimlico, Brasted, Machynlleth and Tybrith, in order to produce a valuable archive document of an amazing, late-twentieth-century success story. But it remained unpublished and is as yet unfinished. The company was, inexorably, being positioned for a further dramatic stage in its development, and Laura was uneasy about the next chapter in their own story.

12

Brussels to the Bahamas

Remaining cheerful in adversity had been Laura's principal virtue since childhood. She expected life to shower her with burdens and how one carried them was the ultimate trial. 'I have myself become rather stoic (that Roman sect who believed in overcoming both pleasure and pain),' she wrote to her eldest daughter in 1982, 'because my own philosophy seems to be that one should accept each and every morning as a new beginning in the surroundings and atmosphere and position in which one's maker (or fate) place one.' As she explained to José, their former Portuguese housekeeper, who was unhappy at being asked to work at the 'Laura Ashley' Catford 'Home Base' after running the Bridal Department at Harriet Street: 'I myself have to live in a foreign country so I know how difficult life can be and how one has to keep cheerful in the circumstances one finds oneself.' She warmed to her theme: 'I am very sad not to see you more often but, as you can imagine, I am pulled about all over the place and I have to try and keep in touch with my children as well ...'

Living apart from her children was Laura's greatest burden; rootlessness came a close second. Added to Bernard's mercurial inclinations was the new imperative of notching up enough flying hours and so breakfast, lunch and dinner would frequently be spent in different towns or even countries. Laura might never have chosen this punishing routine for herself but she did not baulk at it. It amused her to be a jet-set Granny, sitting in the back of the aeroplane doing her needle-work. She cannot have been unaware, from her wide reading of Victorian literature, how symbolic of feminine submissiveness was her chosen activity; but submissiveness she could assume without any difficulty. Much as she hated being torn away from her work, she liked most to be close to her husband, sharing his excitement over his new skill as a pilot. When Laura wanted to be in New York for her grandchild's birthday, Bernard agreed, so long as they flew all the way in the company 'plane via Greenland and Montreal. 'So I am not sure *when* we shall get there,' she reported to Emma with no trace of a whinge.

In spite of an intense longing to see more of her children, she put Bernard's needs first, as she always had. Not that, in a sense, she did not share them. They were still, at heart, the two suburban kids who wanted to break away. A yearning for new adventures and new horizons remained an unassuageable constant for them both. When she felt especially homesick (for her family, not for a particular house) she comforted herself with the thought 'that I am lucky my children are all well and happy', and alleviated the pain by writing as many letters to them all as she could. While Emma was at boarding school she aimed, initially, at one a day; towards the end these dwindled but still averaged one a week. When Emma left school, Laura recognized that she could no longer control her life, especially as she could not offer her a home base in England. Not only did she put up little opposition when Emma decided to move into a flat with a boyfriend, however much she disapproved in general of such a mode of living, she determined to look on the positive side of the arrangement and asked only to be invited to see her daughter's new flat. 'I promise not to be critical of *anything* – it's now your life and I do think it is very important to have surroundings of your own choice because ...' – an extraordinary *cri de coeur* from a woman who headed a major household decoration company – 'I went straight from my family to marriage with Father, I have never had a chance to completely choose my own environment.' She went on: 'I can hardly complain of that when I have so many compensations in other ways. Not many women nowadays are lucky enough to have four children!'

She wrote many letters to Jane too, encouraging her in her various artistic and creative ventures, trying gently to steer her towards a course in life which she felt would increase her happiness. As the company grew larger Jane ceased her photographic activities for catalogues and publicity material. She toyed with the idea of producing exclusive handknit designs and all who saw her work marvelled at her originality. She set up a magazine called *Working Proof* about working people and their activities, also a nightclub called 'The Exchange' on Tuesdays at the Arts Theatre Club in Great Newport Street, which was loosely connected with the magazine. Laura praised the magazine as 'nothing short of a work of genius! ... Her talent is bearing fruit.' Nonetheless the venture did not survive for long. Laura believed that her daughter's sympathies for those in greater need than herself would cost her dearly in emotional pain and suffering. She constantly warned her against supporting those she considered downtrodden. 'Lame ducks are not actually helped. People can be helped best by strong discipline and the need to stand on their own two feet,' Laura told Jane.

She managed to see most of Nick, who was more involved in the business, and therefore was least written to. She trusted his artistic judgement and increasingly referred important decisions to him, persuading her team to consult him rather than her as often as possible. Nick, keen to stamp his own signature on the Collection, saw the revival of the decorative arts which took place during the Twenties and Thirties as a fertile field. He had noticed that one of the greatest successes among the company's 1983 fabrics was a big, loose, splashy print called 'Emma', which he had commissioned. It was not unlike some of the Thirties bold colour prints he so admired and was quite different from the traditional 'Laura Ashley' sprigged prints. Its name had been carefully chosen to appeal to a younger market as by 1983 both Nick and Laura were trying hard to move away from purely Victorian reinterpretations, to turn themselves into 'revivalists' with a wider outlook. Laura was greatly aware of the dangers of becoming stale and was also genuinely excited by the wealth of new ideas in other periods yet to be tapped, which she was suddenly discovering through her travel and exposure to new societies, cultures and places. On the other hand, it was the ideas and morals of the Victorian period which she admired most, and which she knew from the sales figures her customers still looked to her to provide. This was the look which 'Laura Ashley' had appropriated and which was ideally suited to the thousands of Edwardian (or earlier) terraced and semi-detached houses being converted throughout England. Even by the early Eighties, imitators of the country, Victorian look were relatively few in number. Laura could not ignore the argument, often put to her in the most forceful terms, that it was madness to discontinue popular lines, which customers expected to find in 'Laura Ashley' shops, simply because she herself wanted to be more innovative.

It was in this climate that the notion of reproducing some Duncan Grant and Vanessa Bell designs from the Thirties appeared as an inspired exit from a cul-de-sac. It was additional to, but never intended to replace, the core collection. The Charleston Trust the body which administers the Sussex farmhouse where Grant and Bell lived, had wanted to revive the fabric designs for some time as the originals were in danger of deteriorating beyond recognition. In 1982 Nick Ashley approached the Trust. The possibility of reproducing some of their ideas seemed to him a most exciting departure, appealing to his personal tastes and offering the company, for the first time, a source of inspiration from a twentieth-century arts movement. After several meetings 'Laura Ashley' agreed to reproduce faithfully the fabrics needed for the house as their donation to Charleston and also to purchase the copyright for a number of designs which the company hoped to market commercially.*

The main problem in reproducing the fabrics for Charleston itself was colour accuracy. Hems were unpicked to acquire unfaded slithers of cloth but, rather than reproduce the fabrics in their original bright colours, it was decided to find a shade half-way between the original and present state which would not jar with the faded aura of the rest of the house. Considerable research was also undertaken into the type of cloth originally used and Nick scoured Europe to find enough 32-inch width slub rayon, a highly popular material in the Thirties. Eventually he located a few bolts of suitable cloth in Germany. Those fabrics intended to be sold were recoloured, with the scale adjusted slightly, and printed on linen union. Yet every attempt was made to preserve the spirit in which they were originally created.

'What struck us from the very beginning,' commented Deborah Gage, Honorary Secretary of The Charleston Trust, 'was the emphasis that Nick Ashley had laid on quality – just as essential a criterion with

---

* The total package that Laura Ashley made available to the Charleston Trust amounted to £50,000 and included sufficient material of five designs to use in the house currently as well as some to be kept in store to replace the present fabrics when they wore out.

us.' As the project gained momentum, Nick enthusiastically suggested reproducing a collection of accessories to reflect the complete Charleston style. Professor Quentin Bell, Vanessa's son and Virginia Woolf's nephew, designed a plate, a vase, a fruitbowl and a lampbase, all his interpretations of his mother's and Duncan Grant's designs in colours from the 'Laura Ashley' palette. Although Laura herself kept a watchful eye on the project and her approval, as well as that of Angelica Garnett, Vanessa's daughter, was sought before the fabrics were finally printed, she was happier to let Nick control this particular venture. As Nick himself was aware, the more she discovered about the way of life of Bloomsbury in general and at Charleston in particular, the more her misgivings grew about allying herself too closely with a group whose moral standards were, to say the least, far removed from her own.

Although travel fuelled her, in some ways it is hard to imagine how Laura managed to achieve anything for the company in the last two years of her peripatetic life. Friends were always touched by the way she never forgot a handwritten thank-you note in spite of her life constantly being a 'mad rush', or 'wonderfully hectic' with 'masses of socializing and Father in his element between boat, restaurants and friends (there is a constant flow of the latter),' she wrote to Emma in 1983. Andy Garnett, Bernard's friend from the 1950s, and his wife, the writer Polly Devlin, saw more of them than they had done for decades. Now approaching sixty, Laura felt a security that enabled her to view an independent spirit such as Polly with admiration, if trepidation for her liberality. But, Polly believes, 'she would still edit herself before talking to me ... it was tied up with what she thought of as "clever" people outside her world – she was just as clever in her own world – but she was not entirely relaxed.' Lord Montagu of Beaulieu was one of their new friends who stayed with them in France, and 'couldn't be nicer', Sally, Duchess of Westminster and the Marchioness of Bute were two other guests. Laura's excitement at being invited to the Bute Ball was palpable; 'Hooray!' she wrote to her younger daughter in girlish anticipation of the event. She tried to combine all too rare trips home with crucial selection meetings and visits either from her children or to her mother and sister. Bernard's father and Laura's mother were often whisked off in the Ashley 'plane to be present at family occasions. After a birthday tea with Bernard's father and as many other relations as she could muster, Laura returned to her London hotel quite exhilarated and immediately wrote to Emma: 'feeling that almost the most important thing in life is for families to stick together – you can get so much strength from it to help others.' She posted the letter, packed up and then hurried to a small private airfield, where Bernard met her for a weekend in France.

Bernard adored whatever time he could spend in Port Grimaud, on the Côte d'Azur; his boat was a constant source of admiration and he attracted many friends who were first drawn by his magnificent craft. But after five years in France, he was ready for a move and Laura was not spared the waves of unrest. There were many possible places under discussion but towards the end of 1982 they were shown an exquisite French farmhouse high in the hills about an hour's drive from St Tropez. Ever since the children were young, Bernard and Laura had happy associations with this part of France. The beautiful house they were now considering was the former home of the actress, Jeanne Moreau and was hidden among lavender groves, chestnut woods and acres of sweet smelling herbs. This ancient French *manoir*, with its stone foundations, flagged floors and galleried drawing room could be the perfect retreat house, the family home where no business meetings would ever take place. There were hectares of grounds, with wild boar to one side and a swimming pool to the other, and terraced banks of olive trees and clumps of peach, plum and apricot trees in between. No invading press would find them here; no noise from the outside world other than gently trickling water and laughing crickets could possibly disturb their tranquillity.

La Pre Verger was bought and Laura immediately launched into its redecoration. But however much they loved the Mediterranean sunshine, the Côte d'Azur could never be an ideal base for their business. And now too, as preparations were advancing to take the company public, tax advisers were pressing the Ashleys to think about another move; rationalization again demanded that they should have one commercial base for tax purposes, however difficult the international nature of their growing business made this. Brussels, a sophisticated, cosmopolitan city with elegant avenues and shops, gourmet restaurants and delicatessens, had been mooted as a centre several times in the past few years. Previously Bernard and Laura had not felt ready to lead such an urban existence; suddenly, as they both neared sixty, it seemed an obvious choice.

The Belgian capital was geographically convenient for Holland, France and Britain; it was at the epicentre of the European Economic Community should any lobbying or entertaining of diplomats or officials be required and, above all, it had romantic connotations for Laura and Bernard from their post-war courtship. In addition, Bernard had found that customs officials at Brussels Airport had always treated him with maximum courtesy and efficiency and minimal delays; he could find no better reason for choosing their next home. 43 Rue Ducale was, for a change, a town house, built in the late eighteenth century overlooking the Parc Bruxelles. It was probably intended originally to house courtiers and their families and is reputed to have been the French Embassy during Waterloo. Nonetheless, by 1983 it had not been lived in properly for half a century and its many partitions and divisions bore witness to its sometime use as offices. The exterior, an elegant white, stuccoed façade, had survived the centuries remarkably unscathed; although double-fronted, the left-hand side of the courtyard was conveniently hived off for 'Laura Ashley' offices.

The rest of the house was to be restored as a family home with grand interconnecting reception rooms to create the main salon on the first floor. As Laura wished to decorate as much of La Pré Verger herself, she put Michael Howells and Antonia Kirwan-Taylor, a former *Vogue* fashion editor who had just joined the company, in charge of Rue Ducale. 'The interior was just a peeling tip and shambles, a collapsed mountain of plasterwork on the floor,' Antonia recalls of her first view of the house. But among the heaps of rubbish, Laura would often scrabble with bare hands to find a snippet of original wallpaper. In the event she only discovered one suitable original, which she used in her bedroom. Antonia, whose chief responsibility was running the decorator showroom, went to Brussels once a week for six months to oversee the transformation. She well recognized the potential for disagreement in the job but believed that creative friction would have a positive effect. Just when it was nearing completion she noticed an extraordinary change in Laura. 'I always sent her every paint reference and swatch to check but I made a mistake with a paint colour on the beading; I had given the painters a sample to copy that was too pink, not beige enough, and she was furious with me. All of a sudden, just when the fun part of the decoration was to begin, hanging pictures and arranging curtains, I was completely left out of everything. She didn't actually say or do anything nasty but it was clear she was deeply angry,' Antonia recalled. She was not the first to suffer this 'freezing-out' process – Laura was autocratic and believed she had every right to be – but Antonia found it so painful that she resigned, only to be brought back into the company by Nick, who asked her to work in the Home Furnishing Department.

Antonia felt the explanation for Laura's behaviour was simple; she was stretched to the utmost and simply could not find the time to oversee every single detail of this new house. As long as everything was executed exactly as she wanted, this worked smoothly. However, as soon as a small detail went wrong she realized with a pang that this might no longer be her own house, but someone else's and she wanted it back before it was too late.

Antonia was able to make her peace with Laura, eventually, but she missed working closely together as she considered Laura's talent for extracting one successful print from a large bundle was matchless. In 1983 and 1984 the Collection was still dominated by Laura's personal impulses. 'Her approach was as sentimental as it was romantic; it was not just a question of whether she liked the print but it might be that she liked the lady it belonged to or the place it had come from.' As Antonia knew, there was more to her success than that. 'Her eye was extraordinary – and although this brought in some beautiful and original prints it meant things often did not go together. Those in the company demanding that we bring order to the Collection were threatening Laura,' Antonia explains.

The decoration of the Brussels house marked both the apotheosis of her belief in authenticity and the move away from it. She devoured countless books of eighteenth-century interior design and household management in an attempt to discover how the house originally looked and felt, and insisted on eighteenth-century colours for the paintwork. But in another sense it also indicates her flexibility since, under Michael Howells' guidance, she was happy to mix periods and ideas, as long as the flavour of each room was kept intact, rather as if the house were a revolving stage set. One of her latest enthusiasms was Biedermeier furniture and her bedroom took on a much lighter tone by housing a few elegant pieces of Biedermeier fruitwood. The dining room, by contrast, was a recreation of an English Georgian country house, full of dark green and red.

If Antonia detected a note of extreme frustration in Laura's treatment of her, she was probably correct. Echoing the transformation of Rue Ducale was the transformation of the company. Throughout the period of redecoration in Brussels the company, too, was being groomed for its presentation to the public. Laura viewed the inexorable expansion of the company with the concern any parent has watching its own child being removed from its daily care. She accepted what everyone told her was the inevitable progress of a successful company, but could not help worrying about how this would affect her family's role within it. Her own projected role in the new company was never precisely delineated. According to a draft document prepared for the flotation of the company Laura was to be officially designated Deputy Chairman but there was no job description provided. There could not have been. Laura's talents had stretched too far to be gathered in tightly now. She would continue to contribute widely to the company but had no need of labels.

Nor could she ever see the logic in the argument which demanded that the company should constantly grow. 'Laura accepted expansion with unease,' according to John James. 'I don't think she realized what was involved at all, but then perhaps she wasn't exposed to the real problems of a small business because she was always shielded and protected by Bernard,' he added. No one could argue with the fact that the company, once floated, would not be the same creature; that their private lives, once they were accountable to the public, would be invaded and scrutinized, possibly to an unacceptable degree. She already resented the fact that she was recognized as she went about her private business. During a very precious lunch with her mother, sister and Jane in London she had been acutely embarrassed when a young girl rushed over from another table and begged her for a job with 'Laura Ashley' in France. Would this sort of thing now happen all the time, she wondered? But there was time to adjust her sights and if Bernard believed in the rightness of the move she was able to put her trust in him. She also put her trust in God. Laura's spirituality had been an important guide for her throughout her life but in her later years she reverted to the church-going of her younger days. 'It is the moment of greatest peace to me when I enter a church anywhere. For a short time one relinquishes the battle of life with its triumphs and disasters and one is a small voice in the congregation of those gathered together in God's name,' Laura wrote as part of a contribution to a book called *What God means to Me*.* She had no difficulty in worshipping in churches of different denominations; Roman Catholic in France; Episcopalian in the United States and in Brussels she returned to the Holy Trinity in whose choir she had sung at the end of the war. While living in Remaisnil she had often sat alone praying and contemplating, in the little Catholic chapel situated just beyond the château gates but, until recently, part of the château itself. She was sad to see it in such disrepair and wanted to refurbish it. However, she felt as a non-Catholic it might be impertinent to suggest this; the priest who often noticed her there, likewise felt too inhibited to ask her for money.

By 1984 Laura Ashley was enough of a celebrity, and known to have religious leanings, that she was invited to take part in the television programme, *Home on Sunday*. Cliff Michelmore was to interview her about her life and her beliefs and the talk was interspersed with hymns selected by Laura. She recalled for Michelmore, and the thousands of viewers on 1 July 1984, her early life in Dowlais, meeting Bernard and her war service and chose as her first hymn, 'Guide Me O Thou Great Jehovah', sung by the Dowlais Male Voice Choir, of which she had recently been invited to become Vice President. She spoke of her early religious teaching at the hands of Uncle John Lloyd, the simultaneous birth of her first child and the business, and family life when her children were growing up in Wales. Sitting in the *petit salon* of the château at Remaisnil, used for the occasion since Brussels was not yet ready, she spoke movingly of her duty in life, which she said was made quite clear to her from childhood. 'Once I had a child my first duty from then on was to that child. I was only working when they were elsewhere, and when they were very small I was only working when they were asleep and so on.' Michelmore tried to press her to discover whether she ever felt any conflict or difficulties between the demands of family and business. 'No, not really. No, because there are always people to whom you can delegate, who can do a job as well as you can.' Michelmore found Laura, 'absolutely marvellous as a hostess ... extremely cooperative and ... a little sad not to be able to go [to Wales] more often.' He recalled also that Bernard 'insisted on listening to every word that was said.'

* Marshall Pickering Books, 1986.

Religion shored her up and helped her deal with one of her most severe personal blows; the breakdown of her elder son's marriage and subsequent divorce. Hitherto she had always looked upon divorce as an unimaginable horror of the modern world. She felt sadness for her young granddaughter, sadness for her daughter-in-law, whom she liked and with whom she continued to correspond and feel warmly towards, as well as overwhelming sorrow for David. Partly to help her come to terms with this, but also to help her reflect on her own life, she entered a religious retreat in Wiltshire for a few days. She told no one, including Bernard, that she was going, although David, as well as her sister Mary and her old friend, Jeanne Watters knew about it afterwards. As an intensely controlled and private person, keeping a secret of this importance would present no difficulty for her. Although she never referred to it, she evidently derived great support and comfort from her solitary contemplation with the Sisters of Mercy. It was, after all, only taking to its logical conclusion her belief in the necessity of every home providing an oasis of calm. Perhaps she learnt something there about the transience of life which helped her cope so uncomplainingly with the nomadic months which were to follow, when all she wanted was 'my nice settled house in Brussels'.

Bernard and Laura often embarked on impulsive trips. 'They'd have gone on travelling for ever if Bernard had had his way,' according to the company pilot, Malcolm Bland. 'They never had an alarm clock but just decided the night before to go wherever they felt like at that moment,' he recalled. If they found the weather bad when they arrived they would go elsewhere. Laura was never permitted to travel with much more than a wicker basketful of clothes and occasionally they arrived at a destination for which they had neither the correct currency nor attire. Two days in one place was usually enough for Bernard. Bland believed that one of the happiest trips they made was to Scandinavia; 'they just hired bicycles and travelled around with no family and no company pressure'. In March 1984 Bland flew Laura and Bernard to Venice. She had never been there before but knew it would prove a rich source of inspiration. After three days she said she now understood how people could travel to Venice for a lifetime and never be bored. Laura produced a wide range of designs from this trip, called the Venetian Collection, which featured some of the most exotic and lavish gold patterns she had yet created.

Much of the spring and summer of 1984 was spent trying to finish both La Pré Verger and Rue Ducale. But it was marred by two painful intrusions on their privacy. On 12 May 1984, an interview of Nick by Lynda Lee-Potter occupied an entire page in the *Daily Mail* and dropped like a grenade on the house in the South of France where Bernard and Laura were staying when they read it. The tone of the article was not so much criticism of but concern for his parents. 'I am worried about them right now. In the past six months I don't think they've stayed longer than two nights in one place,' Nick was quoted as saying. 'My mother is totally subservient to my father. She says "yes" to everything.' Later in the article Nick was attributed as describing his father as 'unemployable'. 'He's fantastic at working with a team. He'll solve any problem but he has to be king of the jungle ... People stand bolt upright in terror when he appears, but it's respectful terror.' Of Nick himself, Lee-Potter wrote that he was 'totally disarming, frank, a brilliant designer, known to all employees as Nick.' Bernard and Laura were, of course, struck with horror. Their temporary, but real, anger was sharpened by a searing pain occasioned by the thought that they might in any way have done less than their duty to their children. But while their fury with Nick subsided, their repugnance for the British press multiplied.

Some six weeks later, on 7 July, Nick married his long-standing girlfriend Ari, in Beaulieu, Hampshire. To Laura's enormous chagrin, neither she nor Bernard was able to attend. They felt compelled to prove to the Inland Revenue their non-resident status by completing, as they believed for the second time, a whole year out of the country. It was a shattering blow and Laura tried to think of a way round it. In the end she concluded that her thoughts would be with Nick and Ari but that there was too much at stake should she come herself. 'It's usually (in fact always) a question of security for all the families who work for the company. Duty comes first to them,' she tried to explain to Emma. Of course, she still believed in the primacy of the family and for a mother not to be present at a son's wedding was an almost unimaginable sorrow for her. Nonetheless it was a loss she lived with by convincing herself that 'Laura Ashley', the company, was also her family, equally deserving of her attention.

This crisis was compounded a few months later by an article in the *Daily Telegraph* reporting that, in the spring of 1984 Laura had been offered an Honorary Degree of Doctor of Literature from the University of London. The article suggested that she had hoped to accept the degree even if she were not able to come to London in person for the award ceremony. In the event it was not possible for her to visit England and 'as the University does not award Honorary Degrees *in absentia* the degree was not conferred', a spokesman for the University of London stated. Laura wrote a personal letter to the University to explain her difficulty and to make clear how deeply wounding she had found the newspaper report.

Duty to others always headed Laura's list of priorities. But her close friends felt that in one or two ways Laura was, in her last year, clawing back small twigs of independence for herself. She travelled more on her own, hitherto Bernard's prerogative, and in March 1984 took Jane Clifford away with her for a break in St Moritz. Neither of them skied but they walked, chatted and revived themselves in the mountain air. Another friend, Henrietta Dunne, noticed her on holiday later that year with some sharp embroidery scissors surreptitiously snipping out the label of a couture skirt before wearing it. 'Bernard so hates me not wearing company clothes,' she explained. A more direct confrontation threatened when Laura decided finally to cut off her long hair. She had always maintained that she kept it long to please Bernard. But as part of her new, elegantly tailored image she had it cropped to the nape of her neck. It gave her a more severe, if tidier look. In spite of her fears, Bernard offered no criticism when he saw it. During a holiday at the Cliffords' villa in Tuscany, the women in the party often engaged in a Jane Fonda workout programme. Laura used to love exercising in this way – 'I'm sure it's making me have lots of energy,' she wrote to Emma. But one day Bernard passed by and told them to turn off the awful noise. 'Go away if you don't like it,' one of the women told him, and he did. 'I would never dare to have told him that,' Laura confided with a giggle, but promised she would try it in future. Later that summer the Ashleys went sailing off Corsica with the Duchess of Westminster as their guest. When Laura proposed stopping off to visit the local Napoleon Museum, Bernard was distinctly unimpressed. However, as the Duchess sided with Laura in favour of going, a detour was made and Bernard stayed behind.

However strange Laura found the American environment (and she found some American taste 'extraordinarily bizarre') there was much of which she approved particularly the positive outlook, 'the way they tend to effuse about everything', compared with London 'where people are so highly critical'. For that reason she even encouraged Emma to study in the United States. The effect on Laura herself was to make her more English; Americans believed she epitomized English life and England, a view she was not averse to cultivating. The single event which had more than anything else confirmed this role was a 'presentation' (not a fashion show) in November 1983, in Los Angeles, given as a joint benefit for the British Olympic Association USA, and the US Olympic Committee. This was a gala event staged at The Beverly Hilton Hotel in Beverly Hills in which highly romantic Ashley fashions were modelled in an elaborate production choreographed once again by Patrick Libby. The children's collection was modelled by the children of celebrities, including Jane Seymour, Sally Struthers and Lynn Redgrave.

Sarah Callander, fully recognizing Laura's abhorrence of brash commercialism, was careful to make certain that the show was always presented as a 'stage fantasy' with as much emphasis on the historical context of 'Laura Ashley' clothes as possible. The format was similar to the Platt Hall show in Manchester and Laura loved it. The occasion sparkled for her not so much through mixing with so many stars but being treated as one herself. When Cary Grant embraced her afterwards, congratulating her on the show and telling her she was wonderful, she nearly collapsed with pure pleasure. Luckily a photographer was on hand to record the occasion and the resulting shot of Laura and Cary Grant was one of her most treasured possessions. That the presentation had cost £35,000 to mount, more than the company had ever spent on public relations or charity, although relatively little for such a venture, was quickly forgotten.

The charitable benefit, and the rapturous reception she received personally, coupled with a desire to avoid another European winter, conspired to persuade the Ashleys of yet another move, this time to a seemingly incongruous location for Laura Ashley, a rented house in Palm Beach. Bernard had often toyed with the idea of a house in America and Laura concluded that it might be best 'to get it out of our system'. She never enjoyed discussions about money. When they saw a new house, she could simply instruct Bernard; 'If you want it, buy it.' In less than a week after moving in to Palm Beach, by the end of

October 1984, she had rearranged the house the way she wanted it, including the installation of her precious telex machines.

She was continually amused, but never offended by Palm Beach, 'the only town in the world with two Cartier shops, where everything is exotic and like Alice in Wonderland ... It's like nowhere else and I feel very spoiled.' In between Cartier and Gucci were the thrift shops. 'Just imagine what gets thrown out,' Laura enthused to her friend, Mary Henderson, who in January 1984 became a consultant to the company. 'I have bought myself from the thrift shop a wonderful creation for just $50 as well as a $5 cable knit pullover. It's a bit awkward if I'm recognized,' she wrote.

By 1984, Lady Henderson had become not only her closest colleague but her first real friend for years, as Laura emerged through the hedgerows into the open plains of society. Laura had implicit trust in her taste, by which she was undoubtedly influenced, and was able to relax fully in her company, possibly in a way she could not with any of her other colleagues. Mary Henderson saw in Laura only 'naturalness, freshness, charm and humour', and derived great inspiration from working with her.

Laura soon discovered the Episcopal Church of Bethesda by the Sea, and spent much time there. She immersed herself in researching the architecture of Palm Beach and learnt that most of the Spanish revival-style houses were designed by Addison Mizner shortly after World War I. Mizner was commissioned by hundreds of American post-war millionaires who, unable to reach the devastated European Riviera, now chose to winter on the Florida coast. He produced for them his own interpretation of Spanish buildings, recreated as restive and airy American suburban villas. Laura was determined to use their own house as a springboard for new design ideas as well as decorating several of the rooms for the catalogue. For the first time in years she and Bernard spent a quiet Christmas alone, but immediately afterwards her sister Mary came to visit followed by Jane, her old friends Anita Saada and Jeanne Watters, Bernard's former colleague, Peter Brunn, the McNulties and several friends from the company. All of these visitors commented on her remarkable talent as a homemaker; that, if called upon, she could create her own peaceful environment in a desert or a wilderness. Since the house boasted a swimming pool she took advantage of the warm weather to conquer swimming, her oldest fear, and organized regular lessons. Within a month she reported to Emma some news about which she was inordinately proud. 'Swam four widths SOLO', but was dismayed to find that there was more to real swimming than merely staying afloat.

Perhaps as a reward for so much positive thinking, two pieces of news cheered her while in Palm Beach. David had announced he was to marry again: Caroline Pagano, a stunningly beautiful model with a mane of chestnut hair from Boulder, Colorado. And Jane was to have a baby, albeit without marrying the father. Laura had had nearly thirty years to accustom herself to Jane's nonconformist ways and so the news was scarcely a shock. In the past Jane might have worried that her mother did not condone her lifestyle, but, 'How can I judge, when it is so outside my own experience? I hope I don't appear disapproving, which is not meant, rather am I non-plussed in the sort of way I am in any other unknown environment in which I find myself. Perhaps because I have concentrated harder than most on my own exploits (a very Welsh trait) it has made me narrow-minded or at least appear so. In my heart I hate a narrow attitude but often one hates most in others those faults in one's own character one is struggling to overcome.' Laura wrote this tender piece of self-appraisal to Jane in 1982, nearly three years before she found herself welcoming her pregnant daughter to stay with her in Palm Beach. Clearly, by then, Laura had struggled enough to overcome her inbuilt disapproval of Jane's way of life and now lightly told her friends about Jane's news. Jane, relieved, recognized that there was a part of her mother which was proud of her for not being conventional; the bohemian streak of Laura's own younger days had not totally deserted her. After giving birth to four children interspersed with several miscarriages, Laura now found it riveting to discuss pregnancy with her daughter. 'I realize I know nothing about it all and wonder I never noticed all these symptoms in myself,' she wrote to Emma. Laura had never had time for such introspective soul-gazing.

No sooner had she settled in Palm Beach than she found herself touring, first Barbados and then the Bahamas, with Bernard looking for a permanent place in the sun. In January they went to Japan to open the company's first shop in Tokyo and on this trip was allowed to take several suitcases as the Clapham studio had made her an entire wardrobe for the occasion. The new shop was in the Ginza, Tokyo's major shopping area, and was a joint venture with a leading local retailer, Jusco (Japan United Stores Company). Although the clothes were scaled down to suit the Japanese figure, all the other merchandise was the same as that available at any other 'Laura Ashley' shop in the world. It was the most lavish store opening ever, attended by the British Ambassador, Sir Sidney Giffard, and a member of the Japanese royal family. Laura herself was treated as royalty and when somebody asked for her autograph she was dumbfounded. Bernard, Laura and the other VIPs were seated on a dais for the opening ceremony and speeches, with 200 newspapermen in serried rows before them. Afterwards, there was a party for 1,000 people, Jusco's top managers, among whom, Laura noticed with interest but not outrage, there was not a single woman.

On the return journey they stopped at several West Coast locations and returned home exhausted, both suffering minor aches and pains including rheumatism. But the pace did not slow up. During the next few weeks they made continual forays to the Bahamas and other islands as well as to Canada and the US. All the while, Laura was trying to complete the 1986 Home Furnishing collection by carrying wherever she went her 'mobile package' into which she put all her current references, samples and papers. In early April 1985 Laura went to Colonial Williamsburg with Emma, as she had been invited by the Association for the Preservation of Virginia Antiquities to decorate and restore a most intriguing three storey house with a Victorian timber-frame. 'I think we've found the cuckoo in his nest,' Laura exclaimed as she walked inside the house, so well-preserved were its many artefacts. She spent two and a half hours in the attic that afternoon, poring over the possessions of the Armistead family, who had lived there until 1984. She fell upon box after trunk upon cupboard, carefully labelling each piece as she wished it to be placed around the house. When she left she knew a considerable amount of work remained to be done with curtains, wallpapers and pictures, but Miss Dora's House, as it was known, had already won her heart.

Later in April, Laura and Bernard set off for Colorado and David's wedding, the first of her children's weddings she had been able to attend. They trekked west via St Louis, Kansas City and Tulsa before arriving in Denver. Several of their Carno friends and colleagues had been invited but 'farmers from Wales don't think much of the land husbandry here', Laura joked. She was thrilled by the entire proceedings and recounted all the details to her friends. She had been involved in the discussions about Caroline's dress, which Anne Wallwork had designed, and had proposed originally that her daughter-in-law should be a reincarnation of Scarlett O'Hara with a flounced skirt, pinched waist and full sleeves; Laura's idealized picture of a perfect, ultra-feminine, old-fashioned bride. But Caroline decided this was not her style and the long, slim, silk-satin dress, reminiscent of the Thirties and Forties which she eventually chose, suited her perfectly. Laura gave her a magnificent veil of antique Brussels lace as well as copies of *Emma* by Jane Austen and *Wuthering Heights* by Charlotte Brontë. She chose for herself an elegant Chanel suit, which she had bought in Brussels.

In the spring of 1985 she could, at last, return to England feeling as if she had been released from a prison sentence. One of the first visits was to Chatsworth, the magnificent Derbyshire home of the Duke and Duchess of Devonshire. Mary Henderson had recently been there and was convinced that there were dozens of old fabrics hiding under newish covers, waiting to be rediscovered and reinterpreted by Laura Ashley. She pressed Laura to see for herself as soon as possible. When Mr Darcy, in *Pride and Prejudice*, takes Elizabeth Bennett to walk around his estates, it is Chatsworth the author has in mind. Today, as you drive over the cattle grid and round the bend into the parkland dotted with sheep, the intensity of feeling that here is a corner of England where nothing has changed for three hundred years is startling. It represented for Laura the quintessential England she had striven to capture in her work.

'She was so quiet and absolutely charming in the true sense of the word, so straightforward and without any fuss, the very opposite of what one expected a hugely successful business person might look like,' the Duchess recalled of her first meeting with Laura. She and Christine Thompson, the chief seamstress, took Laura first through the magnificent state rooms with their painted ceilings and ornate furniture and then to the rear of the house known as the kitchenmaid's landing and laundry passage. Here, in this more familiar Laura Ashley territory, they pulled out the stiff drawers bursting with enticing bundles of old prints, carefully stored away by some bygone housekeeper. Laura was transfixed. Before starting work she rolled up her sleeves and put on her working smock, a gesture of professionalism which impressed Christine Thompson. In one drawer she found silk tassels and complicated trimmings, borders and braids; in another taffetas and figured damasks or large florals used in the grandest rooms. But Laura's eye soon alighted on several smaller, more delicate prints which had once decorated back nurseries and maids' rooms.

'She was so certain she knew exactly what was right and yet she was completely unbossy about it; she had that unerring sense, not just of good taste, but of what other people want,' the Duchess explained. At the end of the day Laura took away thirty-seven samples to be scrutinized by her team for possible copyright or technical problems in reproduction. Of these, three went into immediate production with others kept as reserves. Only small changes were made such as the background stippling removed and a plain fresh white substituted, but otherwise the new version was remarkably faithful to the old. 'Priory', 'Pot Pourri', 'St Clements' and 'Morning Tracery' were all designs originating from Chatsworth fabrics. Typically, Laura wanted to call these new patterns, not the Chatsworth Collection, which had such a grand ring to it, but the Cupboard Collection. As she bade farewell, she expressed her impatience to return. She had not allowed herself nearly enough time to take in all the treasures of Chatsworth, she said. And there were other possibilities too. Some of the old stone cottages on the estate were ideally suited to be decorated with 'Laura Ashley' fabrics for the catalogue. She struck everyone she met that day as a person bursting with new ideas.

For two days in June, Laura and Bernard stayed in Bristol for the Product Division Conference where Laura could not have failed to notice how cheering was her presence. The climax of the conference was a banquet on the second evening at the end of which appeared, as a surprise, the Dowlais Male Voice Choir. They all sang Laura's favourite songs and hymns and more than one person noticed the tears running down her cheeks. Also at this conference was Dr John Rae, the former Headmaster of Westminster School, who was to run the Ashley Charitable Foundation. The possibility of such a foundation had been mooted many years earlier but now, with the company flotation months away, this was to be activated immediately. Laura and Bernard had to decide precisely who should benefit from such a trust. Bernard favoured a dramatic gesture; funding specially equipped aircraft to fly into India and perform cataract operations. The appeal was obvious; the scheme displayed his grand vision, his excitement with high technology and, above all, the possibility of cutting through government red tape and helping individuals. It was, however, an enormously expensive programme and not without risks. Laura, in turn, proposed a Laura Ashley Museum of Design in an unspecified country house. But this long-cherished hope of hers began to founder in favour of something which could be seen to be more overtly charitable. A third idea, which the former headmaster admits he favoured, was for doing something in the educational sphere.

When Dr Rae left them that evening he agreed to prepare a report on the three possibilities, fully aware that while Laura had vague aspirations towards helping women in some way, the one thing both were emphatic about was that their Foundation was not to get involved in charity balls or similar events. Giving adults a second chance in education was then only a germ of a proposal. 'But it was the most interesting and exciting idea, I thought, with immense potential, especially as no other foundation made that its sole concern,' said John Rae. He never met Laura again, but he was confident that she would have wholeheartedly approved the philosophy behind the Laura Ashley Foundation as it was ultimately known. What might Laura have become with a second chance at education? Within months of the Foundation being established, yet independently of it, her own daughter Jane, then aged thirty-three, put herself through further 'O' and 'A' levels followed by a degree course.

During the summer of 1985 Laura and Bernard were based in Brussels, able to enjoy the beautiful pale yellow, lavender and grey drawing room overlooking the park. They came to England sometimes for design meetings and sometimes for purely business meetings to discuss aspects of the now imminent flotation. It was apparent to several of those involved that Laura was not enjoying the process of taking the company public; one banker judged, quite accurately, that she disliked any man in a suit and being surrounded by such a profusion, she found claustrophobic. Only after she retired to bed could the meeting relax in a less tense atmosphere. Laura was more interested in the 1987 Home Furnishing Collection for which she was full of ideas. It was not until 1985 that she employed a secretary and bought herself a portable typewriter in case she could not always reach a telex machine; after twenty-five years of handwritten notes, she believed no one would take her memos seriously any more unless typed.

Among her final lists of typed notes were suggestions for 'damask tablecloths and napkins as one finds in restaurants', new colours for lining fabric and miniature lining prints, nice linen tea towels, blankets, special prints for bedlinen, finer lace or net and myriad new colours and different fabrics. There was, too, a long list of furniture she wished to see in production. Although she had long since dropped her close interest in 'Laura Ashley' garments, periodically she sent Deborah or Moira long lists of items she needed personally and found lacking in the Collection. Mostly these were classic looks in plain colours and good quality material; a silk shirt, a Chanel-look cardigan and a plain slimline skirt. One day Laura rang Mary Henderson and both women had a good laugh about 'being allowed' to suggest a few OPCs (old peoples clothes) to Nick. Of the three proposed by Laura and Mary, two were adopted in 1985. But she had other requests too. 'I lost my battle to have a special fabric for little patchwork prints (on the Home Furnishings committee) but maybe we can do a flanker with the dress side,' she suggested to Deborah James. Similarly with aprons; if 'Garments' were not prepared to do them, Laura decided they belonged to 'Home Furnishings'. 'I insist we introduce these again,' she informed Antonia Kirwan-Taylor stubbornly, as they were vital for the image. She wanted a white, Victorian style with crossed straps plus tall, matching cook's cap, as well as a green butler's apron. She repeatedly badgered Moira for a classic swimsuit in the range, and was even prepared to accept a synthetic mix for this. Unacceptable, however, was 'the glamour variety – cut low on bosom and high on sides.'

Before Jane went into hospital to have her baby, Laura tried to buy her suitable nightdresses for breastfeeding and was appalled to find nothing that was both practical and pretty. She wrote to Moira: 'I have asked for this so many times and if you don't produce a sample within a month I shall go to the Clapham workroom and make it myself and put it into huge production.'

However much she tried to loosen her grasp, Laura was unable to lose interest in details of the Collection which she knew were so important to the public perception of 'Laura Ashley'. Nonetheless she recognized her own limitations and many who saw her that summer, commented that she seemed exhausted for the first time in her life. She came over to England whenever possible to help Jane prepare for her new baby and had cleared out Jane's flat with an energy and gusto that many twenty-year-olds would envy. She had helped Jane prepare a beautiful cottage in Gloucestershire to move into after the baby was born and she was busy scouring the shops for suitable pieces of furniture for her. It was hardly a surprise to Nick, therefore, when she wrote to him on 24 August formally resigning her position as Design Director and handing over to him. In a letter with more than an echo of Edward VIII she admitted to her son that as her life with Bernard demanded that she was always on the move, 'I cannot do the job as I would want to do it.' It was better, therefore, that he took full control. She was only formalizing what was already fact.

13

England Again

Returning to England in mid-August 1985 for the birth of Jane's baby, Laura took the opportunity to visit a close friend, June Buchanan. The two women had lunch together, reminisced and then returned to the Hyde Park Hotel, where Laura was staying, for tea. While she was out, Laura's address book had been stolen, such items being of great value to the newspapers but, calm though Laura was, she felt a part of her life had been snatched. A day later June invited her for an evening swim at the Hurlingham Club; but, in spite of Laura's progress, she was nervous of swimming at night. 'How awful if you lost me in the dark,' she confided to June. The prospect terrified her and Laura proposed instead driving around London to look at the old haunts where she and Bernard had lived when they were first married. They went to Pimlico and, as they paused outside St George's Square, laughed about the ninety-nine steps and the smell from the oven. 'She just wanted to see it again after all these years, she didn't say why,' June recalled. After that the two women had dinner together, and talked almost exclusively about the past. Laura did let slip that she had been invited to meet Prime Minister Margaret Thatcher in September at a private dinner organized by Lady Henderson. She was looking forward to the occasion enormously.

Jane's baby was born in August. 'Exciting baby – thick black hair!! Looks like David otherwise,' Laura wrote. After the birth Laura returned to Brussels, but planned to come back to England for her own sixtieth birthday the following month. As the birthday fell on a Saturday she was going to spend the weekend with Jane, the baby, her mother and sister at Jane's new house in the Cotswolds. From there she and Bernard would fly to the Bahamas to start work on the latest home they had discovered at Lyford Cay. It was a yellow and white two-storey Palladian-style villa built in 1960 with magnificent sea views interrupted only by a grove of immense palm trees.

Laura made one final visit to Carno before the birthday weekend. Staying this time at the old Aleppo Merchant Inn, strangely after all the years at Rhydoldog, she told Jean Evans, one of her oldest employees and friends: 'I'm here to squeeze several days work into one.' In the next breath she spoke excitedly about the new grandson she was about to see.

On 7 September Al Maclean, the company chauffeur, was despatched to pick up Mrs Mountney and Laura's sister, Mary Coates, from the south coast and drive them to Jane's new house. Laura was coming down by train and Bernard was going to make his own way there after a meeting at Maidenhead. It was past lunch time when the family all met up. Laura wanted to hold the baby immediately and look after him until the maternity nurse arrived to take charge for the rest of the weekend. The little cottage was crammed full of cards and flowers and Jane could not resist asking her father whether he was wondering what they were all for. 'Oh no! It's not our anniversary, is it?' he laughed, whereupon Al told Laura that next year he was going to remind Bernard in advance so that he would never forget her birthday again. 'No, you mustn't do that,' she gently chided him. 'That's part of the fun; the fun is him always forgetting.' That afternoon Jane and her mother went shopping in the nearby village of Moreton-in-Marsh. They pottered around antique shops and Laura, hungry after missing lunch, wanted nothing more than fried fish and chips; her naughty streak, according to Jane. Instead, they had an early supper and then went for a walk, taking Mary Coates and Mrs Mountney to a nearby cottage where they were staying.

'There was no special birthday supper because Mum didn't want a fuss made of her. She loved the high life, but all she wanted for her sixtieth birthday was poached eggs on toast and a new grandchild, that was enough,' said Jane. After watching television for a while, both Jane and Laura went to bed, tired. Bernard stayed down for a little longer, but was in bed himself by about midnight.

In the early hours of the morning he half woke, as Laura got out of bed and left the bedroom, without putting a light on, although the rest of the house was in darkness. She had not been sleeping well for some time and so this was not an infrequent occurrence. Bernard, assuming she had gone to the bathroom or to get some water, dozed for the next thirty seconds at most when he heard a noise like a door slamming. He instantly awoke, put on the bedroom light and rushed out of the bedroom.

'The corridor was in darkness, the only light switch being at the far end of the staircase. The bathroom door, which was between the bedroom door and the staircase, was closed. I called Laura, reached across and put on the corridor light, looked down the staircase and saw my wife lying at the foot of the stairs in a pool of blood,' Bernard was to tell the coroner. He was just about to rush down to her when the nurse appeared and ordered him not to move her but to telephone immediately for an ambulance. Since they had never lived in the area before they had some difficulty explaining to the emergency service exactly where they were. The nurse put Laura into the recovery position while Bernard went out into the night and switched on the car headlights to guide the ambulance. She was taken first to Warwick Hospital and then, when the severity of her injuries became clear, to Walsgrave Hospital, Coventry.

Bernard, dazed with shock, somehow gripped himself to follow. The rest of the family were telephoned and Jane met Emma from Oxford station the next morning. The nurse had advised them, as soon as she had found Laura, that her vital functions were very weak. She had lost consciousness immediately. David flew over from America and by the following evening, the whole family had gathered in Coventry to sit by Laura's bedside. They all knew the worst. 'She just didn't look like herself any more,' said Jane. Bernard sought second opinions in America and investigated the possibility of surgery but all the doctors warned them was that there was little hope.

By Sunday night the press, having discovered where Laura was, was fighting for every detail of the tragic story. There was speculation as to whether the flotation would have to be called off. In these circumstances the Ashleys were only too grateful to friends of Ari who offered them the use of their home in the north of England. Laura survived on a life support machine for ten days. She died in the early hours of the morning of 17 September, never regaining consciousness. The cause of death was officially given as 'diffuse cerebral injury, trauma to the head ... injuries consistent with the deceased having fallen heavily downstairs'. A detective constable told the inquest that the banister brackets at the top and bottom of the staircase were loose, that the stairs were steep and some of the carpet had stretched so that 'a person treading with his full weight on the angle of the step is liable to lose his balance'. In addition, Laura was wearing a long nightdress and there were no lights. The most likely explanation of Laura's fatal fall is that she woke up to go to the bathroom, and, hoping not to disturb the other sleepers, did not switch on any lights, turned towards the stairs by mistake and, in the pitch dark she so dreaded, fell headlong.

*　　*　　*

The funeral took place at Carno Parish Church, a simple Welsh country chapel rebuilt in 1867 on the site of a twelfth-century church, originally used as a sanctuary and refuge for the Knights Hospitallers. Rising behind are the patchwork green hillsides where Laura so often walked alone for peace of mind or inspiration. The day of the funeral was warm and sunny and the small church was packed out. Hundreds more waited outside as the factory and 'Laura Ashley' shops worldwide closed down. Almost everyone who had ever known her in Wales wanted to come and pay their respects. The Vicar, Reverend Dennis Parry, faced with such a swollen congregation, many of whom he had never met, imported an electric organ for the day to replace his own push pedal harmonium. Lord Hooson gave the funeral address and reminded everyone how 'in an age when designers were emphasizing the more savage and tough side of human nature, she pointed to its pretty, peaceful and generous side ... she put forward a style which was simpler, kinder and more romantic than her contemporaries projected'. There were hymns and prayers and then, as everyone followed the bier, strewn with wild flowers, to the graveside, the Dowlais Male Voice Choir which had moved Laura to tears just a few weeks ago sang in Welsh a hymn which they had learned especially for her funeral; many mourners were now noiselessly weeping.

The silence was one of the most striking aspects of the day. Although the church sits on the corner of a busy roadside, scarcely a car went past. The sheep which always nudge the graves pushed closer yet barely bleated. As the cortège finally moved off a single graveside bell tolled.

*   *   *

'Anyone who knew Laura is much richer for having known her,' insisted one of her close friends shortly after her death. 'She was not a fairweather friend who would forget about you in bad times but would always try to help if she could.' Loyalty, to friends, family and the company, was a ruling passion for Laura. It was a quality closely intertwined with her conviction that duty to others came first, and principally, her duty to her husband, from which all other comforts and joys would flow.

'It was one of the best marriages I have ever seen,' commented Sybille de la Borde, who knew them better than most, 'because they really shared each other's lives. So easily bored by outsiders, they were an endless source of fascination to one another; they always had so much to say to each other.' Sybille remembers how at Remaisnil, even when there were no children there, Laura would come back after work, smarten herself up and put logs on the fire for Bernard's return. Even if he had been flying all day and she working, she would prepare the evening meal and then sit and sew or talk, but never with papers working, because he hated that. Just as Jane Austen had to write her novels secretly and hide the manuscripts lest she appeared too professional, so did Laura try to work without Bernard seeing. It was a marriage which their children describe as 'occasionally stormy' and their friends as 'sometimes turbulent' but no one denies that the partnership of Laura and Bernard was a brilliant success. Their interdependence increased over the years. In Victorian novels, marriages were always a question of gains and losses; the achievement of harmony through balance. In Laura and Bernard's case, each brought to the marriage such opposing gifts and characteristics – Bernard so straightforward and rough; Laura gentle and soft but deeply involved in an often tortuous thinking process – yet they complemented each other perfectly. The positive/negative wallpaper and fabric can be seen as a simile for their lives; each alone was decidedly individual and vulnerable, as a partnership they became strong, original and bold.

But Laura as a friend (or wife) and Laura as a businesswoman were two, often quite distinct entities. They were given sharper definition by names or greetings; Laura and LA. Many were convinced that the choice of name signified not only a quite different relationship with that person but different characteristics within herself; LA was an employer, Laura was a friend. Sybille was not the only one to call her LA by day and Laura by evening. John James saw the distinction quite clearly too, but wonders whether Laura herself was aware of it. Was the Mrs Ashley who opposed the suggestion of a crèche for working mothers at the factory the same Mrs Ashley who had brought her daughter Emma into the design studio with a packet of crayons and asked staff to keep an eye on her?

One of the most interesting aspects of Laura Ashley is the continual expansion of her intellectual horizons. This was reflected by an evolution in her work and her beliefs. Always a diligent worker, in youth she saw typing and driving as the most important skills a girl could attain because of the doors they would open. She believed that these skills would enable any girl to be of service to others and, ultimately, lead to a husband and marital bliss. While she never relinquished these goals, and never forsook her belief that women could only be truly fulfilled through a domestic environment, she came to see the value and joy of work for its own sake. 'No wonder I am so keen on Florence Nightingale,' she once wrote to Jane, 'she just worked all the time for her whole life. There is something to be said for that once you have discovered a cause (or an art!).' Laura had discovered both a cause and an art, although she consistently maintained that she was not an artist but an artisan. Modestly, she explained: 'I have simply expressed myself within the disciplined framework in which I have found myself and have never wanted to rebel against that.' It was this disciplined framework which restricted her to reinterpretation of ideas already in existence. She did not think enough of her talent to believe she could ever produce anything better than that which had already been thought of. Thus, when Terence Conran chided her, as he did on occasions, for not giving a greater boost to new, modern and original talent, she felt quite confident in explaining to him that she produced the things that she liked. 'I understand what I am good at. I am comfortable with my image. When the children take over they'll do the new things.' Sometimes Conran pressed her: 'Surely you want to leave some contribution of the age we've lived in?'

'I'm only interested in reopening people's eyes to what they have forgotten about,' she replied. She never lost sight of who she was and never tried to become something she was not.

Laura had a dream of the perfect life, which she believed was applicable to all women, and in her own life managed to live her dream. A happy marriage and a secure home life were not some remote ideal; she genuinely believed she had both. Nor was she saying that true moral happiness lay only in the quiet performance of domestic duty; she believed in romantic love as well, having herself married for love and sexual attraction. Security went without saying. Whilst accepting that she had been atypically fortunate and protected from life's hardships, she wanted to make as much of the dream possible for everyone else. Her guiding light was nostalgia for a better past, her goal the prospect of a better future; through her creation she hoped to combine and produce a 'brand new version of the past'.

Two months after Laura's death, hundreds of eager investors jostled their way towards Barclays Bank in the City of London to try and secure their shares in 'Laura Ashley', their share of the dream. Mounted policemen were on hand to control the thousands of people, some of whom had queued all night to buy the shares. The issue was oversubscribed thirty-four times and the flotation ultimately valued the company at nearly £270 million. Approximately 5,000 'Laura Ashley' staff worldwide were not only given preferential rights to apply for shares in the offer but £1.25 million worth of shares were made available to them at no cost. It was this aspect of the flotation which had appealed most to Laura. As Bernard, now the Chairman of Laura Ashley plc remarked in his first annual report in 1986, 'On average there is now a 'Laura Ashley' shop opening somewhere in the world at least once a week.'

But her legacy is more than the sum total of her shops. Within Laura's lifetime it was clear that, largely thanks to her company, mid-Wales had become a highly credible location for industrial development. Without 'Laura Ashley', farms would undoubtedly have been sold, amalgamated or abandoned and the existence of a rural community would have become a historical footnote.

Laura never took her success for granted and knew how much more remained to be achieved, but she was justifiably proud of all that had been achieved. 'Laura Ashley' deserves a permanent place in British social history on two counts; in the Seventies, countering a strong tide, she made it possible for women to look and feel like women without hindering any of their manifold desires for career and job satisfaction. In their homes, and home was the centre of Laura Ashley's world, she rescued a corner of the past that had belonged to ordinary people and restored it to the descendants of those same people with enhanced value. She maintained the highest standards in her work and in her life and was strengthened by an unshakeable belief that there was a moral purpose in what she was doing that transcended mere commercialism. On these foundations she built an empire.

Index

Ashley, Emma Mary—*cont.*
at Remaisnil party, 158; and Laura's flight to USA, 171; relations with mother, 171, 174–5, 181; studies in USA, 183; and mother's fatal fall, 194

Ashley, Geoff (Bernard's brother), 33–4, 36, 51

Ashley, Hilda (Bernard's mother), 17–18, 28

Ashley, Jane (*i.e.* Laura Jane; Laura's daughter): born, 36; childhood, 41–3; and parent's separation, 52; in Wales, 53; schooling, 67, 69, 90; moves to London, 90; and mother's anxieties, 98; as company photographer, 102–3, 152, 172; relations with mother, 152, 160, 164, 171, 185, 193; and mother's inner life, 159; compared to father, 163; activities and ventures, 172; child, 185, 190–3; takes degree course, 189; and mother's fatal fall, 194

Ashley, Laura (*née* Mountney): fatal fall, 1, 3, 194–5; self-control, 2; born, 3, 6; Wallington childhood, 7; schooling, 8, 11, 14; religious background and practices, 10–11, 23, 178–80; wartime evacuation to Dowlais, 12–14; returns to Wallington, 14–16; Victorian ideals and influences, 15, 67, 136, 172; reading, 15; secretarial training, 15; in Girls' Training Corps, 16; works as shorthand typist, 16; serves in WRNS, 16, 21–5; meets Bernard, 17, 19–21; posted abroad, 23–4; choral singing, 25; demobilized, 25; gives up piano playing, 26; courtship, 26–7; marriage, 28–9; home and family life, 30, 67, 71, 181; at National Federation of Women's Institutes, 30; pregnancies, 33, 35, 36, 43, 56, 69, 91; early fabric printing, 33–6, 40; children, 36–7, 70–1, 90, 152–3, 160, 171, 181; forms company, 37; life in Limpsfield, 41–3; relations with employees, 45, 72–3, 80–1, 87, 96–8, 117–18, 120, 129; early clothing products, 49, 55, 58, 61, 83, 87, 92; marriage relations, 50–1, 160–4, 171, 196; austerity, 51; leaves Bernard and lives in Wales, 51–5, 60, 99; develops Tybrith factory, 57–8, 60; and local labour and goodwill, 60–1,

75–6; and Sixties values, 66–7; authoritarianism, 67, 98, 113–14, 121, 129, 177; and children's education, 67–9, 90–1, 107–8; moves to Clogau, 69–70; hostility to accountants, 83–4, 121–2, 141; opens London shops, 84; print designs, 88; hysterectomy, 91; and Bernard's outbursts, 97–8; stresses, 98; philosophy of women's dress and design, 99–102, 106; puritanism, 101; and Paris shop, 104–5; at Rhydoldog, 106; sells fabric remnants, 108–9; relations with John James, 111–12; at board meetings, 112–13; and professional staff, 115–16, 121; visits France, 116–17; learns French, 117, 168; and effluent disposal, 119; overseas travels, 120, 122; personal dress and style, 121–2, 182, 187; on sales, 121–2; declines offer of OBE, 122–3; documentary film on, 123–4; moves to Remaisnil (France), 125–30; in USA, 133–40; interviews, 135–6, 139, 162; and feminism, 136; print research, 143, 187–8; life and style in France, 143–8, 150–1, 160–1; attitude to publicity, 146; and corporate plan, 149–50; ceases to attend board meetings, 149; punctuality, 150–1; buys from Cambrian Woollen Mills, 153; aids Gallery of English Costume, 154–5; on dress and sexuality, 155–6; attitude to charity, 156; gives parties at Remaisnil, 157–9; inner life, 159, 164; phobias, 163; sailing, 163–4; and interior design, 166–8, buys La Pré Verger, 175; Brussels house, 176–8, 189; dominates Collection, 177; as Deputy Chairman, 178; and public flotation of company, 178, 189; TV interview, 179; religious retreat, 180; travels, 180; and Nick's newspaper interview, 181; offered London University honorary degree, 182; cuts hair short, 182; views on USA, 182–3; Palm Beach house, 183–5; learns to swim, 184–5; and Ashley Charitable Foundation, 188–9; resigns from company, 191; sixtieth birthday, 193–4; death and funeral, 195–6; standards and values, 197–9; *see also* Laura Ashley (company)